Backroad Mapbook

Welcome to the Premier Edition of the Backroad Mapbook for Southwestern Ontario!

D1244512

Inside this guidebook, you will find the most comprehensive outdoor recreation resource available for Southwestern Ontario. This mapbook covers the last remaining portion of Southern Ontario for the Backroad Mapbook Series. From the Golden Horseshoe southwest to Windsor and from Long Point all the way to the tip of the Bruce Peninsula, you will find a lifetime of outdoor activities in this area.

Since it is the most populated part of the province, outdoor recreationists often overlook Southwestern Ontario. In the past decade, however, the region has made monumental strides in establishing outdoor recreation opportunities. In fact, the region is now home to the largest established trail network in the province. Trails like the famous Bruce Trail and the Waterfront Trail have helped make Southwestern Ontario the destination of choice for trail lovers.

Through a strong conservation effort, the region has also established hundreds of public parks and conservation areas. These spaces have been put aside for all to enjoy and provide some of the best outdoor recreation opportunities in the province. Take a trip to the lush marshlands of Rondeau Provincial Park or explore the unique rock formations found in Bruce Peninsula National Park. Outdoor enthusiasts can also experience some of the most accessible river paddling routes in Ontario. Rivers like the Grand River and

the Saugeen River not only offer fantastic paddling they also provide world class fishing opportunities. Whatever your outdoor recreation desires are, there is plenty to choose from in Southwestern Ontario.

The Backroad Mapbook is an explorer's guide that provides a detailed set of maps and information on a wealth of recreational opportunities in the area. Explorers will find the maps extremely useful in finding new areas. We have highlighted the trail systems as well as park and recreation areas in Southwestern Ontario. Along the way, we have noted the points of interest and the infinite recreation opportunities. From fantastic fishing holes to endless trail systems and scenic campgrounds, we provide the maps and information that will make your trip planning easier.

People interested in a particular activity will find the reference section invaluable. Our reference section includes information on lake and stream fishing, paddling routes, multi-use trails (hiking/biking, and off road trails) parks and conservation areas (camping), and winter recreation. Countless hours have been spent researching this book, making it the most complete compilation of outdoor recreation information you will find on the region anywhere. This information can be enjoyed by anyone who spends time in the great outdoors.

If you enjoy the outdoors, we are sure you will have as much fun using the Backroad Mapbook as we did in developing it!

Backroad Mapbooks

DIRECTORS
Russell Mussio
Wesley Mussio
Penny Stainton-Mussio

COVER DESIGN & LAYOUT
Farnaz Faghihi

PRODUCTION

Adrian Brugge
Shawn Caswell
Farnaz Faghihi
Brett Firth
Brad Hudson
Cindy Ly
Grace Teo
Dale Tober
Heather Yetman

SALES /MARKETING
Shawn Caswell

Jason Marleau

WRITERS
Russell Mussio
Jason Marleau

National Library of Canada Cataloguing in Publication Data

Marleau, Jason, 1972-
    Mussio Ventures presents Backroad mapbook : southwestern Ontario. -- Premier ed.

Written by Jason Marleau and Russell Mussio.
"Southwestern Ontario's most complete outdoor recreational guide".
Includes index.
ISBN 1-894556-14-3

    1. Outdoor recreation--Ontario, Southwestern--Guidebooks.
2. Recreation areas--Ontario, Southwestern--Guidebooks. 3. Ontario, Southwestern--Guidebooks. 4. Ontario, Southwestern--Maps, Tourist.
I. Mussio, Russell, 1969- II. Mussio Ventures Ltd III. Title. IV. Title:
Backroad mapbook : southwestern Ontario.

G1146.E63M365 2003   796.5'09713'2   C2003-900934-3

Published by:

5811 Beresford Street
Burnaby, B.C. V5J 1K1
P. (604) 438-3474   F. (604) 438-3470
E-mail: info@backroadmapbooks.com
www.**backroadmapbooks**.com
Copyright © 2003 Mussio Ventures Ltd.

All materials contained within this Mapbook are the property of the publishers and may not be reproduced in whole or in part without the expressed written consent of the publishers

Acknowledgement

This book could not have been compiled without the relentless effort of Jason Marleau. He headed the research and writing effort and did a fabulous job of digging up countless recreational opportunities and describing them in a creative, yet appealing way. This book could not have been created without the hard work and dedication of the Mussio Ventures Ltd. staff, Shawn Caswell, Farnaz Faghihi, Brett Firth, Brad Hudson, Cindy Ly, Grace Teo, Dale Tober and Heather Yetman. Without their hard work and support, this comprehensive mapbook would never have been completed as accurately as it was. We would also like to thank the following for helping with the project: Joanne Kelly , Heather K. Marleau, Carmine Minutillo, Cathie Smith and Richard Smith for their photos and first hand knowledge of Southern Ontario.

In addition, we would like to thank all those individuals, retailers, Ministry of Natural Resources staff and tourism personnel for their knowledge and assistance in the production of this mapbook.

Finally we would like to thank Heather K. Marleau, Allison, Devon, Nancy, Madison and Penny Mussio for their continued support of the Backroad Mapbook Series. As our family grows, it is becoming more and more challenging to break away from it all to explore our beautiful country.

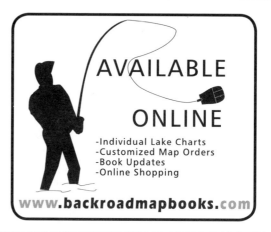

AVAILABLE ONLINE
-Individual Lake Charts
-Customized Map Orders
-Book Updates
-Online Shopping
www.**backroadmapbooks**.com

Help Us Help You

A comprehensive resource such as the **Backroad Mapbook for Southwestern Ontario** could not be put together without a great deal of help and support. Despite our best efforts to ensure that everything is accurate, errors do occur. If you see any errors or omissions, please continue to let us know.

Call (604) 438-FISH (3474)

toll free 1-877-520-5670,

fax 1-604-438-3470

e-mail updates@backroadmapbooks.com

Mail to: 5811 Beresford Street
              Burnaby, B.C. V5J 1K1

All updates will be posted on our web site
www.**backroadmapbooks**.com

Disclaimer

Mussio Ventures Ltd. does not warrant that the backroads, trails and paddling routes indicated in this Mapbook are passable nor does it claim that the Mapbook is completely accurate. Therefore, please be careful when using this or any source to plan and carry out your outdoor recreation activity.

Please note that travelling on backroads and trails is inherently dangerous, and without limiting the generality of the foregoing, you may encounter poor road conditions, unexpected traffic, poor visibility, and low or no road/trail maintenance. Please use extreme caution when traveling logging roads and trails.

Please refer to the Fishing and Hunting Regulations for closures and restrictions. It is your responsibility to know when and where closures and restrictions apply.

Table of Contents

Outdoor Recreation Reference Section

Map Section

Map Key & Legend

www.backroadmapbooks.com

Foreword

The Backroad Mapbook is truly a unique product. No other source covers Southwestern Ontario with as much detail or information on outdoor recreation activities as this book.

The mapbook is simple to use. There are two sections in the book, a reference section and the maps. If you know the activity you are planning, you simply turn to that reference section and find the activity you are interested in. If you are planning a trip to a specific area, you should consult the index to find the appropriate map(s) and look for the various recreation opportunities highlighted.

The maps have been developed and updated using a variety of sources including extensive field research. They are very detailed and show up to date information on the backroads and trail systems of Southwestern Ontario. In addition, we provide a map legend at the start of the maps to show you the region the book covers as well as how to decipher the various grades of roads and symbols used on the maps.

By popular demand from GPS users, we have included UTM Grids (NAD 83) and longitude and latitude reference points. We must emphasize that these are for reference only. This generality is because we have to consult several different sources to create the maps.

Generally, Southwestern Ontario has a well established secondary road system that provides easy access to many outdoor activities. With numerous side roads and trails, a good portion of the region is accessible by vehicle. Some farming roads, however, are restricted to public access. Be sure to pay attention to road signs and please do not trespass.

We emphasize that our mapbook should only be used as an access and planning guide. We have gone to great lengths to ensure the accuracy of this book. However, over time, the road and trail conditions change. Always be prepared!

Please respect all private property and close any gates behind you.

Backroads of Southwestern Ontario

Southwestern Ontario was one of the first areas of the country to be settled. Settlers soon logged the area to create farmland, which is still prevalent throughout the area today. Some of the roads in this part of the province have been in use for over a century. The rolling hills and flat terrain made road construction easier than in most other parts of the province and after the advent of the automobile, the region sprouted roads almost everywhere.

While travellers to Eastern, Central and Northern Ontario can continue to find new logging or bush road networks, Southwestern Ontario offers few if any such systems. Almost every point in this region is accessible by some sort of road. Travellers will find an intricate network of roads that range from freeways to farming roads.

Southwestern Ontario is truly a backroad traveller's paradise. Most of the region's roads are paved or hard packed gravel, which when maintained is the next best thing to pavement. You can pretty much avoid every main highway en route to your destination. For travellers that are not in a rush and simply want to enjoy the countryside, this is a real advantage. In particular, you will find that motorcyclists like to cruise the many paved backroads throughout the region.

Another popular attraction for travellers in Southwestern Ontario is the scenic shoreline roads. Travellers will find roadways skirting the edge of Lake Erie, Lake Huron and the Georgian Bay are some of the most scenic driving opportunities available in the province. In fact, you can almost follow the shoreline from Niagara Falls all the way to Windsor, then north to the tip of the Bruce Peninsula.

The main artery for travel access in Southwestern Ontario is Highway 401. At times it almost seems like the 401 is a part of any travel plans in the region. The super highway stretches from Metro Toronto southwest to Windsor ending at the Ambassador Bridge over the Detroit River. If you want to make good time in your travels it is best to include the large highway whenever possible.

If you are heading north of Highway 401, there are several smaller (two lane) highways that lead north from the 401. Essentially, travellers will find a mix of interconnecting highways that never seem to take you directly to your destination. Instead, you will often have to creatively join a few highways or County Roads together to get where you want to go. With this Backroad Mapbook, we hope we can help you find your way or even better show you what to do along the way.

Freshwater Fishing

(Lake, River and Stream Fishing)

Southwestern Ontario is river country. The region is riddled with a maze of rivers and creeks that wind their way towards the Great Lakes. The Bruce Peninsula is home to many headwater streams that are supplied by cool running water. These streams and the lakes around them often support trout species such as brook trout. As the cool streams eventually flow into the larger rivers, warm water species such as bass and pike become more prevalent.

Over the past few decades, river fishing has become very popular with the establishment of steelhead (sea-run rainbow trout) and salmon spawning runs. During the spring and fall, anglers crowd the rivers for a chance to hook into one of these trophies. The smaller streams, with resident sportfish ranging from trout to bass and pike, offer good fishing throughout the season.

Lake anglers also have a lot of variety to choose from. The Great Lakes have seen tremendous improvements over the years in both water quality and fishing success. Further inland, there are the man-made lakes and reservoirs of the south along with a good selection of interior lakes in the northern portion of this region. Warm water fish such as bass, pike and walleye prefer the marshy, shallower lakes while trout prefer the deeper, cooler lakes in the area.

A few of the more consistent restrictions in Southwestern Ontario are slot size limits and seasonal fishing sanctuaries. A slot size limit is the restriction of what size of fish must be released and what size you can keep from a lake. For example, in Lake St. Clair only one walleye kept out of your total limit can be greater than 46 cm (18 in) in length. The idea is to release fish that are at a healthy maturity and the prime breeding stock of the lake, to give them the opportunity to reproduce. Seasonal fishing sanctuaries are one of the newer restrictions that have been brought into effect on various water bodies in the province. The idea of this regulation is to curb incidental and out of season catches of fragile species such as walleye when fishing for other fish. Each species also has a regulated open and closed season. The closed period usually coincides with the spawning period to allow for regeneration of stocks without angling pressure.

Other regulations that are becoming more prevalent in Southwestern Ontario is catch and release areas along with bait bans and barbless hook. These three regulations on rivers such as the Grand River have helped the river establish a world class brown trout fishery. Expanded awareness of anglers have also increased the practice of voluntary catch and release. With so many anglers out there, catch and release is vital for a healthy sport fishery in Southwestern Ontario. All of these regulations are having positive effects on fishing quality in the region and are in place strictly for the benefit of future angling.

The most popular sportfish in Southwestern Ontario are listed below:

Brook Trout are native in many cooler streams in Southwestern Ontario. They are also known as speckled trout due to the red spots with blue halos on their sides. In streams, they are generally small and rarely reach sizes in excess of 30 cm (12 in), while in lakes they can be found to 1 kg (2.2 lbs) and sometimes larger. Brookies are often a fickle and difficult fish to catch, but one of the most effective methods of angling is fly fishing. Small spoons and spinners tipped with worms can also be productive, and is the recommended set up when fishing for brook trout through the ice. The Ontario record brook trout was caught on a fly in the Nipigon River and weighed a whopping 6.58 kg (14.5 lbs).

Brown Trout are native to Europe and were first introduced into the Great Lakes in 1884 by the United States. Ontario began its own stocking program in 1913 and browns are now resident in many streams. Brown trout are more adaptable to warmer water conditions and can often be found cruising shorelines near stream mouths. Stream browns are best caught on the fly, and can be found over 1 kg (2.2 lbs) in size. Lake run browns are caught mainly by trolling with spoons or spinners. In the Great Lakes these fish have been caught over 10 kg (22 lbs) with the Ontario record brown trout recorded at 15.6 kg (34.38 lbs).

Lake Trout are one of the most sought after sportfish in the province. In Southwestern Ontario a few inland lakes support lake trout, and they are also found in Lake Ontario and Lake Huron. Lake trout grow very slowly and the use of catch and release can go a long way in helping maintain populations. Lakers can grow to sizes exceeding 6 kg (13 lbs) and can be found near the surface in spring but retreat to colder water depths in the summer. Spoons, spinners, or anything that imitates the lake trout's main food source, the minnow, are good choices when angling for lakers. The Ontario record lake trout is 28.6 kg (63.12 lbs).

Largemouth Bass are found throughout Southwestern Ontario in numerous lakes and rivers in the region. The warmer waters of the region make great habitat for this species. In large rivers and lakes, top water lures and flies can create a frenzy of action. Plastic jigs or any minnow imitation lure or fly can also be productive. Largemouth bass are readily adaptable to warm water lakes and generally grow larger than its cousin, the smallmouth bass. The Ontario record largemouth bass is 4.7 kg (10.43 lbs).

Muskellunge are the largest freshwater sportfish in Ontario and can reach over 16 kg (35 lbs) in size. Often referred to as "musky" this warm water predator feeds mainly on other fish as well as frogs, mice, muskrat, and the occasional waterfowl. The best method for finding these large fish is by trolling long plugs and lures in calm bays where they often cruise for food. Fall is the more productive time of year. The Ontario record muskellunge was caught in the Georgian Bay and weighed 29.5 kg (65 lbs). This great fish would not have made it to a record size if not for catch and release angling.

Northern Pike are the cousin of the muskellunge and inhabits weedy, murky waters throughout Southwestern Ontario. Pike are very aggressive and readily strike fast moving spoons and spinners or anything imitating a good meal. Northern pike can be found over 8 kg (17.6 lbs) in size and colourful spoons or flies can be very productive baits. The main food source for this predator is other fish, although they often take frogs, ducklings and small muskrat. Ontario's record northern pike is a 19.11 kg (42.13 lb) lunker.

Pacific Salmon were introduced into the Great Lakes and include pink, chinook and coho salmon. Pink salmon were accidentally introduced into the Current River, a tributary of Lake Superior in 1956, and have since spread throughout the Great Lakes and established spawning runs on many streams in the area. Chinook and coho salmon have been stocked in the Great Lakes since 1873. Despite the healthy spawning runs of both species, the reproduction success has been dismal and the fishery is solely dependent on stocking programs. Trolling spoons or spinners that imitate minnows can take all three pacific salmon species. In streams, the big fish are very spooky, although they will strike brighter coloured flies and lures. The Ontario record pink is 5.9 kg (13.1 lbs), the biggest coho is 12.1 kg (26.64 lbs) and a chinook has tipped the scales at 20.6 kg (45.38 lbs).

Rainbow Trout and **Steelhead** are native to the Pacific Northwest and by 1882 rainbow had been stocked into each of the Great Lakes. The prized trout readily adapted to the environment and by the early 1900's had established reproducing populations in all of the Great Lakes. Today, rainbow trout have also been introduced

into many inland lakes, ponds and streams of Southwestern Ontario. Inland lake trout usually average 35-45 cm (14-18 in) in size. Fly fishing is the preferred method for trout, although small spinners and spoons can be productive. In spring, the Steelhead spawning run in some streams of the Great Lakes basin is North America renowned. Roe sacs are the preferred bait, although the migratory fish will also strike steelhead pattern flies. It is not uncommon to find fish larger than 8 kg (17.6 lbs) in the Great Lakes. The Ontario record rainbow trout is 13.2 kg (29.12 lbs).

Smallmouth Bass are the close cousin of the largemouth bass and occur naturally in hundreds of water bodies in Southwestern Ontario. The smallmouth has a reputation of putting up a great fight when hooked, and can be a very aggressive feeder at times. The feisty fish readily strikes jigs, spinners, spoons and other fast moving lures that look like a good meal. Smallmouth can be found around structure such as shoals, islands and under water drop-offs. The Ontario record smallmouth bass is 4.5 kg (9.84 lbs).

Splake is a sterile cross between lake trout and brook trout and was developed specifically to stock lakes uninhabited by other trout species. Splake grow very rapidly similar to brook trout and to sizes similar to lake trout. Similar to lake trout, splake are most active in winter and in spring just after ice off and will strike shiny spoons and spinners.

Walleye or **pickerel**, are perhaps the most prized sportfish in Ontario due in part to its acclaim as a great tasting fish. The walleye's diet is made up of mainly baitfish, although they do take leeches and other grub like creatures. Jigs are the lure of choice for walleye, either through the ice or during open water season. Walleye travel in loose schools and once you find them, you should be able to catch more than one. Jigging in set locations is a productive method or trolling slowly along weed beds can also entice strikes. Walleye are most active during the darker times of day and early morning or evening are the most productive periods. The Ontario record walleye is 10.1 kgs (22.25 lbs).

Yellow Perch are aggressive feeders and are best caught by still fishing worms with a float. Perch don't grow very big and only average 20-30 cm (8-12 in) in size, although they are fished for their great eating quality. In this regard, they are often compared to walleye. Yellow perch are found in many warm water lakes throughout the province and the Ontario record is 1 kg (2.25 lbs).

Before heading out, be sure to check the Ontario Recreational Fishing Regulations Summary to ensure you are not breaking any laws. Penalties for offences can be severe including large fines, confiscation of vehicles and equipment, or even jail time.

Lakes

From the Great Lakes to small man-made reservoirs, anglers in Southwestern Ontario have an excellent array of stillwater to fish. The Grey/Bruce or northern region is home to the majority of the interior lakes. Further south, many man-made reservoirs and lakes have been created and stocked to provide some fantastic fishing opportunities.

While we have done our best to cover the bulk of the sport fishing opportunities in the region, it is recommended to get out there and explore. Some of the smallest ponds (too small to mark on our maps) or even wetland areas offer some great fishing.

Allan Park Pond (Map 24/E1)
Located at the Allan Park Conservation Area east of Hanover, the Allan Park Pond offers fishing opportunities for stocked rainbow trout. Rainbows average 20 cm (8 in) in size, however larger trout are available. Fly anglers should try a small bead head nymph or even a dragonfly nymph in the spring. Spinners also produce results.

Andrew Lakes (Map 39/A5)
The Andrew Lakes are two secluded Bruce Peninsula National Park Lakes that are located in the southeastern end of the park. The larger **Upper Andrew Lake** is only accessible from the Bruce Trail or by bushwhacking from Emmett Lake. A rough road off Emmett Lake Road can find the smaller **Lower Andrew Lake**. The lakes offer some good fishing at times for smallmouth bass and northern pike. Success rates and sizes of fish caught in Upper Andrew are usually better than in Lower Andrew due to the accessibility.

Arran Lake (Map 33/E6)
This long lake is located east of Port Elgin and can be accessed at the Arran Lake Conservation Area off Side Road 10. The lake is home to a fair population of smallmouth bass and northern pike. Northern pike average 1.5 kg (3.5 lbs) while bass average 0.5 kg (1 lb) in size.

Bass Lake (Map 34/C1)
Bass Lake is a long narrow lake that holds smallmouth bass and a small population of northern pike. Pike are best caught cruising the shallows at dusk. Rainbow trout have been stocked in the lake and are best caught in the spring. Bass Lake is located north of Owen Sound off the east side of County Road 17. Boat access is available from the tent and trailer park for a fee. Check for special season restrictions.

Bells Lake (Map 31/A5)
Bells Lake has been stocked periodically with both rainbow trout and brook trout. The lake is a good destination for anglers to get out in the canoe or float tube. Try stripping in small minnow or dragonfly patterns to hook into one of the trout, which can be 30 cm (12 in) in size. Although fishing can be good on occasion, like all trout lakes, patience is certainly needed. Access to the lake is via the 70 Side Road west of the village of Markdale. There are special season regulations on Bells Lake.

Belwood Lake (Map 25/G7)
The damming of the Grand River created Belwood Lake and the large water body has become a good fishing destination. Some big pike and smallmouth bass live in the reservoir. Pike over 75 cm (30 in) are caught on occasion, while smaller pike in the 3+ kg (6.5+ lb) range can be picked up by trolling or by casting into the shallows as evening approaches. Smallmouth bass average 1 kg (2 lbs) in size, although larger smallmouth can be taken on the fly as well as lures. Fly fishing for smallmouth bass in Belwood Lake has become a popular attraction and there is truly nothing like hooking into a feisty smallmouth with a fly rod. The ensuing fight can be phenomenal. Access to Belwood Lake is from the Belwood Lake Conservation Area.

Berford Lake (Map 36/G6)
Due to the close proximity of this lake to the towns of Wiarton and Owen Sound, the lake receives significant angling pressure. Fishing

success is often slow for smallmouth bass, largemouth bass and northern pike. Bass are usually small in size, although they can certainly put up a good fight. Northern pike in the lake are scattered and range in size, from hammer handle size to the mid 2 kg (4.5 lb) range. Access to this lake is limited, although there are tent and trailer parks available along the lake.

Bluewater Lakes (Map 30/E6)
The Bluewater Lakes are a small chain of cool, clear lakes that are inhabited by brook trout. At the time of writing, it was unclear if access was permitted to the lakes. For locals, however, it is said that success can be quite good in these spring fed water bodies for some nice sized trout.

Boat Lake and Isaak Lake (Maps 33/F1, 36/F7)
These two interconnected lakes are popular fishing destinations. Boat Lake is accessible via the Boat Lake Road southwest of Wiarton or by County Road 13, which travels along the northern shore of the lake. Isaak Lake lies to the north of Boat Lake and can be reached by Isaak Lake Road off the west side of Highway 6. At the end of the road you will find a picnic area with a rough launch. Both lakes are very weedy and fishing can be good for smallmouth and largemouth bass. Both species seem to thrive amid the immense vegetation. Success really depends on if you can keep your gear from getting snagged. Northern pike and walleye also frequent these two lakes. Fishing seems to be hit and miss for pike, as some days they are quite aggressive while other days they are almost impossible to find.

Brantford Bass Ponds (Map 15/B1)
These small ponds are located just east of Brantford via Powerline Road. The ponds hold fair numbers of smallmouth and largemouth bass that average about 0.5 kg (1 lb) in size. Shore fishing is an option, although a canoe can greatly increase your chances for success.

Britain Lake (Map 39/C6)
Set only a kilometre inland form Dyer's Bay of the Georgian Bay, Britain Lake offers fishing for smallmouth and largemouth bass. Bass fishing can be good at times for above average sized bass. While fishing can be quite good, access can be a problem. Most of the lake is surrounded by heavy bush or private land making access difficult. Be sure to respect land owners wishes when visiting the lake.

Cameron Lake (Map 38/G4)
Cameron Lake lies within Bruce Peninsula National Park and is home to walleye and smallmouth bass. Success in the lake can be quite good on occasion for smallmouth, while fishing for walleye is generally fair. Smallmouth can be found up to 1.5 kg (3.5 lbs) in size, although average around 0.5 kg (1 lb). Walleye average about 1 kg (2 lb) in size with the odd 2+ kg (4.5+ lb) fish caught on occasion. Casting and jigging chartreuse or white coloured jigs can be effective. Be sure to check the regulations for special season restrictions before heading out.

Chesley Lake (Map 33/F4)
Chesley Lake is a very weedy lake that lies in a lowland area of the Bruce Peninsula. The lake is inhabited by smallmouth bass, walleye and northern pike. Fishing success for bass up to 2 kg (4.5 lb) in size is good. Fishing for walleye is generally fair for average sized pickerel, while success for pike can be slow at times. Currently there is a sanctuary period on the lake from December 15th to January 31st in order to reduce ice fishing catches. The lake is located east of Southampton just off County Road 14.

Claireville Reservoir (Map 27/C7)
Along with plenty of panfish, a fair population of largemouth bass exists in the Claireville Reservoir. Fishing is slow at times, although it does pick up on occasion. Bass are not usually very big, but the odd 2 kg (4 lb) bucket mouth can be caught. The reservoir was created by damming of the West Humber River near Malton. Access can be found from the Claireville Conservation Area.

Clam Lake (Map 23/E1)
You can find this lake south of Silver Lake and Highway 9 west of Walkerton. The lake offers fishing for smallmouth bass, largemouth bass and northern pike. A private tent and trailer ground is located on the lake and as a result, the lake receives significant pressure throughout the year. Fishing success is rumoured to be fair.

Conestogo Lake (Maps 20/A1, 25/A7)
The damming of the Conestogo River northwest of Kitchener/Waterloo created this popular recreational lake. Anglers visiting the lake can look forward to the opportunity to catch some big northern pike. Pike can reach over 75 cm (30 in) in size and average 3 kg (6 lbs). Fishing is generally quite good, especially in the spring. At this time, pike will cruise along the flooded shoreline areas of the lake and will strike well presented top water flies and lures.

Smallmouth bass fishing on Conestogo Lake can also be good for bass that can reach up to 2.5 kg (5 lbs) in size. Bass congregate near creek mouths and near any sort of underwater structure. Smallmouth can be taken on the fly regularly as they will chase down minnow, leech and other attractor type patterns. For spincasters, crankbaits and jigs can be quite productive. During overcast periods and in the evening, top water poppers and lures can create a lot of action on this lake.

Cyprus Lake (Map 38/G4)
Found within Bruce Peninsula National Park, Cyprus Lake is home to a large campground. As a result, the lake receives significantly more angling pressure than nearby Cameron Lake. Cyprus also offers fishing for both walleye and smallmouth bass. The fishing is usually a little slower but casting and jigging chartreuse or white coloured jigs can be effective. Be sure to check the regulations for special season restrictions before heading out.

Dankert Lake (Map 30/C7)
Dankert Lake is located north of Hanover not far off the west side of County Road 10. The lake is inhabited by a population of smallmouth bass, which provide for fair fishing most of the time. Bass in the lake are not very big but they like to hit hard. Be sure not to trespass.

**hiking
fishing
camping
hunting
archery**

Providing outdoor enthusiasts with serious gear for over 52 years.

Make the outdoors feel like home

AL FLAHERTY'S OUTDOOR STORE

2066 Dufferin Street, Toronto, ON M6E 3R6
phone: 416-651-6436   fax: 416-651-6454
info@alflahertys.com   www.alflahertys.com

Deer Creek Reservoir (Map 8/D2)

South of the town of Delhi, the Deer Creek Reservoir can be found off the west side of County Road 59 at the Deer Creek Conservation Area. Fishing in the reservoir is quite good for panfish, while a population of largemouth bass also exists in the water body. Using light tackle and gear can make fishing this reservoir a lot of fun. Try jigs and smaller sized spinner baits for success. The odd brown trout is also caught on occasion.

Durham Town Pond (Map 30/G7)

This small pond is stocked with brook trout that can be caught in the 20 cm (8 in) range. The pond is found right in town at the conservation area. Small bead head nymph flies and spinners work well in the spring and fall.

Emmett Lake (Map 39/A4)

Some big northern pike can be found in this Bruce Peninsula National Park lake. Fishing for northerns can be good at times and there is always a chance to catch a pike over 5 kg (10 lbs) in size. Fishing can be even better for smallmouth bass that range between 0.5 & 2 kg (1 & 4 lbs). Access to Emmett Lake is from Emmett Lake Road off Highway 6.

Eugenia Lake (Map 31/E5)

Brown trout, brook trout and rainbow trout have all been stocked in Eugenia Lake at one time. Today, rainbow trout are the only species that are being stocked. There are occasional reports of brook trout being caught but rainbow seem to provide most of the action, especially during the spring and through the ice in winter. In the spring, try trolling a small spoon like a Little Cleo or work a minnow type fly pattern towards shore.

Smallmouth and largemouth bass also inhabit Eugenia Lake in significant numbers. Fishing for bass in the lake is usually good for fish that average 0.5-1 kg (1-2 lbs) and can be found up to 2 kg (4.5 lbs) on occasion. Bass can be taken on the standard spincasting tackle such as spinner and jigs, while top water lures can be a lot of fun on this lake. Check for special season regulations before heading out.

Fairy Lake (Map 21/D2)

Right in the town of Acton, Fairy Lake offers fishing opportunities for panfish and bass. Largemouth bass are the main bass species found in the lake and fishing can be good on occasion. Largemouth average 0.5-1 kg (1-2 lbs) in size and can be found bigger. During slow days, try something subtle like a tube jig or a leech type fly pattern. A canoe can greatly add to your success on this lake.

Fanshawe Lake (Map 13/A3)

Fanshawe Lake is a man-made reservoir created by the damming of the Thames River. The main sportfish species found in the lake are smallmouth and largemouth bass. Bass can reach up to 2 kg (4.5 lbs) but average around 1 kg (2 lbs). Try using a tube jig on slower days worked along bottom structure. For fly anglers, a big leech pattern with some crystal flash can be effective. The lake also holds some good size northern pike and walleye. Pike average 60 cm (24 in), but can reach over 90 cm (36 in) in size. If you catch a tagged walleye, please report the catch to the conservation area office. The lake is readily accessible north of the city of London. The main access is from the Fanshawe Conservation Area.

Feversham Town Pond (Map 31/G5)

Near the town of Feversham, anglers can try their luck in the stocked trout pond. The pond is stocked regularly with brook trout and fishing can be good at times for fish over 20 cm (8 in) in size. Try a small spinner or silver bead head nymph fly pattern.

Flesherton Community Pond (Map 31/D6)

This small pond is stocked with brook trout that provide for good fishing, especially in the spring. Brookies are usually caught in the 20 cm (8 in) range, although bigger trout are available. Small bead head nymph flies work well in the spring and fall. The pond is accessible off County Road 4, just south of Flesherton.

Francis Lake (Map 34/B1)

Anglers will find fair to good fishing on occasion for smallmouth bass that average 0.5 kg (1 lb) in size. Bigger bass are hard to find. Northern pike can also be found in the lake, although fishing is often slow. Decent sized pike have been reportedly caught in the lake, but they are generally small. There are a number of cottages and camps on Francis Lake and access is limited. Be sure to ask permission before crossing any private lands.

George Lake (Map 39/A5)

George Lake is home to a fair population of smallmouth bass, largemouth bass and northern pike. Some good size bass are caught in the lake regularly. Access to George Lake may be limited since a portion of the lake lies within the Cape Croker First Nations Hunting Ground. Please check locally before trying to access the lake.

Georgian Bay (Maps 34, 35, 36, 37, 38, 39)

Over the past century, fishing in Georgian Bay has become a mutli-million dollar industry. So popular is this fishery that many forget the bay is part of Lake Huron. The bay offers healthy populations of popular game fish such as lake trout, rainbow trout, chinook salmon and walleye. Trolling for these species is the most common and effective way in finding success throughout the year. In the spring rainbow and chinook cruise along the limestone shorelines as they prepare for their journey up one of the many spawning streams in the region. Shore anglers can cast a bag of roe with a strike indicator and wait for big trout or salmon to swing by. One area in particular that is good for finding these offshore cruisers is between the towns of Collingwood and Meaford.

Georgian Bay is also home to some very good smallmouth and largemouth bass fishing. Bass in the 2-3 kg (3-6 lb) range are common and they can be caught in the many bays and sounds such as Owen Sound, Melville Sound and Colpoy's Bay. Try a tube jig or crayfish imitation along rocky shore structure or underwater rock piles for big smallmouth. Large northern pike are also caught throughout Georgian Bay, especially along shoreline structure areas in the spring and fall periods.

Gillies Lake (Map 39/D5)

Much of the property surrounding Gillies Lake is privately owned; however, there is a tent and trailer park on the lake that will allow access for a fee. Anglers can expect to find smallmouth bass and lake trout in the lake. Fishing is best for smallmouth bass as they hold up in certain areas around the lake. Try flipping jigs along rock walls and other structure to find ambush ready smallmouth. Lake trout are both natural and stocked. While it is possible to hook a lake trout from shore by casting in the spring, action is best when trolling silver spoons with a downrigger, especially during the summer. Please practice catch and release if you land a native trout. Other trout species have been stocked in the lake in the past, but there have been no recent reports their survival. Be sure to check the regulations.

Gould Lake (Map 33/G3)

Gould Lake is a weedy, marsh like lake that is located southeast of Sauble Beach. Smallmouth and largemouth bass are found in the lake in fair numbers, while success for walleye and northern pike can be slow at times. Bass average 0.5-1 kg (1-2 lbs), while walleye and northern pike tend to be smaller than average. There are cabins and camps along the shore of Gould Lake. Access is best via the tent and trailer park located off County Road 14.

Guelph Lake (Map 21/A2)

Perhaps one of the most overlooked fishing spots in the region is Guelph Lake. The lake is home to a healthy population of bass and also sports a decent northern pike population. Since the lake is a reservoir, there is plenty of old stumps and other underwater debris creating ideal habitat for big bass. Smallmouth bass can be found in the deeper waters around the lake and can be enticed with presentations of tube jigs or other deeper type lures. There is also plenty of shoreline structure to hold largemouth bass. Try flipping spinner baits or even top water flies and lures along the shoreline during dusk and overcast periods. Some big bass in the 1.5 kg (3.5 lb) range are caught regularly in Guelph Lake. While casting for bass, many anglers also hook into the odd northern pike. Pike fishing in the lake is generally fair for pike that average around 45 cm (16 in) in size. The lake is accessible from the Guelph Lake Conservation Area.

Habermehl Lake (Map 30/D7)

This small lake can be found north of Hanover and is accessible north of Concession 6. The lake is home to a fair smallmouth bass population and can provide some entertaining fishing especially with a fly rod. Try stripping in small minnow patterns or even bug patterns like a dragonfly nymph. Please respect private property.

Heart Lake (Map 27/A7)

Heart Lake is stocked regularly with rainbow trout, which provide for some fair to good fishing at times. Fly fishing is a fine way to try to hook into one of these feisty rainbows. For spincasters, small spinners also work well. Heart Lake also holds a good population of largemouth bass that average about 0.5-1 kg (1-2 lbs) and can reach up to 1.5 kg (3.5 lbs). During the summer months, largemouth bass are the main sportfish caught as rainbow become less active when the water warms. The lake is accessible from the Heart Lake Conservation Area.

Holstein Pond (Map 25/A2)

The Holstein Pond is located north of Mount Forest off County Road 109. The small pond is stocked with brook trout and fishing can be good, especially by fly fishing in the spring. Brookies are usually caught in the 20 cm (8 in) range.

Irish Lake (Map 31/C6)

Rainbow trout are stocked in Irish Lake every few years and provide for fair to good fishing throughout the season. Rainbow average around 22 cm (9 in) in size and are best caught on the fly with a small bead head nymph pattern. For spincasters, a small spinner can be productive as well. A population of smallmouth bass share this lake with the trout and sometimes can dominate the action. Most bass are quite small. Access to this lake is found off the Artemesia-Glenelg Townline. There are special season regulations on this lake.

Tall Tales

LIVE BAIT & TACKLE

WILD TURKEY & DEER HUNTING GEAR

Minnows, Worms, Leech's
Maggots, Wax Worms

Complete Selection of Fishing Tackle

310 King St. E. (at Eagle) Cambridge, ON N3H 3M8
(519) 650-3465 www.talltales.on.ca

Island Lake (Orangeville Reservoir) (Map 26/D4)

Located just outside the town of Orangeville, Island Lake can be accessed at the Island Lake Conservation Area found along the southeastern shore of the lake. Fishing in the lake is generally fair for largemouth bass and northern pike. Bass in the lake can be found along shoreline structure such as docks and submerged trees and average around 0.5-1 kg (1-2 lbs) in size. Pike can reach over 60 cm (24 in) in size and are often caught by bass anglers working the shoreline. Pike will cruise shoreline areas, especially in the evening, in search of food. Try spinners and bait for both species or on slow days, tube jigs can work well for largemouth.

Jack's Lake (Map 32/E2)

As part of the Nottawasaga River system, Jack's Lake holds walleye during certain times of the year. Northern pike, smallmouth bass and largemouth bass are also found in the lake in consistent numbers. Since the lake is actually an extended portion of the Nottawasaga River, access is limited to mainly canoes and other small water craft.

Lakelet Lake (Map 24/C4)

You can find Lakelet Lake west of the village of Clifford via the Fordwich Line (County Road 30). A number of tent and trailer parks are located on the lake and a few offer access to the lake for a fee. Fishing in the lake is fair for decent sized smallmouth bass.

Lake Erie (Maps 1, 2, 3, 5, 6, 7, 8, 9, 15, 16, 17)

Once considered a shallow, murky polluted waterbody, Lake Erie has certainly been cleaned up over the past several decades. Today, it is one of the cleaner Great Lakes, and as a result, the sportfishing industry is thriving. The main sportfish anglers are after in the lake are walleye, but lake trout and coho salmon are quite popular as well. Lake trout are restricted mainly to the eastern portion of the lake, while coho runs have been established along both the south and northern shores.

The most overlooked fishing opportunity on Lake Erie is its bass. The big lake is home to some of the best smallmouth and largemouth bass fishing in the province and perhaps Canada. Big bass, upwards of 3 kg (6 lbs), are common. The best way to find success for bass is to locate structure such as underwater rock formations or even man-made debris like a shipwreck. Work a tube jig or crayfish imitation along these areas and you will certainly have success.

There is plenty of big water to fish in Lake Erie and anglers often overlook the shoreline areas. Big bass and northern pike can be found roaming the many bays and weedy shore areas such as Rondeau Bay and Long Point.

Lake Huron (Maps 10, 11, 18, 23, 29, 31, 32, 33, 34, 35, 36, 38, 39)

The sheer size of Lake Huron has helped it remain one of the cleanest Great Lakes. The lake draws thousands of anglers to its waters annually, many who visit the Georgian Bay. Most anglers are after the salmonids: rainbow trout, lake trout, chinook salmon and pink salmon. During the spring, the feeder streams into the lake are home to some of the largest salmon and rainbow trout runs in the Great Lakes. At this time, some areas literally see hundreds of anglers line the banks in search of big trout and salmon.

In the open water, trolling with down rigging equipment is popular for lake trout, rainbow trout and chinook salmon. The lake produces some big fish with many reaching over 5 kg (10 lb) in size. Some nice sized brown trout can also be caught along the Huron/Bruce County areas. Only lake trout are natural to the lake, while brown trout and pink salmon have established naturally regenerating populations. All of the other trout and salmon species have been introduced and stocking is required to maintain the quality fishery.

Walleye are another popular sportfish sought after in Lake Huron, but few anglers realize that there is also a good fishery for bass and pike. Areas around Owen Sound, Tobermory, Meaford, Collingwood and Wiarton offer some of the best bass fishing opportunities in the province.

Lake Lisgar (Map 14/A7)

Set right in the middle of the town of Tillsonburg, Lake Lisgar is a warm water lake. While panfish and carp are the main species found in the lake, there are opportunities to hook into a marginal sized largemouth bass.

Lake Ontario (Maps 16, 17, 22, 28)

Lake Ontario has gone through a tremendous transformation over the past 20 years. In the not too distant past, sportfishing in the lake was all but dead. Natural lake trout stocks had dwindled, and walleye and northern pike had lost large portions of their range. However, with the introduction of non-native species, the lake has flourished and now makes up a considerable portion of Southern Ontario's sportfishing opportunities. Rainbow trout, brown trout and pacific salmon are well established and offer some of the best fishing opportunities in the province. In fact, when the rainbow trout and chinook salmon run into feeder creeks, anglers from around the province come for a chance to catch a big fish. Along with significant northern pike and bass populations, the shoreline areas of the big lake have plenty to offer anglers. Lake trout fishing near the mouth of the Niagara River has also become one of the best areas in Ontario to catch large lakers.

Lake St. Clair (Maps 1, 2, 4)

With the cities of Detroit, London and Windsor so close, it is amazing how resilient Lake St. Clair remains. The big lake remains a good destination for a day out on the water. The main sportfish pursued by anglers is walleye. With some luck and patience, good size walleye can still be found in the lake. Perch are also a big draw to the lake, especially in the winter for ice fishing.

Perhaps the best but least known fishery available in Lake St. Clair is its bass fishery. Both smallmouth and largemouth bass are found in the lake in good numbers. If you can find the right holding areas, the fishing will rival any bass lake in Ontario. Any sort of underwater rock structure or shoreline structure is sure to hold bass. Bass in this lake often reach 2 kg (5 lbs) in size.

Lake St. Clair is also known to hold northern pike and big muskellunge. Musky provide for good fishing if you know where to look, while

northerns are often caught along shoreline structure. Pike do reach 10 kg (22 lbs) in size on occasion. Be sure to check the regulations thoroughly before fishing in Lake St. Clair, as a number of special regulations apply.

Lake Scugog (Map 28/G1)

Although we only capture a portion of Lake Scugog in this book, it is worth mentioning since it is one of the more productive fishing areas in Southern Ontario. The large lake is very weedy, allowing for good fishing for largemouth and smallmouth bass that average in the 1 kg (2 lb) range. Largemouth are more abundant in the southern portion of the lake. Walleye fishing can be good, especially during the extensive ice fishing season, for fish averaging around 1-2 kg (2-5 lbs). Yellow perch are in abundance and fishing for perch is also good during ice fishing season. Lake Scugog is also renowned for its muskellunge fishing that can be quite good at times. Muskellunge are the largest fish in the lake averaging 3-4 kg (6-9 lbs), although every year a fair number of 10 kg (20 lb) musky are caught. To find out more about this lake, be sure to pick up a copy of "Fishing Ontario for the Kawarthas". It highlights this and several of the better lakes in the area with invaluable depth charts and other handy information.

Louise Lakes (Map 30/E6)

Northwest of Durham, the Concession 6 Road travels right between these two lakes. While you can access the lakes form the road, please be sure to respect landowner's wishes. Fishing in the lakes is fair at times for average sized smallmouth bass. Fly fishing for these smallmouth with a light fly rod is a lot of fun.

Markdale Town Pond (Map 31/B5)

The Markdale Town Pond is accessible off County Road 12, south of Markdale. The pond is stocked with brook trout and fishing can be good, especially in the spring. Brookies are usually caught in the 20 cm (8 in) range, although bigger trout are available.

Marl Lakes (Map 30/D7)

This chain of small lakes is located just north of the town of Hanover. The lakes were once known as smallmouth bass and trout lakes, although the dominant sportfish these days is largemouth bass. Largemouth are actually doing quite well in the lakes and fishing is fair to good at times for average sized bass. Try top water flies and lures during overcast periods or in the evening to entice exciting breakwater strikes.

Martindale Pond (Map 17/B1)

Martendale Pond is a large, marshy water body located in the northwest end of St. Catherines. While shoreline fishing opportunities do exist, it is best to get out there in a small boat or canoe to really work the shoreline areas. Anglers will find plenty of panfish, smallmouth and largemouth bass as well as northern pike. If you are looking for bass or pike, try working the weed structure.

McCullough Lake (Map 30/F4)

McCullough Lake is inhabited by natural populations of northern pike and smallmouth bass, while it is also stocked with splake. The brook trout/lake trout hybrid, splake, provides good fishing at times, especially in the winter. Try jigging small silver spoons through the ice for both splake and northern pike. Splake are usually caught in the 30 cm (12 in) range, while there are some nice sized pike available in the lake. During the summer, smallmouth bass add to the action and average about 0.5 kg (1 lb) in size. For smallmouth, spinners and jigs work well or try fly fishing with a clauser minnow or top water popper. To reach the lake, take McCullough Lake Road west off Highway 6, south of Owen Sound.

McNab Lake (Map 34/B2)

Northern pike and largemouth bass can be found in this Grey County lake. The lake is quite marshy, providing the perfect cover for the fish. Through research of the region, mixed opinions were offered on McNab Lake and the actual fishing quality is sort of a mystery. The lake is located northwest of Owen Sound, although access is limited. Be sure to ask permission before crossing private land.

Miller Lake (Map 39/B7)

Fishing in Miller Lake is generally fair for smallmouth bass but can be slow for northern pike at times. Bass average around 0.5 kg (1 lb), while pike are normally in the 45 cm (18 in) range, although can definitely be found bigger. The lake is quite large as it is over 3 km (1.9 mi) in length and has a number of camps and cottages along its shoreline. There are a few tent and trailer parks that offer launching for a fee. Alternatively, the picnic area along the east side of the lake can be used for canoe access.

Minkes Lake (Map 30/F4)

Surprisingly, this small lake has a population of northern pike. The lake is located just north of the larger McCullough Lake, although access is limited. Be sure to ask permission from private landowners before heading out to the lake.

Morrison Dam (Map 18/D6)

A small reservoir has been created by the Morrison Dam along the Ausable River east of Exeter. The reservoir holds a population of smallmouth bass that can be quite active on occasion. Although the bass are not usually large, they often put up a great fight. The reservoir is also stocked every few years with rainbow trout. Rainbow average about 25-30 cm (10-12 in) in size and can be taken on the fly or with lures.

Mountain Lake (Map 34/B1)

Anglers visiting Mountain Lake can expect to catch smallmouth bass and the odd walleye. Fishing for smallmouth is regarded as fair and can be good at times for bass that average around 1 kg (2 lbs) in size. Look for smallies along shoreline structure and even near man-made structures such as boat docks. Walleye fishing is often slow but the prized sportfish can reach up to 60 cm (24 in) in size. Jigging can be effective at times or try a slow troll with a worm harness for ambush ready walleye. Access to Mountain Lake is off Concession 17 Road or from the tent and trailer park located along the north shore of the lake.

Mountsberg Reservoir (Map 21/D4)

Visitors to the Mountsberg Conservation Area west of Milton can enjoy fishing in the reservoir. The reservoir is quite marshy in areas and is home to a population of largemouth bass. Fishing is fair at times for bass that can reach over 1.5 kg (4 lbs) in size. Fishing with top water flies or lures can create a flurry of action during summer evenings.

Musselman Lake (Map 28/B2)

North of the town of Stouffville anglers can find Mussleman Lake off the 9th Line Road (County Road 69). The lake is a popular spot with three tent and trailer parks surrounding the lake. Smallmouth bass and largemouth bass inhabit the lake, although fishing is usually slow for below average sized bass. Panfish make up the bulk of the action and can be a lot of fun with a fly rod.

Nottawasaga Bay (Maps 31, 32, 35,)

The Nottawasaga Bay is a part of the Georgian Bay portion of Lake Huron and is renowned for its recreation opportunities. Fishing near the many river and creek mouths can be quite productive for chinook salmon and rainbow trout, and to a lesser degree brown trout. The bay also holds good populations of yellow perch along with the odd pink salmon, coho salmon, lake trout, and splake reported annually. During spring and fall, the Nottawasaga and Pretty River areas offer good fishing for rainbows and chinook to 15 kg (33 lbs) in size. The Collingwood Harbour and pier area offers good fishing for smallmouth bass to 2 kg (4.5 lbs) and walleye averaging 2 kg (4.5 lbs).

Otter Lake (Map 39/C6)

Surrounded by heavy bush or private land, access to Otter Lake is difficult. As a result, bass fishing can be good at times for above average size smallmouth and largemouth bass. Please respect land owners' wishes when visiting these lakes.

Pearl Lake (Map 30/C7)

Pearl Lake is stocked periodically with rainbow trout, which provide for

FISHING ONTARIO
Collection of Best Fishing Lakes

Eastern Ontario

Kawarthas

Muskoka

Depth Charts
Fishing Tips
Access
Hatches
Stocking

To Order
visit your local retailer or contact:
phone: **(604)-438-FISH**
toll free: **1-877-520-5670**

www.backroadmapbooks.com

generally fair fishing. A population of smallmouth bass also inhabits the lake and success is also normally fair. Spinners as well as streamer type fly patterns can work for both species. Pearl Lake is located north of Hanover, not far off County Road 10. The lake is surrounded by private property and permission is required to access it.

Pinehurst Lake (Map 20/G7)

Pinehurst Lake offers fishing opportunities for panfish and bass. Largemouth bass are the main bass species found in the lake and fishing can be good on occasion. Bass average 0.5 kg (1 lb) in size but can be found bigger. Top water presentations, such as fly poppers and popping minnow type lures can create a frenzy of action. The lake is accessible south of Cambridge off the east side of County Road 75 at the Pinehurst Lake Conservation Area.

Pittock Reservoir (Map 14/A2)

This large reservoir near Woodstock was created by the damming of the Thames River. The Pittock Conservation Area along the northeast side of the reservoir provides good access. Fishing in the reservoir can be quite productive at times, especially for smallmouth and largemouth bass. They are active feeders throughout the reservoir and average 1 kg (2 lbs) in size. Northern pike also exist in the lake and can reach over 90 cm (36 in) in size on occasion. While shore fishing is possible, a canoe would increase your chances for success dramatically.

Professor's Lake (Map 27/B7)

Professor's Lake lies in the north end of the suburb of Bramelea. The lake is accessible from a small marina along the eastern shore and offers fishing opportunities for panfish and largemouth bass. While panfish are quite abundant, the odd largemouth bass in the 1 kg (2 lb) range is caught on occasion.

Puslinch Lake (Map 21/A5)

The main sportfish found in the lake are smallmouth and largemouth bass. Bass can provide for some decent action at times and are a lot of fun to catch with a fly rod. Muskellunge once roamed this lake, although today northern pike have taken over their role as the dominant predator in the lake. Fishing is slow to fair for pike that can reach up to 2 kg (4.5 lb) in size. Remarkably, a natural population of walleye also remains in Puslinch Lake. Fishing for walleye is slow and it is highly recommended to release any walleye caught to help maintain the species.

Robson Lakes (Maps 31/A3, 35/A7)

The Robson Lakes are a collection of small lakes found southeast of Owen Sound. The lakes are stocked with splake, the brook trout/lake trout hybrid and are also inhabited with northern pike. Northern pike are usually small in size and fishing is usually fair. Both pike and splake will hit under the ice and are active springtime feeders. Splake are usually a little more active at these times but are harder to find in the summer. Pike, on the other hand, will be active during overcast periods and in the evenings during the summer.

Rockwood Pond (Map 21/C2)

Rockwood Pond is stocked annually with rainbow trout, which provide for some decent fishing opportunities throughout the year. Smallmouth bass can be found below the dam and pond at the conservation area. Bass are usually small, but can put up a great fight when hooked.

Silver Lake (Map 23/E1)

You can find this lake off the south side of Highway 9 west of Walkerton. The lake offers fair fishing for smallmouth bass, largemouth bass and northern pike. A private tent and trailer ground is located on the lake and as a result, the lake receives significant pressure throughout the year.

Sky Lake (Map 36/F6)

Anglers visiting Sky Lake can expect to find fair to good fishing at times for smallmouth bass. Bass average 0.5-1 kg (1-2 lbs) and can literally be found almost anywhere in the lake. Walleye and northern pike are also found in Sky Lake in fair numbers. Pike sometimes shock bass anglers by veraciously striking bass flies/lures. The weedy nature of Sky Lake provides ideal habitat for all of these species; however, it also makes consistent fishing success a real challenge. Anglers are advised to use top water or weedless lures and flies.

Spry Lake (Map 36/E7)

Due to the close proximity and easy access to Spry Lake from Wiarton, the lake receives significant angling pressure throughout the year. Smallmouth bass and largemouth bass are the main species found in the lake and range from 0.5-1 kg (1-2 lbs) up to 2 kg (4 lbs). Northern pike are also found in the lake but fishing is regarded as slow. For better success on the lake, work the shallows near any type of structure, especially during dusk or overcast periods.

Valens Reservoir (Map 21/C6)

Valens Reservoir is a man-made lake that offers fishing opportunities for largemouth bass and northern pike. Bass average around 0.5-1 kg (1-2 lbs) in size, while northern pike have been known to reach the 75 cm (30 in) range. Fishing for both species is best during overcast periods or in the evening at dusk. Top water lures and flies can be a lot of fun on this lake. The reservoir is found east of Cambridge and is surrounded by the Valens Conservation Area.

Waterford Ponds (Map 14/G6)

Access to the Waterford Ponds can be found at Izzy's Conservation Area west of the town of Waterford. The ponds offer good fishing at times for some nice sized largemouth bass. Bass average around 1 kg (2 lbs) but can reach up to 2 kg (4.5 lbs). Tube jigs and other jigs are the standard, although larger presentations such as a crankbait or spinner bait often will find the bigger bass.

Wawanosh Lake (Map 23/D5)

Fishing success in Wawanosh Lake is regarded as fair to good at times for northern pike and smallmouth bass. Bass average 0.5 kg (1 lb) in size, while pike can reach over 2 kg (4.5 lbs) on occasion. Spinners can be productive for both species while fly anglers will find any bright minnow pattern can work well. Access to the lake is via the Wawanosh Lake Conservation Area west of Wingham.

Wilcox Lake (Map 27/G4)

Wilcox Lake is a headwater lake to the East Humber River and offers fishing opportunities for panfish and largemouth bass. Bass in the lake average 1 kg (2 lbs) in size and are reported to reach up to 2 kg (4.5 lbs). The lake is located south of Aurora off King Road.

Wilcox Lake (Map 31/D7)

Wilcox Lake is stocked regularly with brook trout, which provide for good fishing at times during the spring and through the ice in winter. During the summer months, fishing slows considerably before picking up again in the fall. Fly anglers can have plenty of success at this lake, as brookies will aggressively take fly presentations in the spring. Try a minnow type pattern or even a mid sized bead head nymph. Check the regulations for the special season on this lake.

Wilder Lake (Map 25/A1)

Wilder Lake has been heavily stocked with brook trout and as a result fishing success can be good at times. Fly anglers can have a lot of fun at this lake, as brookies are very aggressive during the spring, just after ice off. You can get them on the fly and on lures in the summer, although they are often lethargic during the day. In the evening brookies will often move closer to shore in search of insects.

Smallmouth bass are also found in the lake in fair numbers. Bass are usually small, although they can surprise you occasionally. A few flies that may do well here are a simple bead head nymph or a larger fly like a leech. Spincasters will often have success for both trout and bass with small spinners. Be sure to consult the fishing regulations for the special season available on Wilder Lake.

Wildwood Lake (Maps 13/D1, 19C7)

Wildwood Lake was formed by the damming of the Thames River just east of St. Mary's. Fishing for smallmouth and largemouth bass can be good at times, especially during overcast periods or in the evening at dusk. Largemouth are the main bass species found and they can be a lot of fun on this lake. Look for heavy shoreline structure such as logs or other types of debris and cast a jig or spinner bait nearby to entice ambush ready bass. Largemouth have been known to reach up to 2 kg (4.5 lbs).

If you are looking for big fish, Wildwood Lake also offers a healthy population of the northern pike. Pike can be found in the 75+ cm (30+ in) range, although average around 45-60 cm (18-24 in). Try trolling a gold spoon along shorelines, especially in the evening.

Williams Lake (Map 30/G4)

The Williams Lake Conservation Area lies along the southeastern shore of Williams Lake and provides access to the lake. The conservation area is notable for its sandy beach and outdoor recreation opportunities, which includes fishing. The lake is stocked regularly with brook trout and also holds a natural population of smallmouth bass. Fishing for brookies can be good in the spring just after ice off or even through the ice in the winter. Smallmouth bass begin to hit just after the season opens and can be taken on a variety of presentations. Try a small attractor type fly patterns or smaller spinners for both species. Special season regulations apply. Check your regulations before heading out.

the fishin' hole

"Everything for Sportfishing"

Get your FREE Fishing Catalogue!

Call 1.800.661.6954

Edmonton, Saskatoon & Winnipeg

"Shop Online!" www.thefishinhole.com

Streams

The best opportunities for sportfishing in Southwestern Ontario are found in the region's rivers and creeks. Many of the larger rivers offer spring steelhead (sea-run rainbow trout) runs and fall salmon runs that can produce some big fish. There are also runs of brown trout along with resident brook, brown and rainbow trout. In the slower, meandering streams, warm water species like bass and northern pike are common.

While some rivers are quite popular and can be overcrowded at times, there are plenty of smaller hidden streams out there for anglers to explore. The main obstacle to the streams in this region is access. The majority of land in the region is private and public access is often limited. The best way around this issue is to fish near road crossings or by asking permission for access. Whatever you do, please do not trespass.

Below we have covered the main river and creek systems in Southwestern Ontario, but there are many more feeder streams out there that offer fishing opportunities. A large number of feeder streams, especially in the Niagara Escarpment area north of Highway 401, are home to populations of brook trout or brown trout or both. The best way to find these hidden gems is to get out and explore.

Ausable River (Maps 10/inset, 11/E1-G3, 12/A3-C1, 18/C7-G5)

The Ausable River is better known for its bass and northern pike, although a run of chinook salmon does enter the river each fall. The river is accessible from many locations and flows through the heart of Grand Bend on its way to Lake Huron.

Bannockburn River (Map 18/F4-C3)

A fair population of smallmouth bass can be found in the Bannockburn River. Bass average around 0.5 kg (1 lb) in size and can be a lot of fun to catch on the fly or with a light spincasting outfit. A population of northern pike also exist in the river, although pike are usually small and fishing is spotty. Some areas you can find decent numbers of pike, although they are scattered. The river is accessible from the many bridges southeast of Bayfield.

Batteaux Creek (Map 32/B3)

The Batteaux Creek is also known as the Batteaux River and is rumoured to have a resident population of brook trout. During spring, the steelhead run can be good if water levels permit. These sea-run rainbow can reach up to 5 kg (11 lbs) in size although are usually found smaller.

Bayfield River (Map 18/G4-A3)

The Bayfield River offers good fishing for smallmouth bass throughout the summer months, although its big attraction is its runs of steelhead and salmon. Steelhead migrate up the river in good numbers in the spring, while chinook and a fair run of coho run in the fall. Unlike some other area rivers, the Bayfield is not overly busy. There are also a few local feeder creeks that see both steelhead and salmon migration. Some of these streams have resident brook trout. Be sure to check the regulations on this river before heading out.

Beatty Saugeen River (Maps 25/B1-24/D1)

A decent run of steelhead that average over 2 kg (4.5 lbs) in size is available on the Beatty. After spawning season your best bet is to head to the upper reaches of the river where most of the resident brown trout are found. There is a spring fishing sanctuary on this river.

Beaver River (Map 31/G5-F1)

Beaver River flows north from the rolling hills of the Beaver Valley to Nottawasaga Bay at Thornbury. The river below the dam in Thornbury is a busy spot during the spring steelhead runs. The migratory trout can be a lot of fun to catch, as long as you have room to fight it. The dam area is not quite as busy during the chinook salmon run in fall. Above the dam and south into the Beaver Valley anglers can look forward to fishing for the river's resident brook trout and brown trout.

Belle River (Map 1/G3)

This rural river flows north from near Cottam into Lake St. Clair at the town of Belle River. Since the shoreline of the river has been extensively deforested for farming, the quality of fishing has been adversely affected. Anglers can find some success near the mouth for the odd northern pike as well as smallmouth and largemouth bass.

Big Creek (Maps 14/D4-8/F4)

Big Creek is home to perhaps the largest spring steelhead run on Lake Erie. Over the years habitat rehabilitation has definitely helped to improve this fishery. The long stream is also home to many other species. Brown trout are also found in the creek during their summer migration and there are a few resident browns found periodically. Around Delhi, brook trout are being reported, while smallmouth bass and the odd northern pike are mainly found closer to Lake Erie. Check the regulations before fishing Big Creek as there is a winter/spring fishing sanctuary on the entire creek and a fall sanctuary period on a portion of the creek.

Big Otter Creek (Maps 7/G1-8/A3, 14/D4-A7)

Although the Big Otter Creek begins northeast of Tillsonburg, it is lower reaches of the creek that offer better fishing for the smallmouth bass. The stretch south from the village of Richmond through Port Burwell Provincial Park and into Lake Erie offers bass that average around 0.5 kg (1 lb) in size. The odd northern pike and largemouth bass can also be found in the river.

Bighead River (Maps 30/G2, 31/B1, 34/G7, 35/B4)

Entering Lake Huron and Nottawasaga Bay in the town of Meaford, the Bighead is a popular fishing destination. In the spring there is a fantastic steelhead run that attracts hundreds of anglers. Big steelhead are mainly caught using roe and a float, although ardent fly anglers can have success. It is quite a challenge to land one of these feisty steelhead as they will literally launch out of the river and take off up and down the river to try to get loose. In the fall, the action continues as there is a significant chinook salmon run available. The odd steelhead can also be caught at this time. Angling options also exist upstream for resident brown trout and brook trout. Please practice catch and release with these beautiful steelhead and resident trout. Check for sanctuary times.

Black Creek (Map 18/D5)

Black Creek is a tributary of the Ausable River and has a small population of northern pike. The pike in the river are not very big, although they can be fun to catch with light fishing gear. The creek is part of a spring fishing sanctuary.

Blyth Brook (Map 23/D7)

Blyth Brook is a rehabilitated stream that sees a decent steelhead and chinook run. In spring, the sea-run rainbow can be found over 2 kg (4.5 lbs), while in fall the big chinook can easily reach 5 kg (11 lbs). Fishing with roe sacs is the preferred method. During the summer months, the resident brown trout and brook trout populations can certainly be entertaining. Use light gear to catch these smaller trout and you are sure to have some fun.

Bourgoyne Creek (Maps 33/E7 & 29/G3)

West of Port Elgin, Bourgoyne Creek has a fair population of resident smallmouth bass. Bass in the creek are usually small, although they can be a lot of fun to catch on light gear. The creek flows through private land for most of its entirety, but access is provided at the few road crossings over the creek.

Bronte Creek (Maps 21/C5-22/B6)

North of Lowville, Bronte Creek offers fishing for resident brown trout and brook trout. However, the main attraction to the creek is the spring steelhead and fall salmon runs. In fall, anglers can expect decent runs of chinook salmon mixed in with the odd coho. There is also a summer brown trout migration as well as some smallmouth bass that can be caught closer to Lake Ontario. The only downfall of this river is the fact that the lower reaches flow through heavily developed areas making the scenery not so pleasing. There are also portions of the creek that are currently closed to fishing as well as a fall to spring sanctuary period. Check the regulations.

Carrick Creek (Map 24/D2)

This small cool running stream is home to a fair population of brook trout. Brookies in the creek average around 20 cm (8 in) in size and will take flies and worms. Small bead head presentations can work quite well. The creek flows into the South Saugeen River south of Hanover.

Catfish Creek (Map 7/F1-D3)

In the lower reaches of Catfish Creek, there are largemouth bass averaging around 0.5 kg (1 lb) in size. Of course larger bass are caught regularly. The creek flows south from near Aylmer to Lake Erie at Port Bruce. A popular access area is from the Archie Coulter Conservation Area west of Aylmer.

Clavering Creek (Maps 36/G7-33/G2)

From the north end of Boat Lake, Clavering Creek flows south eventually entering the Sauble River east of Sauble Beach. The creek offer fishing opportunities for brown trout and brook trout. Brookies in the creek are usually small, although some nice size but finicky browns live in the creek.

Colpoy's Creek (Map 37/A6)

This small stream flows south into Colpoy's Bay. The creek is home to a population of brook trout and rainbow trout. The trout are generally small in size and fishing is slow to fair. Flies and small hooks with worms both provide results. A portion of this creek is closed to fishing. Be sure to check the regulations.

Conestogo River (Maps 25/D6-20/D3)

This big river flows south from the town of Arthur all the way into the Grand River north of Kitchener/Waterloo. The river is home to good populations of northern pike and smallmouth bass. The larger pike are actually caught where the river has been dammed to make Conestogo Lake, while smallmouth bass average 0.5-1 kg (1-2 lbs) throughout the system. The best sections of the river are from just north of Conestogo Lake all the way to where the river meets the Grand River.

Crane River (Maps 39/C4-38/G7)

The lower stretches of the Crane River, west of Crane Lake, support a variety of trout. Fishing is fair for small brook trout, rainbow trout and the odd brown trout, which all average 20 cm (8 in) in size. Try small nymph flies or small spinners.

Credit River (Maps 26/D4-22/D3)

The Credit River is best known for its good spring steelhead and fall chinook salmon runs. During these periods anglers crowd the urban Mississauga stream to get a crack at catching the big fish. Other than the spawning runs, the lower portions of the river also offer fishing opportunities for largemouth bass, smallmouth bass and the odd northern pike.

As you venture further north out of the city, several more angling opportunities arise. Resident brook trout can be found in many of the river's tributaries including the **Black Creek, Upper Credit, West Credit** and **Little Credit Rivers.** Resident brown trout also begin to appear north of Huttonville and can be found in the Upper Credit River. To help maintain the fragile trout fishery on the Credit, several special regulations such as slot sizes and artificial lure regulations have been established. Be sure to check the regulations before heading out.

Deer Creek and Pearl Creek (Map 30/C7)

Pearl Creek flows from the headwaters at Pearl Lake into Deer Creek, which flows east to west into the Saugeen River southeast of Paisley. The creeks are mainly inhabited by northern pike and smallmouth bass. Pike are often hammer handle size and bass average around 0.5 kg (1 lbs). There are also reports that there are sections of both creeks that still have resident brook trout.

Detroit River (Map 1/B1-A5)

It is kind of a surreal site to see people fishing the Detroit River between the city of Windsor and the towering buildings of Detroit City. Despite decades of industrial development and the fact the river is one of the largest shipping lanes in the world, the river continues to provide sportfishing opportunities. The main attraction to the river is its walleye fishing. Fishing is generally fair for walleye that average 1-2 kg (2-5 lbs) in size. Northern pike and smallmouth bass can also be found in the river and in some areas fishing for bass can be quite good. Access to the river is available from numerous marinas and docks along both sides of the river. Special walleye limits are in place, check the regulations for details.

Duffins Creek (Map 28/E4-6)

This creek once was supported a healthy population of brook trout along its northern reaches. Today, it can be hard to find these elusive fish, but they are still found in areas. Further south, the main fishing draw to the creek is the spring steelhead run. Big brown trout also migrate along the lower reaches in the late spring/early summer. Alternatively, anglers can look for smallmouth bass and the odd northern pike in these lower reaches near Pickering Beach.

Eighteen Mile Creek (Map 23/B2)

The Eighteen Mile Creek is also known as the Eighteen Mile River. No matter what you call the stream, a good population of smallmouth bass inhabits it. While the bass are not very big, there are good pockets of these feisty fish, especially closer to where the creek enters Lake Huron. Smallmouth stick close to cover, such as shoreline habitat, and in deep holes. Try flipping a jig or casting a streamer fly pattern into these areas.

Fish Creek (Maps 18/G7-11/A1)

Fish Creek flows south into the North Thames River south of St Marys. The creek is home to a warm water fishery, including a fair number of average size smallmouth bass. Fly rods and light spincasting equipment can enhance the fun in this creek.

Fromosa Creek and Kinlough Creek (Maps 24/B2-23/G2)

These two creeks are located south of Walkerton and are small cool running streams. The creeks offer slow fishing for brook trout. Brookies average around 20 cm (8 in) in size and will take both flies and worms.

Gleason Brook (Map 37/B7)

Flowing west from Gleason Lake into Colpoy's Bay, this small stream receives significant pressure from trout anglers throughout the year. Both brook trout and rainbow trout can be found in the stream and fishing is regarded as slow to fair. Since access to the brook is limited by private property, be sure not to trespass. Consult your regulations for closures.

Grand River (Maps 14, 15, 16, 20, 25, 26)

Over the past decade, the Grand River has become one of the most popular outdoor recreational rivers in Southern Ontario. The hard work of volunteers and local organizations has transformed the river into a world class angling destination. Special regulations, including catch and release areas and bait bans, have also helped the river become one of the great rivers to fish in Ontario. We have portioned the river into sections for an easier read on where and how to fish the Grand.

Belwood Lake to Elora Gorge (Maps 25/G7-20/F1)

Below Belwood Lake and through the Elora Gorge a fantastic brown trout fishery has developed. The river is a fly anglers dream as brown trout over 2 kg (4.5 lbs) can be caught by ardent anglers offering well presented flies. Caddis hatches are quite prevalent, especially in the early summer but nymphs will often provide your best chance at hooking a big brown. These elusive trout will feed off the top periodically, mainly as evening approaches, and there is nothing better than catching a chunky trout off the top.

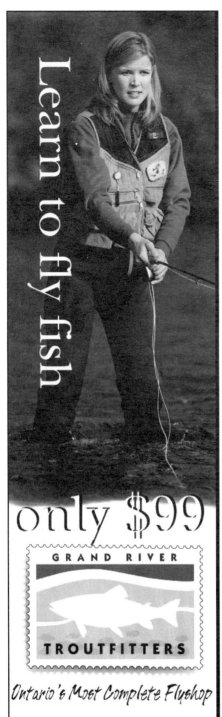

Learn to fly fish

only $99

GRAND RIVER

TROUTFITTERS

Ontario's Most Complete Flyshop

For more information
(519)787-4359
790 Tower St. S. (hwy#6)
Fergus, ON N1M 2R3 Canada
www.grandrivertroutfitters.com

Public access points have been established throughout the area.

Elora Gorge to Kitchener (Map 20/F1-F5)

As the river progresses south toward Kitchener, the fishery enters a transition zone from a cool water river to a warm water fishery. In this stretch brown trout, smallmouth bass and northern pike can be found. Your best bet for brown's are in the upper reaches closer to the gorge, although they have been reported on occasion as far south as Waterloo. The smallmouth bass fishery in the Grand is quickly becoming one of the best bass fisheries in the region. Feisty smallmouth will aggressively take streamers, woolly buggers and other attractor flies, as well as top water presentations. If you can master the presentation, crayfish imitation flies can be deadly. Work the flies off bottom and strip in quick medium turns to entice bass to suck them in. Anglers will find the best pike fishing during the spring. Bigger flies and lures such as a large streamer or spinner will often attract larger pike.

Kitchener to Cambridge (Map 20/F5-G6)

Although this portion of the Grand is not the prettiest, some good fishing is available. Smallmouth bass fishing can be quite good at times in the summer, especially at dusk. Top water flies, such as poppers, or lures, such as a Zara Spook, can create havoc out on the water. While a few pike can be caught in this stretch, your better off fishing for crappies if you are looking for a change from smallmouth.

Cambridge to Lake Erie (Maps 20/G6-16/D7)

The section north of the Penman Dam in Paris to Cambridge is a good area for smallmouth bass. Fishing for smallmouth is best in the summer and fall months for bass that average around 0.5-1 kg (1-2 lbs) in size. Northern pike are also found north of the dam in fair numbers and are best found in the spring.

South of Paris, the fishery begins to offer more variety. Along with northern pike and smallmouth bass, anglers can also catch walleye and migrating species. Closer to Paris, anglers can occasionally hook into a migrating brown trout or steelhead in the spring or fall. The areas below Wilkes Dam provide the best opportunities to hook into a spring steelhead as well as walleye.

Please Note: In order to maintain and enhance the fishing quality of the Grand River, there are several special regulations in place on large tracts of the river. Consult your regulations before heading out.

Gully Creek (Amp 18/A2)
This small creek was once in rough shape, but recently the stream has been rehabilitated and resident trout populations are making a comeback. Anglers can expect to find small brook trout in the 20 cm (8 in) range. Small nymphs on a light fly rod can be a lot of fun on this small creek. Check for sanctuary areas and times.

Holland River (Map 27/A3-E1)
The Holland River is a weedy, almost marsh like stream that flows north from near Cedar Mills to Lake Simcoe (in our Cottage Country mapbook). The river offers some good fishing in areas for largemouth bass that average 1 kg (2 lbs) in size as well as northern pike averaging about 45-60 cm (18-24 in). A boat or canoe can definitely increase your chance for success in this meandering stream.

Holmesville (Hopkins) Creek (Map 18/C1)
Also known as Hopkins Creek, this small stream flows northwest into the Maitland River near the settlement of Holmesville. The creek has been rehabilitated over the past number of years and sees a decent run of steelhead in the spring and chinook salmon in the fall. Resident brown trout and brook trout round out the fishing possibilities in the creek.

Humber River (Maps 26/F3-22/F1)
From its more remote countryside beginnings west of Cedar Mills, the Humber River and its tributaries flow south eventually through metro Toronto and into Lake Ontario. Most of the river has been environmentally abused and fishing opportunities are quite limited. However, there are good spawning runs of brown trout, steelhead and chinook salmon. The mouth of the river and its tributaries near Lake Ontario also provide slow to fair fishing for largemouth bass and the odd northern pike when the spawning fish are not running. Be sure to check your regulations before heading out.

Indian Creek (Map 34/D2)
Over the years, Indian Creek has suffered from over use. Brook trout inhabit portions of the creek, although success is hit and miss. A steelhead run is also present in the spring. The creek is part of a spring fishing sanctuary to enhance spawning success.

Judges Creek (Map 36/E3)
Judges Creek is a cool stream that is accessible from a number of road crossings. Fishing for small rainbow and brook trout can be fair at times. Try using a small bead head nymph or spinner. There is a special summer season on this creek.

Kettle Creek (Map 13/E6-7/A2)
This warm water creek stretches south from near the Lake Whittaker Conservation Area all the way through St. Thomas and eventually into Lake Erie at Port Stanley. Fishing in the creek is best in the lower reaches for smallmouth and largemouth bass. The odd brown trout is also caught around Port Stanley.

Kintail (Kerry's) Creek (Map 23/A4)
Also known as Kerry's Creek, this small stream is home to a resident population of small brook trout. But it is the steelhead run in the spring

that is the main attraction for anglers to the creek. These migratory rainbow trout average around 2 kg (4.5 lbs) in size. The creek is located north of Goderich and flows through the village of Kintail

Little, Middle and South Maitland Rivers (Maps 23/G6, 24/D7, 18/D1)

These three rivers are tributaries of the Maitland River. Kids can have a great time fishing in these rivers, as there are plenty of panfish available. Anglers can also enjoy fishing for average size smallmouth bass along most stretches of the rivers. The South Maitland River flows north from Seaforth, while the Little Maitland and Middle Maitland Rivers flow west meeting the main Maitland River at the town of Wingham. Be sure to check the regulations for special regulations that apply to these rivers.

Lyons Creek (Map 17/C5)

Lyons Creek is a Niagara Region creek that flows east into the Welland River near the Niagara River. The creek offers fishing opportunities for largemouth bass that average about 0.5 kg (1 lb) in size but can be found larger. The bulk of the fishing opportunities exist closer to where the creek flows into the Welland River.

Maitland River (Map 23/G4-A7)

Perhaps one of the most scenic areas to fish in Southern Ontario, the Maitland River is also an ideal fly fishing river. The wide river has runs of both steelhead and salmon. Almost any portion of the river between Wingham to the mouth at Goderich can provide decent results. The sea-run rainbow enter the river in good numbers in the spring, and there is a smaller winter run starting in mid fall. Chinook and a small run of coho salmon run up the river in the fall and can be a lot of fun for anglers.

Other angling alternatives include smallmouth bass and sampling the many feeder streams for brook trout and brown trout. Smallmouth can be found almost anywhere in the big river, although fishing is better east of Wingham. A number of restrictions are in place on the Maitland, check the regulations for details.

Mill Creeks (Maps 29/F4, 33/C7)

South of Port Elgin, both **Mill Creek** and **Little Mill Creek** are accessible from one of the many road crossings over the small streams. In the upper reaches, anglers can expect to find a few brook trout, while smallmouth bass begin to appear closer to Port Elgin. Smallmouth provide the best action on the creeks and are readily found near the mouth of Mill Creek along the Saugeen River.

Naftel's Creek (Map 18/A1)

Despite the size of this creek, it has a decent steelhead run in the spring and chinook run in the fall. A few small resident brook, brown and rainbow trout can also be found in the creek during off run periods. The creek is located north of Bayfield and is accessible from a road crossing. Currently this creek is open for any type of fishing from early May to the end of September.

Niagara River (Map 17/E1-G7)

Cascading over Niagara Falls and stretching between Lake Erie and Lake Ontario, the Niagara River is one of the most famous rivers in North America. The river is often overlooked for its recreational opportunities due mainly to its sheer power and size. However, over the past few decades anglers have begun to tap into this great angling resource. Anglers can fish for steelhead in the spring and chinook and the odd brown trout in the fall. There is even the chance to hook into a lake trout in the fall. Not to be outdone, smallmouth bass fishing can be very good during the summer months. One caution, however, the river is quite powerful and should be taken seriously by both boaters and shore anglers. Check for special regulations.

Nine Mile River (Map 23/C4-A5)

Nine Mile River can be very crowded with anglers during the productive spring steelhead and fall chinook salmon runs. Since the upper portions of the river have tight overgrown banks, anglers concentrate on the lower portion and overcrowding can be a problem at times. A small coho run also occurs in the fall. Alternatively, there are also a number of feeder streams (Dickies, Petterson & St. Helens Creeks) that flow into the river offering resident brook trout. Be sure to consult the regulations for closures.

Nith River (Maps 14, 19, 20)

The main sportfish found in the Nith River is smallmouth bass. Bass average about 0.5-1 kg (1-2 lbs) in size and are best found in the lower reaches of the river. However, over the past decade, some spawning steelhead have begun to make their way up the Nith. In the future, this popular fishery may blossom on this river.

North Penetangore River (Map 29/E7-B7)

Flowing east to west through the heart of Kincardine and into Lake Huron, this small river is host to a decent spring steelhead and fall chinook salmon run. The best way to catch both species is to drift a roe sac with a float. The big fish will readily strike the sacs as they pass by. A resident population of brook trout is said to remain in the stream.

North Saugeen River (Map 30/F4-A5)

The North Saugeen River flows east to west from around Highway 6 to where it meets the larger Saugeen River at the town of Paisley. The extreme eastern stretches of the river have a resident population of brown trout and brook trout. The portion closer to the Saugeen River boasts fair fishing for smallmouth bass and northern pike. Both pike and bass are relatively small, although the action can be rewarding.

Nottawasaga River (Map 32/G6-E2)

The Nottawasaga River has many characteristics. The river is home to spawning walleye in the fall and early spring as well as fabulous steelhead and chinook salmon spawning runs. While the walleye are off limits during much of their spawn, they are caught periodically after the spring season opening. The steelhead run begins in the fall and can be fished throughout the river shown in this mapbook. Steelhead in the river are known as some of the largest and strongest in Ontario and can put up a tremendous fight when hooked. Add big chinook salmon to the mix and fishing on the Nottawasaga can be quite good during the early fall. If that is not enough, the river also boasts resident smallmouth bass and northern pike closer to Nottawasaga Bay. Before heading out be sure to check your regulations as there are special sanctuary areas and periods on this river.

Otter Creek (Map 24/B2)

This small stream flows north through the town of Mildmay and eventually dumps into the Saugeen River south of Walkerton. The creek offers fishing opportunities for brook trout and brown trout. Try using a small grey bodied bead head nymph for brookies or leech patterns for bigger browns.

Penetangore River (Maps 23/D1-29/B7)

The Penetangore River sees a fair run of steelhead in the spring and chinook salmon in the fall. During off spawning periods anglers can enjoy fishing for the river's resident smallmouth bass. Bass average about 0.5 kg (1 lb) in size, although they can certainly be found larger. Try spinners or jigs for bass success.

THE GRAND RIVERS MOST COMPLETE SELECTION OF FISHING TACKLE

SAGE
G. LOOMIS
FENWICK
ST. CROIX
LAMPSON
ISLANDER
3M MASTERY

SHIMANO
DAIWA
QUANTUM
ABU GARCIA
MITCHELL
BERKLEY
LOWRANCE

NATURAL SPORTS
1572 VICTORIA ST. N. KITCHENER 519-749-1620

Pottawatomi River (Map 30/D1)

The Pottawatomi River is a short river that flows from south to north passing through the city of Owen Sound. The river has a marginal resident trout population, along with a spring steelhead and a fall chinook run. The spawning fish can reach some nice sizes, with steelhead over 5 kg (10 lbs) and chinook over 7 kg (15 lbs) not uncommon. The Pottawatomi Conservation Area southeast of the city is a popular angling spot. Special sanctuary periods are in place on this river to protect stocks. Check the regulations before heading out.

Pretty River (Map 32/B3)

From the Pretty River Valley Provincial Park, this river flows through the Niagara Escarpment into Nottawasaga Bay near Collingwood. The river sees a run of spawning steelhead during the spring and is home to a resident population of brook trout. Access to the river is limited in many areas due to a combination of private property and geographical barriers. Check the regulations for special restrictions.

Rankin River (Map 33/F1)

Northeast of Sauble Beach, the Rankin River flows from the southern end of Boat Lake south into the Sauble River. The smaller river has a fair to good population of smallmouth bass, largemouth bass and northern pike available for anglers. During spring, anglers can catch the odd walleye or try their luck for the steelhead that run up the river in marginal numbers.

Rocky Saugeen River (Maps 31/C5-30/G7)

Decent sized brook trout and brown trout can be found in the Rocky, although fishing varies greatly from section to section. As with most rivers, the help of a local will really improve your luck. Both fly fishing and spincasting can be successful on this river.

Rouge River (Map 28/C6)

The Rouge River is an urban stream that offers some good migratory fishing opportunities. Steelhead run up the river in good numbers in the spring and are the main attraction of anglers. Brown trout also migrate up the river in fair numbers from the spring to the early summer, while in the fall anglers can expect good runs of chinook and coho salmon. The Rouge is benefiting from habitat restoration, which should have a positive impact on the sportfishing for decades to come.

St. Clair River (Maps 4/C2, 10/C6)

The St. Clair River flows from Lake Huron through the city of Sarnia south to Lake St. Clair. The river is part of the St. Lawrence Seaway that sees a lot of industrial traffic. Boaters should always pay attention when out on the river. Fishing in the river varies from area to area, although the portions near Walpole Island and Sarnia are a favourite among anglers. Access to the river is available along the US side and Canadian side from several marinas and local dock areas.

Although, smallmouth and largemouth bass can be found throughout the river system in good numbers, the biggest attraction for anglers on the St. Clair River are its walleye. Fishing is usually a little slow for nice size walleye. Northern pike are found in parts of the river, while muskellunge also roam certain areas at different portions of the year. Some big pike can be caught with some consistency in the areas around Sarnia. The odd chinook salmon is also caught in the river periodically. Slot sizes and special possession limits have been introduced to help fish stocks. Check the regulations for details

St. Helens Creek (Map 23/D5)

This rehabilitated stream is home to a fair population of brook trout and brown trout and sees runs of both steelhead and chinook. Fishing for these big fish can be quite good in areas. Most anglers prefer to use the standard roe sacs with a float, but fly anglers are finding some great action with bright coloured flies on occasion.

Salem Creek (Map 24/B4)

Native brook trout can be found in this small creek north of Wroxeter. Brookies average around 20 cm (8 in) in size and are best caught on the fly using small nymphs or even bead headed nymphs. Spincasters can also find good success with the old hook and worm. The creek

can be fished from near road crossings but please be aware of private property in the area.

Sauble River (Maps 30/D4-33/E2)

The Sauble River is a big river that stretches from the countryside south of Owen Sound north to eventually enter Lake Huron at Sauble Falls. The river is home to a marginal steelhead run in the spring and a chinook salmon run in the fall. A small population of coho also run during the fall, but catches are limited. The short section below Sauble Falls sees most of the action from the migratory species. Resident smallmouth bass and northern pike can also be found near the mouth as well as in portions of the upper river throughout the year.

Saugeen River (Maps 24/E2, 29/G4, 30/F7, 31/D7)

The Saugeen is one of the largest rivers in Southwestern Ontario and is a very popular spot among steelhead and salmon anglers. The river can be crowded during the spring and fall running periods, although there is usually a spot to cast a fly or drop a line. Fishing for steelhead is regarded as fair and can be good at times during the spring. Chinook salmon fishing is slow to fair with a few good days in the fall. Perhaps some of the best areas to fish the river are upstream all the way to Walkerton. The river receives significantly less pressure along these areas. The sea-run rainbow in the river can exceed 75 cm (30 in) and the chinook can top 10 kg (22 lbs). During off spawn periods, resident brown trout and smallmouth bass can be found in the river. To enhance and maintain fish populations, several special restrictions are in place on the river. Be sure to check your regulations.

Sharpes Creek (Map 23/B7)

Sharpes Creek is part of the Maitland River watershed and enters the big river east of Goderich at Benmiller. Over the past decade rehabilitation efforts along the creek have re-established trout habitat. Brook trout can now be found in many areas of the creek and provide for fair fishing at times. Access to the creek is available at one of the many road crossings.

Snake Creek (Maps 30/D5-29/G3)

Northern pike and smallmouth bass make up the majority of the fishing opportunities along the Snake. Anglers will find the areas closer to the

Saugeen River a little more productive. During the fall, chinook salmon begin to run. Runs can be quite good some years and can last a number of weeks depending on seasonal climate and water levels. Access is available from the various road crossings over the creek.

South Saugeen River (Maps 25/F1-24/D1)
This large river stretches from the countryside west of Shelbourne, all the way west to the Saugeen River at Hanover. The river offers fair to good fishing opportunities for smallmouth bass and northern pike. In some areas where the river is quite wide, decent sized bass and pike can be found. A known hot spot is the area near Ayton. Try a multi purpose lure such as a spinnerbait or jig for both bass and pike.

Speed River (Maps 26/A7-21/A2)
The Speed River flows south through Guelph Lake and the city of Guelph before entering Eramosa River. Fishing the Speed can be good in sections for smallmouth bass. In particular, the sections just below and above Guelph Lake can be quite good at times for average sized smallies. Northern pike also frequent the river in areas.

Spring Creek (Maps 39/B7-36/A1)
This Bruce Peninsula stream has a population of rainbow and brook trout available despite flowing through a number of marshy areas. Anglers will need to locate the nice holes that trout like to hide in. Try flipping a well presented nymph fly pattern or worm into these pools for success.

Styx River (Map 30/G5-E7)
Both brook trout and northern pike can be found in the Styx. Of course the two species are never in the same areas. The portion of the river closer to the Saugeen River is the main holding area for small pike. It is reported that the odd smallmouth bass can also be found along with the northern pike.

Sydenham River (Maps 4/F4, 5/D2, 11/G7, 12/E3)
This big river offers fishing opportunities for walleye, northern pike and smallmouth bass. Fishing is best for pike and bass, as walleye have been hit hard over the years. Northern pike can be found in the 60 cm (24 in) range, while smallmouth average about 0.5-1 kg (1-2 lbs). Try working shore structure such as weed areas or fallen trees for both bass and pike. The river flows west from near London all the way to the St. Clair River at Wallaceburg. There are numerous boat and fishing access opportunities along the river. Check the regulations for sanctuary periods/areas.

Sydenham River (Map 30/G4-E1)
A run of chinook salmon can be expected up the Sydenham River in the fall. These big fish provide decent fishing opportunities mainly around Owen Sound. Some big brown trout can also be found in the river, but they can be a challenge to catch. For browns, try flies or a small fluorescent Mepps or Blue Fox.

Teeswater River (Maps 23/G2, 24/B4, 29/G6, 30/A6)
A few brook trout can be found in the upper reaches of the Teeswater, although they are difficult to find in most cases. As the river approaches

the Saugeen River, warm water species such as smallmouth bass and northern pike begin to appear. Some good sized smallmouth can be found. Bass can be found up to 1.5 kg (3.5 lbs), while pike are usually kept in the 45 cm (18 in) range. Of course, bigger fish are out there.

Thames River (Maps 2/E1, 4/G7, 5/D5, 6/C1, 12/E6, 13/D5, 14/A2, 19/G7, 20/A7)
This big river was an important trade and travel route for natives and eventually settlers. The river is the sight of many thriving communities, which in time have put environmental stress on the river system. Over the past decade or so, efforts to clean up the Thames have come a long way, although there are portions that remain unpleasing to the eye.

Fishing in the big river varies greatly from section to section although the most consistent sportfishing is found throughout the stream for largemouth and smallmouth bass. Bass can be found up to 2 kg (4.5 lbs) in size in some areas. Northern pike are also found throughout most of the river and can be found in decent sizes at times. Below the Springbank Dam near London, anglers will also have the opportunity to fish for walleye. Success for walleye is usually slow. Be sure to check your regulations for special restrictions before heading out on the Thames.

Tricks Creek (Map 18/C1 to B2)
This small creek is home to a small resident population of brown trout and brook trout. Some nice sized browns can be caught in the creek, although they are finicky. The best time to try for browns is after a heavy rainfall. At this time, they are more likely to venture out from their cover after well presented flies and spinners. During the spring and fall, the creek also comes alive with spawning steelhead and chinook. The sea-run rainbow can reach good sizes and are a real thrill to hook into. Tricks Creek flows south into the Bayfield River from north of the town of Clinton.

Twenty Mile Creek (Map 15/G1-16/G2)
Twenty Mile Creek flows atop the Niagara Escarpment from south of Hamilton east all the way to Lake Ontario at Vineland. The portion closest to the lake sees a decent spawning run of chinook salmon in the fall. Fishing for salmon can be good at times for some big fish.

Welland River (Map 15/G3-17/E4)
Plenty of panfish can be caught in the Welland but it is the smallmouth bass, largemouth bass and northern pike most anglers are after. While pike and bass can be found almost throughout the river, the larger fish tend to be found east of the Welland Canal. Bass can reach up to 2 kg (4.5 lbs) in size, while pike are caught in the 60 cm (24 in) range periodically. Try working tube jigs off bottom structure or spinner baits along shore structure for both pike and bass.

Whitemans and Horner Creeks (Map 14/E2)
Brook trout once thrived in these small Southwestern Ontario streams. Unfortunately, habitat degradation has limited brook trout to small pockets along the creek and fishing is often slow. Brown trout on the other hand, were introduced into the creek over thirty years ago and they are thriving. Fishing is fair to good at times for some nice size browns. The creek is best fished on the fly after heavy rains. Since the removal of the Lorne Dam over a decade ago, the system has also been experiencing increased spring steelhead migration. Enhanced regulations have been established along a large portion of the stream to improve fishing quality. Check the regulations for details.

Willow Creek (Map 32/G3)
Some good size brown trout are found in Willow Creek. The creek hosts a spawning run of big browns, and there is a fair population of resident browns found throughout the stream. Resident browns can be quite finicky and are best fished for after a good rain or during overcast periods. Rainbow trout also inhabit the creek. Try a terrestrial fly, such as a grasshopper or flying ant, during the heat of summer for some exciting top water action. Check the regulations for special sanctuary periods.

Paddling Routes

(River, Ocean and Lake Paddling)

Despite the easy access and ability to pick and choose the length of travel, most of the river routes in Southwestern Ontario are rarely used. Even the Grand River, which is one of the most popular paddling destinations in the region, receives limited use compared to some areas like Algonquin Park. Other fantastic river paddling opportunities include the Saugeen River and the Rankin River. The only downfall of a lot of these routes is that camping is limited, although if you plan ahead, you can easily arrange to stay in a nearby campground or even a bed and breakfast.

In addition to the easily accessible river routes, there are many lush wetlands and bay areas that are ideal for touring. Open water kayaking is becoming popular in these areas as well as along the shorelines of the Great Lakes. There simply is not a better way to explore an area than to see it from the water.

Trip equipment is very important to help reduce fatigue and increase enjoyment. For long tripping with numerous portages, a good lightweight kevlar canoe is recommended. This helps increase your endurance and reduce the physical stress of numerous portages. Good planning is also essential to minimize your weight and maximize your comfort. If planning is not done properly, an enjoyable trip can easily become hard work. Experienced canoeists have a good idea of how far they can travel in a day, although in general, during 4-6 hours travel time you should be able to cover 10-20 km or about 7cm-13 cm on our maps. Of course, a number of factors must be accounted for when estimating your rate of progress, such as the number and difficulty of portages, wind on large water bodies, and of course your physical condition.

River Routes

We have used the International River Classification system to grade whitewater areas on rivers:

Grade I: Novices in open canoes or kayaks. Riffles and small waves with virtually no obstruction.

Grade II: Intermediate paddlers. Maneuvering is required. Medium rapids, channels can be clearly spotted without scouting.

Grade III: Advanced Paddlers. Rapids can swamp open canoes. Waves are unpredictable. Scouting should be done before approach. Skilled maneuvering is required.

Grade IV: Expert paddlers; closed canoes & kayaks only. Long, challenging rapids with obstructions requiring maneuvering. Eskimo roll ability is recommended. Good swimming skills. Scouting required.

Grade V: Professional Paddlers; closed canoes or kayaks only. Scouting always required. Long, violent rapids through narrow routes with obstructions. Eskimo roll ability essential. Errors can be fatal.

Please remember that river conditions are always subject to change and advanced scouting is essential. The information in this book is only intended to give you general information on the particular river you are interested in. You should always obtain more details from your local merchant or expert before heading out on your adventure.

Bayfield River Route (Map 18/E3-A2)

Put-in/Take-out: While it is possible to put into this river almost at any road crossing west of Seaforth, the main access is from the Hannah Line Road crossing. It is possible to take-out at almost any road crossing, but most paddlers choose to use either the Clinton Conservation Area, off Highway 4 southeast of Clinton, or the town of Bayfield.

The Bayfield River Route is a moderate canoe route that travels through mainly agricultural areas from Seaforth to Bayfield. From Seaforth to Clinton, paddlers should expect some grade I-II type water with the odd sweeper or logjam to avoid. This is by far the most strenuous and challenging portion of the route and usually takes much longer to complete than the section from Clinton to Bayfield. To finish the trip within a full day (7-10 hours) it is recommended to take-out just south of Clinton and pre-arrange for accommodation nearby. The section from Clinton to Bayfield usually takes just over a half a day to travel. While grade II water is encountered along this section, the majority of the fast water is found upstream. This route is usually only passable during the spring runoff period in April and May. Be sure to check on water conditions before planning your trip.

Beaver River Route (Map 31/E2-D3; E2-F1)

Put-in/Take-out: North of the village of Kimberly, the access area for the upper portion of the Beaver River is located at the end of a rough access road that branches off the west side of County Road 13. To the north, take-outs are located at any of the road crossings over the river. The main and last take-out along the route is found at Heathcote at the County Road 13 crossing.

At the put-in, the Beaver River Route begins with a quick but manageable flow and quickly slows to a relaxing pace. The river passes through the Beaver Valley sporting forested shorelines home to a variety of small mammals and birds. The route is quite peaceful throughout its entirety, broken up by the odd short lift over or portage around logjams. The only fast water on the route other than at the put-in is a grade I-II portion located between the 18th and 21st Side Roads. If you do not feel up to running this stretch, there is a short portage available along the west side of the river. After the portage, the route soon finishes by flowing into the hamlet of Heathcote.

For experienced paddlers, the lower portions of the Beaver River north of Heathcote to Lake Huron offer grade II-IV whitewater opportunities in the spring. Inquire with a local paddling outfitter for current conditions and more detailed info on the Beaver River whitewater opportunities.

Big Creek Route (Map 8/E4)

Put-in/Take-out: Located near Long Point, the main put-in for the Big Creek Canoe Route is located off the south side of County Road 60. To shorten your route, alternate access points are available off a few of the roads that cross the creek to the south. The take-out area is located at the crossing of County Road 59 over the Big Creek Marsh. You can park off the side of the road or at the nearby marina.

The Big Creek flows south from near Woodstock all the way to Lake Erie. The portion of the creek that is easiest to navigate by canoe is the section south of County Road 60, west of Long Point. While some ambitious and experienced paddlers have paddled the creek from Delhi, the upper reaches are very unpredictable in regards to logjams and sweepers. In the early spring after the main thaw and rainfalls, logjams and sweepers can be a major problem along the entire creek. The amazing thing about this creek is that much of the route is lined with thick Carolinian forest. Amid a region that is made up of mainly farmland and irrigation canals, it is amazing to see such a wild area.

Your best bet is to time your trip shortly after the spring flood period or later in the year around mid September. During the heat of summer, the water level along the creek can be drastically low, making water travel almost impossible in areas. At the best of times, there will always be a few carryovers or short portages required to navigate the creek. In general, this route is easy to travel during favourable water levels, with grade I difficulty water and should take about four hours. During high water this creek can be as difficult as grade II-III.

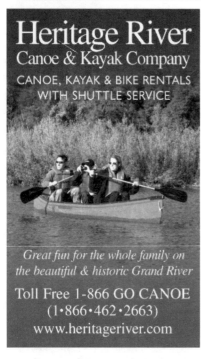

Heritage River
Canoe & Kayak Company
CANOE, KAYAK & BIKE RENTALS WITH SHUTTLE SERVICE

Great fun for the whole family on the beautiful & historic Grand River

Toll Free 1-866 GO CANOE
(1•866•462•2663)
www.heritageriver.com

Bighead River Route (Map 35/C4)

Put-in/Take-out: The put-in for this whitewater paddling route is located at the County Road 12 Bridge over the Bighead River south of Oxmead. The take-out for the route is located in the town of Meaford at the first bridge.

The Bighead River Route offers grade II+ whitewater during the spring runoff period. The run is approximately 9 km (5.6 mi) in length and is suitable for experienced whitewater paddlers only. The route passes along mainly forested shorelines and is not usually runable after spring. Be sure to scout the river before you paddle the route.

Credit River Route (Map 26/F7-20/G1)

Put-in/Take-out: The main access point to this canoe route is from the village of Terra Cotta north of Georgetown. You can put-in near the County Road 19 (Winston Churchill Boulevard) crossing over the Credit River. Parking can be tricky as there really is not much room near the bridge, but the local inn may grant permission upon request. It is possible to take-out at most of the road crossings downstream, although the best spots are located off Wildwood Road in Glen Williams, County Road 23 in Georgetown or at the Ecology Park in Norval.

From Terra Cotta, the Credit River is an interesting paddle as the river passes through some forested sections en route to Glen Williams. Before reaching Glen Williams the river passes underneath a few local roads and passes under Wildwood Road. Shortly after Wildwood Road, be prepared for the 100 m (328 ft) portage located off the east side before River Road. A small concrete dam lies across the river creating a small rapid, which can be run by experienced canoeists. From River Road, the river passes by the remains of a paper mill originally constructed in the late 1830's. Further downriver, the route also passes by the remains of one of Ontario's first hydroelectric dams in the late 1800's. After the hydro station the river soon slows it's pace, eventually reaching the take-out off the west side of the river at the ecology park.

This moderate grade II-III river is best travelled during late spring and early summer when floodwaters have subsided but the heat of summer has yet to reduce river flow to unmanageable levels. During ideal water conditions, you will encounter a few easy rapids and sweepers. In high water this river can be dangerous for inexperienced whitewater paddlers.

Grand River Paddling (Maps 14, 15, 16, 20)

Designated as a Canadian Heritage River, the Grand River is a river intertwined in the history and development of Southern Ontario. For thousands of years, native peoples thrived along the river using it as a food source, as well as a transportation and trade route. Named 'O:se Kenhionhata:tie' by Mohawk natives, the river continued to play an integral role in developing the region after the first European settlers arrived.

Today, the Grand River has grown to be one of the most important outdoor recreation destinations in southern Ontario. Below we have broken down the Grand River into sections that can be paddled in approximately 6-9 hours. There are many alternate access points that can shorten or lengthen the route chosen. Most of the river is easy to paddle, although there are portions of the river that are challenging. For more detailed information and up to date water conditions you can call the Grand River Conservation Authority at (519) 621-2763.

Elora Gorge to Waterloo (Map 20/F1-E4)

Put-in/Take-out: The Elora Gorge Conservation Area marks the beginning of the Grand River Route. The conservation area is accessible off County Road 21 south of Elora. To split this section in half, an access/take-out is available in West Montrose off County Road 86. The main take-out for this section is available in Waterloo (Bridgeport) off the east side of the river at the Bridge Street Bridge.

Beginning at the Elora Gorge Conservation Area, this portion of the route can be done in a full day (approximately 8 hours). From the conservation area, the route passes along a scenic part of the river towards West Montrose. The West Montrose Covered Bridge, about half way along this section, is quite the site. Built in 1881, the bridge is the last covered bridge in Ontario and is also known as the 'Kissing Bridge'. From the Kissing Bridge, the river flows south to the city of Waterloo past the junction of the Laurel Creek to the take out/access at Bridge Street.

Bridgeport to Cambridge (Map 20/E4-G6)

Put-in/Take-out: South of the Bridge Street access, there are two alternate access points available in north Kitchener. One is available at Bingeman Park off Victoria Street (Highway 7) and the other is further east along Victoria Street at the Victoria Street Park. The take out/access in Cambridge is located at Riverbluffs Park off George Street.

Expect to take approximately 7 hours to travel from Waterloo to Cambridge. Water levels are usually sufficient, although in the heat of summer, it may be necessary to walk your canoe through some areas. From Bridge Street, the route flows along the eastern limits of the cities of Waterloo and Kitchener before passing the suburb of Freeport. South of Freeport be prepared for the portage around the water treatment plant dam along the west side of the river. Look for the portage after passing under the King Street (Highway 8) Bridge. After the portage, the route passes by the Deer Ridge Golf Club and soon after past the Pioneer Memorial Tower. The pioneer tower was constructed in 1926 as a commemoration to the first settlers that arrived in the area in the early 1800's. The route is quite peaceful along this portion of the river with plenty of shoreline foliage home to plenty of birds and other wildlife. This portion of the route ends along a scenic stretch of the river in Cambridge, where some fantastic limestone bluffs are displayed.

Cambridge to Brantford (Map 20/G6-1/A2)

Put-in/Take-out: South of Cambridge, an access to the river is available off Highway 24. Look for a gas station off the east side of the highway near the Cambridge to Paris Rail Trail trailhead. Alternate access points are marked on Map 20, while the take out/access in Brantford is available at the Brant Conservation Area along the west side of the river.

The Cambridge to Brantford stretch is one of the most challenging sections of the Grand River to travel. The river drops approximately 46 m (150 ft) between the cities creating a strong flow. There are also man-made obstacles and rapids that portages have been built around. In all, this stretch of river should take 8 to 9 hours to paddle. Along the way, one of the sights to keep an eye open for is the Old Stone Mill off the east side of the river near the village of Glen Morris. The mill is best spotted in the early or late part of the year when foliage is at its lowest.

You can start this section from Riverbluffs Park in Cambridge, but it may be easier to simply tie your canoe to your car and head around the Parkhill Dam and access the river further downstream at Highway 24. The Parkhill Dam portage lies off the west side of the river and is a set of stairs that climb from the river. Also, this portion of the river between the park and the dam is susceptible to dangerous high water levels in the spring or other runoff times, making an even better case for bypassing this section altogether. Further south, just past the Spottiswood Bluffs south of Glen Morris, there are grade II or II+ rapids during high water. Experienced whitewater paddlers can run these rapids. Many choose to travel around the rapids and access the river again off Willow Street in Paris south of Penman's Dam. Penman's Dam is another obstacle to avoid. Be sure to pull out before the CNR bridge at the portage off the east side of the river to bypass the dam.

Brantford to Caledonia (15/A2-F3)

Put-in/Take-out: South of the Brant Conservation Area, an alternate access point is available off Ballantyne Drive in southwest Brantford. While there are a number of access points between Brantford and Caledonia, the main access is found on the east side of the river before the Caledonia Dam. Look for the take-out just under the railway bridge. You can portage through the small park to the other side of the dam.

While it is possible to travel through Brantford along the Grand River, it may simply be easier to bypass the Wilkes Dam and the Indian Dam remnants by putting in off Ballantyne Drive. Otherwise, from the Brant Conservation Area you must first portage around Wilkes Dam by cutting through the park. To bypass the Indian Dam remnants you need to paddle through a shallow gap along the west bank. After the Indian Dam, the river takes you around a large oxbow. The oxbow takes about 3 hours to paddle and leads into the Six Nations Reserve territory. Terrain along this part of the river is made up of a mix of shore foliage and open field with little development between Brantford and Caledonia. The trip from Brantford to Caledonia takes approximately 8 hours to complete.

Caledonia to Cayuga (Map 15/F3-G6)

Put-in/Take-out: The main access to this portion of the Grand River route is from below the Caledonia Dam. The take out/access in the village of Cayuga is at the public boat launch off Ouse Street.

This part of the Grand River route is rich in history as the river passes by many century homes en route to Cayuga. The route also passes by remnants of the old Grand River Navigation Co. canals and locks. The locks were once an integral part of transporting goods along the Grand River and many communities thrived in the early 1800's. While this is the shallowest section of the route, it is usually passable throughout the year.

Cayuga to Lake Erie (15/G6-16/D7)

Put-in/Take-out: The main access is found at the village of Cayuga at the public boat launch available off Ouse Street. The take-out in Port Maitland is off the west side of the river at a formal boat launch. Plenty of parking is available at the launch sites.

The last leg of the Grand River Route leads to Lake Erie and is a very easy paddle. The river widens significantly and paddlers can enjoy the views of the wetland habitat along the way. There is little, if any, current available to aid your progress and the only disruption of your leisurely paddle is the Dunnville Dam and Weirs. The dam is a dangerous spot for paddlers and can be bypassed via a portage at Weir 4 of the Byng Island Conservation Area. To reach Weir 4, take the first channel off the west side of the river. A boat launch ramp is available for take-out and it's a short portage through the conservation area around the dam. After Dunnville, the only disruption to a relaxing paddle to Lake Erie is the odd boater.

Lower Thames River Route (Map 12/F5-5/A7)

Put-in/Take-out: Although there are numerous access areas to the Lower Thames River, one of the uppermost access points is located in the southwest end of London at Springbank Park.

Springbank Park lies off the north side of Commissioners Road West. Parking and canoe access is available at the park. Alternate access points are available at almost any road crossing over the long course of the river between London and Chatham. Conservation Areas such as the Big Bend Conservation Area, the Dutton-Dunwich Conservation Area and the Delaware Conservation Area all make suitable take-out areas.

The Lower Thames River is a river rich in history. The river has been home to native peoples of the region for over 11,000 years and was integral in helping establish a major trade and transportation route for the first settlers. Over the past century, the river was the base for industrial growth from Chatham to London and parts of the river were heavily developed and abused by industry. In the past decade, however, much of the river has been cleaned up, making for a more naturally scenic waterway for people to enjoy. Although sections of the river remain developed, the majority of the river travels through a mix of farmland scattered with shoreline vegetation.

The best time to travel the Lower Thames is after high water in late May to June or after fall rains in late September to October. Much of the river during this time is easy to paddle with very little current and few log jams. During the heat of summer (July, August and early September) portions of the Thames can be very low and log jams and sand bars are more prevalent. The difficulty of the river during medium to low water is grade I but it can swell to grade II-III in areas during flooding periods. Due to the lack of campsites and crown land along the Thames River, rustic camping is not an option for canoeists. If you are interested in an overnight trip, it is possible to organize your trip by pre arranging overnight accommodation. Private campgrounds/trailer parks and bed and breakfasts are all found near the river.

Mad River Route (Map 32/G4)

Put-in/Take-out: The access to this route is located at the County Road 10 Bridge over the river just west of Angus. The take-out is located along the Nottawasaga River at the Edenvale Conservation Area north of Highway 26.

The Mad River Route is a lesser-known route in Southern Ontario due mainly to its frustrating nature at times. During the summer months the water levels retreat to near impassable conditions. Even at moderate water levels, the river is not a fast flowing route and there are numerous logjams and other obstacles making travel in some sections arduous. The route eventually opens up into the dynamic Minesing Swamp expanse. Although the paddling is easy, navigation becomes a problem. Paddlers can get a little lost in the swamp during the spring, as there is no clear cut channel in areas and everything is flooded. Be sure to bring along a compass and a topographical map for this part of the trip, as you are sure to need it.

Currently, the route is regarded as moderate in difficulty due to the many water obstacles and the navigation required in the Minesing Swamp. Allow a full day to complete this trip and pack extra clothes and food just in case you don't make it out when planned.

Maitland River Routes (Map 23/F5-A7)

Put-in/Take-out: The eastern access point to the Maitland River is from in the town of Wingham. West of Wingham, the

after the initial runoff period, the river makes for a pleasurable canoe route. Some years, the river level can also be adequate during the late fall. From any of the access areas, the Nith River is an easy paddle. The main obstacles encountered along the river are the odd submerged log pile and a few grade I riffles. Surprising to most paddlers, the river flows through quite a secluded environment. Paddlers can expect sections of field shoreline as well as forested and marshy sections.

Nottawasaga River Route (Map 32/G5-E2)

Put-in/Take-out: This portion of the Nottawasaga River can be accessed from several different points. The Angus access is the most popular put-in for the route and is located at the Nottawasaga Conservation Authority office off County Road 90. North of Angus, an alternate put-in is located near the end of McKinnon Road. The Edenvale access doubles as a take-out and lies off of Highway 26 at the Edenvale Conservation Area. The end of the route is found at the Schooner Parkette at Wasaga Beach.

Beginning in Angus, the route is generally easy (grade I-II) and travels through the magnificent Minesing Swamp. The Minesing is a biodiverse wetland with many unique qualities, including one of the largest Great Blue Heron colonies in Ontario. The swamp also boasts many rare bird species and plants such as Hackberry Trees that are usually found in more southern areas of North America. Even walleye are found to spawn on vegetation instead of a gravel type bed in the swamp. From the swamp the route travels past the Edenvale Conservation Area where the river has formed a deep gorge, and a formal camping area is found. Rustic camping is possible in the Minesing Swamp, at a well-used site about 2.5 km (1.6 mi) upstream from Edenvale. From Edenvale the route travels its final stretch, past Doran and Jacks Lakes, to Wasaga Beach Park and the Schooner Parkette take-out.

Rankin River Route (Map 36/F7-33/F1)

Put-in/Take-out: The main access for this route is at the Red Bay Road Bridge while the main take-out is located at Sauble Falls Provincial Park along the southern shore of the river. An alternate take-out, to avoid the faster water, is at the Boat Lake Conservation Area.

The Ranking River Route is as close as you can get to a lake route in Southwestern Ontario. The moderate, full day trip passes across two large lakes before entering the main river portion of the trip.

Beginning from just north of Isaak Lake, the Rankin River meanders slowly through a marsh-like setting. Isaak Lake is about 4 km (2.5 mi) in length and the shoreline is heavily lined with reeds and other wetland plants. The lake gradually narrows into the river, which leads to the Boat Lake Conservation Area. This is the site of the historic native Peninsula Portage that was used for over two thousand years by local natives wishing to travel from the Georgian Bay to the east shore of Lake Huron. The portage was vital in bypassing travel around the Bruce Peninsula.

From the conservation area, the route travels into and across the large Boat Lake. Over 4 km (2.5 mi) later, the route begins to speed up as it begins to follow a faster portion of the Rankin River. Along the stretch from Boat Lake to Sauble Falls Provincial Park, the river is regarded as grade I-II water and there is a short portage around a dam. About 1.5 km (0.9 mi) south of the dam, another short portage is required to pass a dangerous chute. After the chute, the river passes under the Rankin Bridge Road eventually meeting the take-out at Sauble Falls Provincial Park.

Sauble River Route (Map 33/F2)

Put-in/Take-out: Paddlers can begin this route from almost any road crossing over the Sauble River south of Sauble Falls Provincial Park. To keep the route within about a half a day, it is best not to put-in any further south than the Silver Lake Road Bridge. The take-out for this route is at the provincial park. Plenty of parking and camping opportunities are available at the park.

The Sauble River southeast of Sauble Falls is a slow meandering river

---

Amberly Road (County Road 86) crossing is another popular put-in. The Wingham to Benmiller portion of the route ends at the Benmiller Dam in the town of Benmiller. The whitewater section starts after the Benmiller Dam and ends at Highway 21 in Goderich.

From the town of Wingham to Benmiller, the Maitland River offers just the right mix of meandering water with faster sections. This portion of the river can be completed in two full days, but most of the river shoreline is private and accommodation must be pre arranged. It is a peaceful paddle that travels through a farmland region with open fields dominating much of the landscape. Paddlers should be wary of the odd sweeper or logjam, the occasional grade I rapid and wire fencing that may be placed over the river from farmers. Also, water levels can be quite low in mid summer making paddling quite difficult.

The Maitland River Route can be continued downstream from the other side of the Benmiller Dam. This section of river is one of the few whitewater areas in Southwestern Ontario and is a favourite with whitewater enthusiasts. In the spring, the river offers grade II whitewater opportunities with some challenging ledges and pools for play boaters. The run is about 14 km (8.7 mi) in length and ends at Highway 21 in the town of Goderich. A portage is required at the Falls Reserve Conservation Area. The short 50 m (164 ft) hike will take you around the falls. Shortly after the spring thaw, water levels begin to drop in late spring/early summer and the route becomes unrunnable.

Nith River Route (Map 20/C7)

Put-in/Take-out: Since the Nith River is a slow flowing river almost any bridge over the river makes a decent access area. To make a nice day trip, two of the recommended access points are from Township Road 14 or Township Road 12. The take-out can also be varied, although most paddlers tend to take-out at Township Road 12 before reaching Highway 401. Parking is available off the side of any of these roads.

The Nith River is not a heavily travelled route due mainly to its low water levels during the summer months. However, in the late spring, making for a fantastic family river route. Regardless of where you choose to put in, the route remains calm as it works its way north towards Sauble Falls. Although the river flows through a predominantly farming region, there is very little development along the shore and most of the shoreline is forested. If you look closely, you may even see a deer hiding in the bush or taking a drink from the river.

Saugeen River (Maps 24/D1-30/A6-29/G2)

Put-in/Take-out: While there are numerous access points available at road crossings over the river, the three main access areas for the Saugeen River are located near the towns of Hanover, Walkerton and Paisley. In Hanover, the river is accessible from Hanover Park. In Walkerton, parking and a canoe launch are available at Lobies Campground located off Young Street North. In Paisley, the best access is outside of town off County Road 3. The end point for the route is found at the Denny's Dam Conservation Area near Southampton.

The Saugeen River Route is a long distance route that can be started in Hanover. The route is very mellow, slowly flowing west towards Walkerton. This is due mainly to the three dams located on the river. Although this section is an easy paddle, be alert for the three short portages around the dams.

From Walkerton, the river picks up its pace and passes over some grade I-I+ riffles en route to Paisley. This section is the most challenging portion of the route, but is still relatively easy for paddlers with river experience. Although farmland is the main feature of this part of the province, most of the river shore remains wooded and heavily forested in some sections. At times, it may feel like you are on a secluded wild river despite being relatively close to civilization.

Past Paisley, the river calms somewhat, although the odd riffle and fast water is still encountered. From Paisley to Denny's Dam Conservation Area is about 43 km (26.7 mi), which is possible to paddle in about 8-12 hours. To shorten this part of the route you can plan to take-out before Denny's Dam at any one of the road crossings over the river.

The best way to plan this route is to set up your accommodations well before your trip. Breaking the route into three or four days is recommended to ease the physical stress of the route. Many paddlers choose to begin the route in Walkerton to avoid the portaging upstream. For experienced paddlers, a recommended weekend trip is to start at Walkerton, camping at the Saugeen Bluffs Conservation Area the first night. The next day, the route can be finished to Denny's Dam Conservation Area. Each day will take approximately 8-10 hours out on the water. Be sure to check locally for water levels, as the route can be dangerous in very high water and impassable in sections during very low water conditions.

Upper Thames River Route (Map 14/A1)

Put-in/Take-out: Paddlers can access the Upper Thames River from the river crossing by County Road 29 or in the village of Innerkip. The take-out is located at the Pittock Conservation Area off the east side of the river north of Woodstock.

The Upper Thames River Route is a short, easy route that takes about half a day to travel. The route meanders past Innerkip and the Pittock Conservation Area to Woodstock. Near Woodstock the river widens significantly forming the Gordon Pittock Reservoir. The reservoir offers lake type paddling in the heart of the city. Near the reservoir dam, turn around and head back to the conservation area take-out to finish the route. To extend the trip, it is possible to portage around the dam, although the river on the west side of the dam flows past some heavy industrial sites making for a less than appealing trip.

From Innerkip, the route is about 16 km in length if you travel all the way to the Gordon Pittock Reservoir Dam and back to the conservation area. The best time to travel the river is after high water levels in late spring/early summer. During the summer, the water level can be quite low creating hindrances to smooth canoe travel. During medium water levels this route is an easy paddle, although it can turn into a grade II river during high water.

Mussio Ventures staff

Lake Paddling

Our difficulty rating of the lake routes is as follows:

Easy: For novice canoeists, with short, easy portages or none at all. Lakes along the route are smaller reducing wind problems.

Moderate: For intermediate canoeists, with a number of portages and a few that may be more rustic and/or longer.

Difficult: For advanced canoeists, with longer portages and/or portages that may be difficult to find or are grown over. Wilderness orientation skills may be required. Some challenging river travel may also be a part of the route.

Bruce Peninsula Kayaking (Maps 36/F1, 36/A2, 37A3, 38/D3, 39/D4)

Put-in/Take-out: Basically, any marina can act as your staging ground for kayaking around the Bruce Peninsula. Paddlers looking to explore Fathom Five National Park are best to launch from Tobermory. To explore the west shore of the Bruce Peninsula a good spot to launch from is Stokes Bay, while Lion's Head and Hope Bay are good staging areas for exploring the east shore.

The Bruce Peninsula offers some of the best kayaking opportunities in Ontario. The shoreline is very rustic in nature and makes a very interesting paddle. Paddlers can explore rock caves, old shipwrecks and quiet scenic bays home to plenty of wildlife. One caution, however, is that much of the peninsula is heavily exposed and waters can become extremely dangerous during even moderate wind conditions. Be sure to check conditions before you head out and certainly let someone know your intended route and approximate return time. Due to the large water body involved and the potential for rough seas, only experienced paddlers in closed canoes or kayaks should attempt to paddle this area.

Guelph Lake Paddling (Map 21/A2)

Put-in/Take-out: From the city of Guelph, take Victoria Road northwest to Conservation Road and head northeast. Conservation Road leads to the Guelph Lake Conservation Area and put-in areas.

Guelph Lake is by no means a canoe route, but it does provide a great location for a nice paddle just outside of the city. Bring along the dog, the canoe or kayak and pack a lunch to enjoy a lakeside picnic. Several picnic tables are scattered throughout the conservation area.

Long Point Paddling (Map 8/G3-9/D4)

Put-in/Take-out: Access to this marvellous wildlife area can be found at the Long Point Provincial Park east of the village of Long Point. To reach the park, follow Long Point Road (County Road 59) south from Highway 3 east of Tillsonburg.

Long Point is a large wetland that juts out into Lake Erie south of Port Dover. The Long Point National Wildlife Area and Long Point Provincial Park protect the majority of area and there are endless coves and inlets to explore. The point stretches over 30 km (18.7 mi) and both canoeists and kayakers can paddle along the shoreline during calm waters. This is one of the wildest areas in Southwestern Ontario and paddling enthusiasts can enjoy exploring this intricate wildlife area. During calm waters, the paddling is regarded as easy, however be sure to check the weather prior to departure as Lake Erie can become extremely dangerous for a small craft in even moderate seas.

Luther Marsh (Map 25/F4)

Put-in/Take-out: West of Orangeville, the Luther Marsh can be found by following County Road 25 to Concession Road 6-7. Head west to Side Road 21-22, which travels north to the marsh access area. There is plenty of parking available at the marsh and it is possible to put-in from a few areas nearby the parking areas.

The marsh is home to hundreds of bird species, which makes this area one of the most important wetlands in Southern Ontario. Canoeists and kayakers can enjoy an easy leisurely paddle around this lush wetland environment to get an up close and personal experience of this magnificent nature area. Be sure to bring along a camera, as there are always plenty of opportunities to snap a great picture of waterfowl and other wetland habitants.

Minesing Swamp Canoe Route (Map 32/G4)

Put-in/Take-out: The access point to the route can be found off of Geo Johnston Road just south of the village of Minesing (found just east of our maps). You can park anywhere off of the road and portage your canoe down to Willow Creek. Alternate access points are found along the Nottawasaga River off County Road 90 or near the end of McKinnon Road. Most of the access points along the Minesing also double as take-outs. If you are using a shuttle system, one of the more popular spots to take-out is located near the bridge of Highway 26 over the Nottawasaga River or at the Edenvale Conservation Area north of the bridge.

The 6,000 ha Minesing Swamp is one of the most important wetlands in the world. The swamp is home to hundreds of bird species, including one of the largest blue heron colonies in Ontario. The Minesing and all its biomass act like a sponge for the outlying areas by sucking up moisture from the spring thaw and helping to control local flooding. During the spring, water levels in the swamp rise to create a large water body easy to paddle. The Minesing is often compared to the Florida Everglades and hours can be spent examining its unique surroundings.

The Willow Creek meanders through the heart of the swamp passing thru the magnificent flooded forest. The most difficult part of exploring the swamp is that its immense size and lush forest cover make getting disoriented quite easy. To help navigate the route it is highly recommended to bring along a topographic map and compass.

Rondeau Bay Paddling (Map 3/F1)

Put-in/Take-out: Access to this large paddling area is available from Rondeau Provincial Park southeast of Blenheim. Access is provided from the provincial park or from one of the marinas found just north of the park.

Rondeau Bay has long been a play area for local boaters and paddlers. The bay is well protected from the strong winds often experienced on Lake Erie, making the bay suitable most of the time for canoes and kayaks. From the park the best way to explore the bay in is to follow the shoreline in a circular fashion. Along most of the shoreline, especially the shore of Rondeau Provincial Park, paddlers will experience some of the most lush shoreline ecosystems east of Leamington. There are also plenty of waterfowl and birds to see. During calm waters, it is an easy day paddle. Be sure to be alert for large boats travelling to and from Lake Erie near Shirley Point.

Parks

(National and Provincial Parks, Conservation and Protected Areas)

Southwestern Ontario has a diverse public park system ranging from provincial parks and natural reserves to national parks and conservation areas. In a region that is the most developed part of the province and perhaps the country, there remains a solid commitment by all to preserve the natural history and environment of the area. Pretty well every park offers its own unique feature and offers visitors a chance to experience the Great Outdoors.

What many people do not know is that Southwestern Ontario is home to a well established system of public campgrounds. Over a dozen parks and thirty conservation areas offer camping in the area. Combined with hundreds of privately owned campgrounds, there are plenty of camping options available. An added feature of Southwestern Ontario parks is that they are often much more developed than in other parts of the province. At some areas, you can enjoy outdoor pursuits like hiking and fishing or simply relax by the sandy beach or pool.

Crown Land or backcountry camping is popular in many parts of Ontario, although in Southwestern Ontario the opportunities are very limited. Private citizens own most of the land and provincial parks, conservation authorities or local governments often manage any remaining Crown Land. Your best opportunity for rustic camping can be found at the Bruce Peninsula National Park north of Owen Sound.

Since parks and conservation areas are usually used as a base for other recreational pursuits in the area, we recommend cross referencing with the other sections of this book to learn more about what to do in the area. Other sections describe the lakes you will be fishing and paddling on and the trails you will be walking and skiing on.

Provincial Parks, Nature Reserves & National Parks

Park fees vary from park to park and are separated into day-use and overnight fee systems. As of fall, 2002, day-use fees range from $6.50-$12 and overnight camping fees range from $17 in the off season to as high as $28 for premium sites with shower facilities. Reservations are usually available and cost about $9 or $10 per reservation. The off-season varies from park to park, although it is generally from the end of the second weekend in October to the beginning of the last weekend in April.

Camping is a very popular activity and the parks with campgrounds see heavy use during the summer. Reservations are highly recommended. For more information on the national parks system visit their website at www.parkscanada.ca. To reserve Ontario Park campsites call (888) ONT-PARK or online at www.OntarioParks.com.

Bayview Escarpment Provincial Nature Reserve (Map 35/B2)[⚏][🛈]

Located just south of the Meaford Department of National Defense Area, the Bayview Provincial Nature Reserve helps protect a portion of the Bayview Escarpment. There are no facilities available at this park, although hiking trails are available to explore the reserve. Some crevice caves can be explored at this 439 ha (1,084 ac) reserve.

Black Creek Provincial Park (Map 36/C2)
[🚻][⛴][⚏][🚣][🛶]

Black Creek Provincial Park lies west of the village of Lion's Head and is accessible via an access road off the west side of Stokes Bay Road. The 335 ha (827 ac) park is day-use only but there are private campgrounds in the immediate vicinity. Visitors mainly come to the park for its fantastic beach area.

Boyne Valley Provincial Park (Map 26/C1)[🚻][⚏][🐟][🛈]
Noted for its tall stands of healthy hardwood, Boyne Valley Park offers a few scenic walking trails, including a portion of the Bruce Trail. The trail provides access to a nice lookout over the rolling fields and meadows in the north portion of the park. Anglers or nature lovers also frequent the park to revel in the tranquility of the Boyne River.

The 431 ha (268 ac) park is a non-operating park and other than the trails, there are no amenities.

Bronte Creek Provincial Park (Map 22/A5)
[🏊][⛴][⚏][🚲][🚣][🐟][🛈]

Set amid the sprawl of urban development, Bronte Creek Provincial Park is a welcome escape from the toils of civilization. This park is unique due to its massive swimming pool and the Spruce Lane Farm. The farm is the focal point of the park and is surrounded by orchards and farmland that is still worked with Victorian era (late 1800's) tools such as a horse and plough. For the kids, the Children's Farm provides youngsters the opportunity to visit a variety of farm animals. Other outdoor recreation opportunities available include hiking along the fitness trail, fishing, and biking along the park's road system. Indoors, the park's visitor centre is a great place to learn more on the many natural and historical features of the region and the recreation complex offers lighted tennis courts, shuffleboard, basketball and volleyball courts.

For the camper, there are 365 sites (all provide electrical hook ups), showers, flush toilets, laundry and a boat launch. Campsites are often full throughout the summer but usually quieter the rest of the year. The park is found between Oakville and Burlington, off the east side of Burloak Drive north of Highway 403 (Queen Elizabeth Way). For reservations call (888) ONT-PARK. For more information call (905) 827-6911.

Bruce Peninsula National Park (Maps 38/G4, 39/B5)
[🏊][🚻][⛴][⚏][🚲][🏕][🚣][🐟][🛈]

Bruce Peninsula National Park is one of the most spectacular public parks in Ontario. As a protector of one of the last wild spaces of Southern Ontario, the park certainly deserves a spot as one of Ontario's premier public parks. Despite the lure of the park's crystal clear Georgian Bay shoreline and the sheer magnificence of the Niagara Escarpment, the park has managed to remain a truly diverse and wild destination. As a testament to the park and the region, wild animals such as black bears continue to call the peninsula home.

The main access to Bruce Peninsula National Park is from the Bruce Trail or from Highway 6. Along Highway 6, visitors can reach a number of day-use areas, such as the Singing Sands beach area and Emmett Lake, as well as the Cyprus Lake Campground. The rugged interior of the park is accessible from a few roads off Highway 6, but the only way to reach the interior campsites is via the Bruce Trail. Peak activity in the park is generally from mid June to mid September when the temperatures are warmer outside. Paddlers can enjoy exploring the Georgian Bay shoreline or the smaller interior lakes such as Emmett or Cyprus Lakes. Other popular outdoor activities at the park are biking along the many park roads, swimming or simply exploring the many natural wonders of the park. For more information on the Bruce Peninsula National Park call (519) 596-2233 or e-mail bruce_fathomfive@pch.gc.ca

Backcountry Camping

Perhaps one of the most exhilarating ways to take in the natural wonders of the park is by backcountry camping. There are two designated backcountry camping areas. Both the High Dump and Stormhaven area offering nine campsites with two tents permitted per site. The backcountry areas can only be reached by trail from along the Bruce Trail and offer basic facilities such as a composting toilet and food storage boxes. Be sure to use the storage boxes to avoid unwanted visitors to your site such as bears or racoons. Campers without prior registration/reservations must register at the main park office to use interior campsites. For reservations call (519) 596-2263 *Please note that under no circumstances are open fires permitted in the interior of the park. Cooking can only be done with a camping stove.*

Cyprus Lake Campground

The hub of the park is formed around the campground on Cyprus Lake. The campground is home to 242 campsites and offers two beach areas, running water, toilets, as well as picnic areas. During the summer, the campground can be quite busy and reservations are highly recommended before your arrival. For reservations call (519) 596-2263

Cabot Head Provincial Nature Reserve (Map 39/D4) ⌂ ⌂

This large 4,514 ha (11,150 ac) nature reserve is scattered around the Cabot Head of the Bruce Peninsula. The Cabot Head is home to varied terrain, which includes wetlands, cliffs, slopes and a diverse shoreline environment. Access is limited but there is road and trail access to the spectacular lighthouse. Alternatively, boaters can explore the shoreline region or hike inland to get a closer look at the natural wonders of this reserve.

Craigleith Provincial Park (Map 31/G1) ⌂ ⌂ ⌂ ⌂ ⌂

Set on the shores of Nottawasaga Bay of Lake Huron, this 66 ha (163 ac) park is popular during the summer months. However, in the spring and fall the cool winds off the bay scare away the majority of would be campers. It is at this time that anglers will find the large rainbow trout in the lake more willing to bite. Of the 157 campsites set amid mature stands of conifer trees, 72 offer electrical service suitable for trailers. Other facilities available at the park include a playground, showers, flush toilets and a day-use picnic area. The park is found west of Collingwood off the north side of Highway 26. For reservations call (888) ONT-PARK. For more information on the park and its facilities call (705) 445-4467.

Devil's Glen Provincial Park (Map 32/B4) ⌂ ⌂

Devil's Glen was once a fully operating park that now sees most of it visitors by Bruce Trail hikers. The old access road is gated and the only facilities are a boardwalk trail that leads down to a lookout over the Mad River Valley. The small park is only 59 ha (146 ac) in size and is located south of Collingwood off County Road 124.

Duncan Crevice Caves Provincial Nature Reserve (Map 31/E3) ⌂ ⌂

South of Thornbury, this nature reserve helps protect a scenic high elevation portion of the Niagara Escarpment. The highlight of the 161 ha (398 ac) reserve is the crevice caves that have slowly developed over time. The Bruce Trail passes through the reserve but it is the scenic side trail that provides the best view of the area.

Earl Rowe Provincial Park (Maps 26/G1, 32/G7) ⌂ ⌂ ⌂ ⌂ ⌂ ⌂

Amid the rolling hills and valleys of Southern Ontario, Earl Rowe Park is a popular destination park. There are 365 campsites, 163 with electric

Symbols Used for Parks and Trails	
⌂	Campsite /Trailer Park
⌂	Road Access Recreation Site
⌂	Trail or Boat Access Recreation Site
⌂	Day-use, Picnic Site
⌂	Beach
⌂	Boat Launch
⌂	Hiking Trail
⌂	Mountain Biking Trail
⌂	Horseback Riding
⌂	Cross Country Skiing
⌂	Snowmobiling
⌂	Mountaineering /Rock Climbing
⌂	Paddling (Canoe /Kayak)
⌂	Motorbiking /ATV
⌂	Swimming
⌂	Cabin /Hut /Resort
⌂	Interpetive Brochure
⌂	Fishing
⌂	Viewpoint
⌂	Wheel Chair Accessible
⌂	Downhill Skiing
⌂	Snowshoeing
⌂	Diving
⌂	Golfing
⌂	Sailing

hook ups, as well as flush toilets, showers and laundry facilities. One of the main attractions to the park, especially during the summer heat, is the football field size swimming pool. Canoe, paddleboat and kayak rentals are also available at the park for visitors to explore the reservoir. Add in a few short trails, nice picnic areas and the Boyne River for fishing or bird watching, and you can see why the park is such a great destination. The park can be accessed just west of the town of Allison off of Highway 89 and is open from early May to mid October. For campsite reservations call (888) ONT-PARK. For more information call (705) 435-2498.

Fathom Five National Park (Map 38/C2) ⌂ ⌂ ⌂ ⌂ ⌂ ⌂

The islands of Fathom Five National Park are some of the most unique natural formations in North America. They are very peculiar and were created by the endless crashing of waves along their shores over thousands of years. The park not only protects the islands that dot the waters, but also the fragile marine ecosystem that lies below. Natural wonders like remnants of ancient trees lie submerged in the park bottom. Some of the tree specimens have been carbon dated back over 7,000 years when ancient lake levels were drastically different. The park is also home to some of the oldest living cedar tree specimens in Canada. There are many specimens hundreds of years old with one in particular on Flowerpot Island that is 850 years old, making it the oldest known tree in Canada.

Diving is a popular recreational pastime at Fathom Five National Park as there are over a dozen shipwrecks available for underwater exploration. Alternatively, you can take a glass bottom boat tour from Tobermory out to a few of the sights. Other recreational opportunities that exist at the park are kayaking and exploring Flowerpot Island. Flowerpot Island is the only island in the park that is open to visitors and offers a boat dock, campsites and hiking trails. The dock is suitable for small boats, while there is another dock that is for the tour boat only. There are only six campsites available, each suitable for two tents, which fill up quickly. The Marl Trail and Loop Trails travel past many flowerpot rock formations, past natural cave formations and to the lighthouse. For campsite reservations call well in advance at (519) 596-2503 or for more information call (519) 596-2233. *Please note that under no circumstances are open fires permitted in the interior of the park. Cooking can only be done with a camping stove.*

Fish Point Provincial Nature Reserve (Map 2/G7) ⌂

Located at the southwestern tip of Pelee Island, this reserve is a favourite spot of bird watchers. The point is home to a large variety of shorebirds and other wetland type birds, including the black crowned night heron. The unique landscape of the reserve is comprised of sand dunes and a wild deciduous forest, which includes rare plants and wildlife such as the prickly pear cactus and the giant swallowtail butterfly. A small parking area found near the southern end of West Shore Road allows visitors a chance to observe from afar.

Forks of the Credit Provincial Park (Map 26/E6) ⌂ ⌂ ⌂ ⌂ ⌂

Set along the Niagara Escarpment, one of the main natural features of the Forks of the Credit Provincial Park is a fantastic waterfall that can be viewed from one of the park's trails. The Bruce Trail also travels though the park. Other than hiking, cross-country skiing and snowshoeing are popular trail uses in winter. The park can be reached via County Road 11 south of Orangeville, where washrooms and a small picnic area are found.

Hockley Valley Provincial Nature Reserve (Map 26/D3)

This 378 ha (934 ac) nature reserve is located north of Orangeville off County Road 7 and is part of the Niagara Escarpment Biosphere Reserve. Visitors to the park can enjoy the fantastic escarpment scenery available here via the Bruce Trail and the many side trails in the area.

Hope Bay Forest Provincial Nature Reserve (Map 36/G3)

The 353 ha (884 ac) nature reserve protects a portion of the Niagara Escarpment north of the small village of Hope Bay. The reserve is accessible via the Bruce Trail, which follows a large stretch of escarpment providing a number of picturesque views of Hope Bay.

Ira Lake Provincial Nature Reserve (Map 36/C1)

Ira Lake Nature Reserve can be found via a rough access road off the west side of Highway 6 south of Tobermory. The 30 ha (74 ac) reserve protects a portion of Bruce Peninsula deciduous forest and has no visitor facilities.

Inverhuron Provincial Park (Map 29/C5)

Open from early May to mid October, this day-use park is a favourite spot with sun seekers. The long sandy beach makes the perfect spot for a summer swim and picnic. The park also has a boat launch available for visitors to launch a boat onto Lake Huron. Washrooms and picnic areas round out the amenities available at this 288 ha (711 ac) park. For more information call (519) 389-9056.

Ipperwash Provincial Park (Map 11/D1)

Ipperwash Provincial Park was once a popular summer camping destination, although it has been closed for some time due to a native land dispute. At this time, access is not permitted to the park. For up to date information on the status of the park, please call (888) ONT-PARK or visit www.OntarioParks.com.

James N. Allan Provincial Park (Map 16/C7)

South of Dunnville, the James N.Allan Provincial Park is accessible off the south side of King's Row Road. The day-use only park lies along the northern shore of Lake Erie and has a small beach area to enjoy. While the majority of the beach is made up of pebbles, there is about a 100 m (328 ft) section of beach comprised of fine sand.

Johnstone Harbour-Pine Tree Point Provincial Nature Reserve (Maps 38/G7, 39/A7)

This 929 ha (2,295 ac) nature reserve is comprised of a few separate pieces set along the west coast of the Bruce Peninsula. The park protects a portion of a mature jack pine forest, which is an important wintering area for local deer. Johnstone Harbour Road provides access to a few areas of the reserve, although there are no facilities at this park.

John E. Pierce Provincial Park (Map 6/E4)

Found in the Carolinian forest region of Southern Ontario, the park was established in 1957, after the Pierce family donated the property to the Ontario government. This day-use park is open from June 1st to October 14th and offers a picnic area, hiking trails and a visitor centre for all to enjoy. A natural feature of the park is its 30 m (98 ft) high cliffs that provide great views of Lake Erie. If you are lucky, you may spot a bald eagle from the cliffs soaring above. Visitors can also visit the nearby Bacus Page Museum to learn more about the rich history of this area. The park is accessible off Currie Road (County Road 8), south of the village of Wallacetown. For more information on the park and its facilities you can call (519) 874-4691.

Komoka Provincial Park (Map 12/E5)

West of the city of London, Komoka Provincial Park lies along the east shore of the Thames River. The non-operating park can be reached off Gideon Road and offers a fine set of trails to explore. Hikers, bikers and, in winter, cross-country skiers can enjoy the trails that traverse past regenerating farmland to the mixed forest by the Thames River.

Lighthouse Point Provincial Nature Reserve (Map 2/G5)

Set at the northeast tip of Pelee Island, this small 96 ha (237 ac) park helps protect what little is left of Pelee Island's natural environment. The reserve is comprised of a mix of lush wetland and deciduous forest, vital to the protection of the rare Blue Racer snake. But the highlight of the area is the remains of the lighthouse constructed in 1834. The reserve can be explored by boat or on foot off the north end of the East Side Road. To reach Pelee Island you must cross Lake Erie by boat or ferry from Leamington or Kingsville.

Lion's Head Provincial Nature Reserve (Map 36/F2)

Named after the unique rock formation along its shore, the 526 ha (1,2998 ac) reserve is also home to ancient white cedars, which can be found along the cliff edge. Unlike the giant ancient red cedars of the west coast, these cedars are surprisingly small for their age. Nonetheless, it remains truly amazing that they have survived so long without human interference. The reserve is accessible via the Bruce Trail and is located east of the small village of Lion's Head. The Bruce Trail passes along the shoreline cliffs providing a number of spectacular views of the Georgian Bay.

Little Cove Provincial Nature Reserve (Map 38/E4)

This small 16 ha (40 ac) nature reserve is accessible via Little Cove Road or the Bruce Trail southeast of Tobermory. The reserve is surrounded by the Bruce Peninsula National Park and was established to protect a portion of the rugged shoreline of this part of the Peninsula. Some of the natural features that visitors can explore at the reserve include steep cliffs, a cobble beach and a few sea caves.

Long Point Provincial Park (Map 8/G4)

Long Point is a 40 km (24.8 mi) long sandspit that juts out into Lake Erie. The area is an important migratory birding area and during the spring and fall the point is often crowded with birds. In the spring the sheer amount of waterfowl seen in the area is impressive. The small 150 ha (370 ac) park gives visitors a chance to explore the area from the campground or beach areas. The full service park offers 254 campsites, 78 with electric hook ups, showers, flush toilets and laundry facilities. The fabulous sandy beach is very popular on hot days while paddlers can often be seen exploring the many coves and channels of the wildlife area. Other amenities that visitors will enjoy are the park store, boat launch, playground and picnic areas. The park is accessible off County Road 59, south of the town of Port Rowan and is open from early May to mid October. For more information call (519) 586-2133.

THE NATIONAL PARKS AND NATIONAL HISTOIC SITES OF CANADA — LES PARCS NATIONALETIES LIEUX HISTORIQUES NATIONAUX DU CANADA

Bruce Peninsula National Park of Canada

Fathom Five National Marine Park of Canada

Box 189, Tobermory, Ontario
N0H 2R0

For Information:
Call: (519) 596-2233
Fax: (519) 596-2298

Canada

Parks Canada   Parcs Canada

Canada

Reservations are highly recommended during the summer and can be made by calling (888) ONT-PARK.

MacGregor Point Provincial Park (Map 29/D3)

South of the town of Port Elgin, MacGregor Point Provincial Park lies along the coast of Lake Huron. The full service park is a popular summer camping destination with 140 electrical sites and 220 regular sites. Campers can enjoy many creature comforts such as showers, flush toilets and laundry. Most sites are set in the forest cover of the park with all sites within a short walk from the shore of Lake Huron. Outdoor activities that can be enjoyed at MacGregor Point include hiking on one of four trails, biking and swimming. In the winter months, portions of the hiking trails double as cross-country ski trails and visitors can even camp overnight in Yurts. Yurts are canvas shelters that are set on wooden decks and are available for rent throughout the year, although they are a favourite with winter campers. Be sure to stop in at the park visitor centre as it provides more information on local history and the natural environment of the park. If you plan to visit the park during July or August, it is highly recommended to make prior reservations by calling (888) ONT-PARK. For information on other park facilities call (519) 389-9056.

Mono Cliffs Provincial Park (Map 26/D2)

The 732 ha (1,808 ac) Mono Cliffs Provincial Park is part of the Niagara Escarpment Biosphere Reserve. The area is known for its unique rock formations including talus slopes and crevice caves. Visitors will find a parking lot with toilets and scenic walking trails to enjoy. The Bruce Trail passes through the middle of the park. Please stay on the trails as the natural features in the area can be easily damaged.

Noisy River Provincial Nature Reserve (Map 32/B6)

This small 378 ha (934 ac) nature reserve protects a portion of the Niagara Escarpment and a stretch of the Noisy River including the scenic Lavender Falls. The diversity of land along this section of the escarpment includes grassy meadows, cliffs and wetlands. The Bruce Trail travels through the reserve and a rustic shelter is available off the trail for hikers to use.

Nottawasaga Lookout Provincial Nature Reserve (Map 32/A3)

The Nottawasaga Lookout Nature Reserve is found on the Niagara Escarpment and home to the Singhampton Cave. The Bruce Trail travels through the park and some great views of the area can be found from along the trail. This provincial reserve is located south of Collingwood off the Clearview Line.

Ojibway Prairie Provincial Nature Reserve (Map 1/A2)

Located within the western city limits of Windsor, this nature reserve was established in order to protect what remains of the natural Southern Ontario prairie ecosystem. Prairie type areas are believed to have covered large portions of Southern Ontario, but after the arrival of European settlers most of the countryside was tilled for farming. Today, this 90 ha (222 ac) reserve offers a chance to hike through the prairie grass and past open woodlands, also known as savannah. In the late spring and summer, hundreds of wildflowers dot the reserve. Visitors can also further their nature education at the visitor centre found next to the reserve.

Pinery Provincial Park (Maps 11/E1, 10 inset)

The 1,000 campsites available attest to the popularity of Pinery Provincial Park. Most of the sites lie in a forest setting, but there are some unique sites set in the sand dune part of the park. Pinery also has 12 canvas yurts available for rental. These are a favourite with cross-country skiers during the winter. The sandy beaches are the main draw in summer but there is plenty more to do. Trails travel past an Oak savannah, which is home to mature oak tree forests that are set on the fragile sand dune soils, while many people prefer to paddle or fish in the nearby Ausauble River Channel. During the winter, cross-country skiing, tobogganing, snowshoeing and winter camping make going outdoors in the cold that much more fun. Pinery is a full service campsite offering electrical hook ups, showers, flush toilets and laundry facilities. Other amenities include the interesting visitor centre, the park store, canoe/kayak rentals and bike rentals. For more information call (519) 524-7124. Campsite reservations are highly recommended during the summer months and can be made by calling (888) ONT-PARK.

Point Farms Provincial Park (Map 23/A6)

Set atop a bluff along the shore of Lake Huron, this park was once the site of the Victorian era Point Farms Hotel. The hotel/resort was constructed in 1870 and was a favourite with visitors from the nearby United States and Southern Ontario until 1924.

Today, the area is the home of Point Farms Provincial Park, which offers 200 campsites for visitors, which includes 131 electrical sites. Other amenities at the park include showers, laundry and a visitor centre. Hiking enthusiasts will enjoy over 6 km (3.7 mi) of trails, which double as cross-country/snowshoe trails in the winter. But swimming and picnicking are the popular pastimes at the park, as the beach area makes a great hot summer day destination. The park is open from early May to mid October. For campsite reservations call (888) ONT-PARK or for more information on Point Farms call (519) 524-7124.

Point Pelee National Park (Map 2/F7)

Point Pelee is one of the most important inland wetland areas for migrating bird in North America. Throughout the year, the area is home to hundreds of bird and animal species, but it is during spring and fall when the area really comes alive. It is at this time that the migrating birds stop en route to their distant destinations. Over two thirds of Point Pelee National Park is comprised of marshland, and it is the largest marsh in the Great Lakes basin. This marvel of nature is home to amphibians, fish, insects, mammals and birds of all kinds.

Visitors to Point Pelee can get a close up view of the marsh and its wildlife by hiking along the famous Marsh Boardwalk. The boardwalk is one of the longest in the country and is a great way to explore the wetland. Another fantastic way to explore the wetlands is by canoe. If you like, a guided paddle is offered during the summer, and will take you through the marsh in a large freighter canoe. Other outdoor activities available at Point Pelee include a large selection of hiking trails, biking along the many park roads and over 20 km (12 mi) of sandy beach to explore or relax on. If you do not have your own bike, bicycles can be rented from April to October. In the past, Point Pelee was a very popular camping destination park. So much so that the park eventually has to heavily restrict camping in order to limit the stress on the park's natural environment. While camping is permitted, it is only available to groups. Organized youth groups, such as scouts or student groups visiting for educational purposes are permitted throughout the summer. During the fringe periods, adult groups are permitted. Camping opportunities are limited and reservations must be made in advance. Call (519) 322-2365 for reservations or for general park information, such as migration information, the park info line is available 24 hours a day at (519) 322-2371.

Port Bruce Provincial Park (Map 7/E3)

This small 5 ha (12 ac) park lies along the northern shore of Lake Erie next to the small village of Port Bruce. The park is a day-use only park that is mainly used for its boat launching facilities. Other facilities available at the park include a playground, picnic area, washrooms and a sandy beach. The beach area is a favourite spot during the heat of summer and can be quite busy at times. The park is open from June 1st to September 2nd. For more information call (519) 874-4691.

Port Burwell Provincial Park (Maps 7/G3, 8/A3)

While Long Point and Rondeau Provincial Parks are renowned bird watching areas, Port Burwell is often overlooked. The park comes alive in the spring and fall with over 85 species of migratory birds passing through the area. Hike the park's trails or simply take a stroll along the 2 km (1.2 mi) sandy beach area to further explore the park's natural beauty. The park is also home to 232 campsites set amid a Carolinian forest. Amenities include 123 electrical sites, a boat launch, park store, showers, flush toilets and laundry. Port Burwell Provincial Park is open from early May to mid October and is located south of the town of Tillsonburg. More information on the park can be obtained by calling (519) 874-4691. For campsite reservations call (888) ONT-PARK.

Pretty River Valley Provincial Park (Map 32/A3)

Southwest of Collingwood the Pretty River Provincial Park is accessible off the north side of County Road 31. This 808 ha (1,996 ac) non-operating park protects a portion of the Niagara Escarpment complete with crevice caves to explore. Part of the Bruce Trail travels through the park and visitors can enjoy fishing and hiking in the summer or cross-country skiing and snowmobiling in the winter.

Rock Point Provincial Park (Map 16/E7)

Rock Point Provincial Park lies next door to the small Lake Erie village of Port Maitland. As a shoreline park, Rock Point attracts a number of interesting wildlife species. Along with birds, the migratory monarch butterfly visits the park in significant numbers during the month of September as a stopover en route to Mexico. Another interesting natural feature of the park is the large display of fossils that can be easily spotted in the limestone shale along parts of the park shoreline. Some of the outdoor activities available at the park are hiking along the 2.5 km (1.6 mi) park trail, swimming and paddling in the nearby Grand River and camping. Park facilities include showers, flush toilets, picnic areas, a park store, a beach area and laundry. The park is open from early May to mid October and has 81 electrical and 97 regular campsites. This park is quite busy during the summer and it is recommended to reserve your campsite prior to arrival by calling (888) ONT-PARK. Call (519) 674-1750 for more park information.

Rondeau Provincial Park (Map 3/F1)

As the home to one of the largest Ontario tracts of Carolinian forest, Rondeau Provincial Park is an interesting place to explore. The park was established in 1894 as Ontario's second provincial park and today is one of the most popular parks in the system. Visitors can hike or bike through the expansive forest setting. If you prefer water activities, Lake Erie is easily accessible from a number of areas around the park. There are over 12 km (7.5 mi) of sandy beach areas along the eastern shore, while canoeists and other boaters can explore Rondeau Bay. The bay is a lush wetland that is home to wildlife and hundreds of birds, especially during the spring and fall migration. Winter activities at the park include cross-country skiing, ice fishing and skating on Rondeau Bay.

Plenty of amenities are available at Rondeau as this full service park offers flush toilets, showers, a visitor centre, park store and laundry. Campers have 110 regular and 152 electrical campsites to choose from. Most sites are set in the campground located at the northern end of the park. If you have a boat, there is a boat launch providing access to Rondeau Bay and Lake Erie. The park also hosts a variety of guided hikes, canoe excursions and interpretive programs. The park is open year round and can be reached via County Road 15 south from Highway 401 near Ridgetown. Be sure to call (888) ONT-PARK if you plan to camp at the park during the summer. More information can be obtained by calling (519) 674-1750.

Sauble Falls Provincial Park (Map 33/E1)

Set along the scenic Sauble River, the natural highlight of the park is Sauble Falls. The falls were once the backbone for generating electricity and power for a local timber mill. Today, the park is home to 152 campsites, 46 electrical services, as well as flush toilets, showers, a day-use picnic area and laundry facilities. During the spring, a popular attraction to the park is the rainbow trout that make their way up the falls to spawn. Anglers and viewers flock to the area to witness this force of nature. Hiking enthusiasts will enjoy the Sauble Trail, which passes through a mixed forest to a lookout over the falls. The nearby Rankin River and Sauble River Canoe Routes are another intimate way to explore the area. The park can be accessed off County Road 13 north of Sauble Beach, and is open from the last weekend in April to the last weekend in October. Call (519) 422-1952 for more information or (888) ONT-PARK for reservations.

Selkirk Provincial Park (Map 15/F7)

Selkirk Provincial Park is a 73 ha (189 ac) park that lies along the northern shore of Lake Erie. Visitors can hike the 2 km (1.2 mi) trail through the forest, marsh and meadows of the park or simply laze at the sandy beach area. Facilities available at Selkirk include 80 regular and 62 electrical campsites, flush toilets, showers, a picnic area, a park store and laundry. If you have a boat, there is a boat launch onto Lake Erie. Located east of the City of Simcoe, the park is open from early May to late October. For campsite reservations call (888) ONT-PARK or for more information call (519) 674-1750.

Short Hills Provincial Park (Map 17/B3)

Short Hills is designated as a natural environment park and is located southwest of the city of St.Catherines. Access to the park is available off the west side of Cataract Road or off County Road 69. The park is home to a series of multi-use trails. While there are hiking only designated trails available, there are also trails suitable for mountain biking and horse back riding.

As Authentic As All Outdoors!

© AZ CARDS

SOJOURN

a seasonal experience

✦ Technical Outerwear ✦ X Country Skis & Snowshoes
✦ Clothing & Hiking Boots ✦ Travel Essentials & Books
✦ Camping Equipment ✦ Canoes & Kayaks
✦ Rentals Available ✦ Climbing Equipment

31 Commerce Park Dr, Barrie
(705) 739-9694
510 First St., Collingwood
(705) 446-1990

www.sojournoutdoors.ca

Smokey Head-White Bluff Provincial Nature Reserve
(Map 36/E1, 39/E7) ⬚ ⬚

North of the village of Lion's Head, the Smokey Head-White Bluff Nature Reserve can be reached via the Bruce Trail. The park is home to some magnificent 50 m (164 ft) high cliffs. Over the years, sea caves and other interesting rock formations have formed by waves smashing into the cliffs. Visitors can enjoy a hike through the upland forest and along the ridge, which provides great views of the Georgian Bay.

Trillium Woods Provincial Nature Reserve (Map 13/G3)
⬚ ⬚

Situated between Ingersoll and Woodstock, this small 10 ha (25 ac) reserve lies near the northern limit of the Carolinian forest region of Southern Ontario. To find the reserve follow County Road 12 east or west to the Trillium Line. The reserve lies along the west side of Trillium Line north of County Road 12. The main feature of this reserve is its abundance of rare white trilliums. Many of the trilliums here sport green pin stripes and other variations of the stripe and are a rare find. An easy 1 km (0.6 mi) trail is available to the public in order to explore the reserve. Be sure to stay on the trail to avoid trampling fragile plants and please do not pick any of the flowers. Plant removal is prohibited and punishable by law.

Turkey Point Provincial Park (Map 9/A2) ⬚ ⬚ ⬚

Located southwest of the town of Port Dover, Turkey Point lies along the northern shore of Lake Erie. The park is a popular summer destination and is a full service park. Park visitors can choose from 104 electrical campsites and 131 regular sites while enjoying the comforts of showers, flush toilets and laundry facilities. Outdoor activities that can be enjoyed at Turkey Point include hiking through the park's Carolinian forest, swimming and golfing. The park is the only provincial park in Ontario that is home to a 9-hole golf course, complete with club rentals. If you plan to camp at the park during the summer, it is recommended to make reservations by calling (888) ONT-PARK. For more park information call (519) 426-3239.

Wasaga Beach Provincial Park (Map 32/E2)
⬚ ⬚ ⬚ ⬚ ⬚ ⬚ ⬚ ⬚

As the name implies, the main attraction of this day-use park is the 14 km (9.7 mi) long white sand beach on Nottawasaga Bay. The beach and bay make a great place for all forms of recreation including swimming, wind surfing, beach volleyball, picnicking or cycling along the park's beach bike path. The beach is not the only recreation area in the park. The dunes area is designated a natural environment area and offers over 26 km (16 mi) of hiking trails that double as cross-country ski trails in winter. Canoeing and fishing are also available on the Nottawasaga River. Wasaga Beach is one of the most popular summer destinations in Southern Ontario. For a little peace and solitude in this beautiful area, try visiting the park in the off-season. Call (705) 429-2516 for more information.

Wheatley Provincial Park (Map 2/D5) ⬚ ⬚ ⬚ ⬚ ⬚ ⬚

Located along the northern shore of Lake Erie, Wheatley Provincial Park is a busy park home to 220 campsites, hiking trails and sandy beaches. Campers will marvel at the Carolinian forest setting while enjoying comforts such as electric hook ups, showers and flush toilets. To further explore the Carolinian environment of the park, you can hike along one of the park's hiking trails or simply take a stroll along the sandy beaches of Lake Erie. A major natural attraction of this park is the migrating birds that can be viewed here during the spring and fall periods. If you plan to camp at Wheatley Provincial Park it is recommended to make a reservation prior to arrival by calling (888) ONT-PARK. The park is open from mid April to mid October. For more information please call (519) 25-4659.

Conservation Areas

Over the past fifty years, conservation areas have become an important part of preserving our natural and historical heritage. In a region like Southwestern Ontario, where the demands on the environment are quite large, conservation areas have become an integral part of the outdoor recreation system. While many conservation areas have been developed to provide basic outdoor recreation opportunities, a large number focus primarily on habitat maintenance and restoration. Camping opportunities do exist at a number of areas, but most sites remain day-use areas that usually offer picnic sites and/or trail systems.

Below we have included a description on the more popular and well-developed conservation areas in Southwestern Ontario. However, due to the sheer number of areas, with more being added annually, we did not provide a complete list. Many of the sites not listed below have few, if any, facilities. In most cases, these smaller conservation areas are peaceful locations that provide a chance to get out and enjoy nature. For more information on these remaining areas it is recommended to call the local conservation authority for that area.

A.W. Campbell Conservation Area (Map 11/F7)
⬚ ⬚ ⬚

The A.W. Conservation Area is a small natural area east of the town of Alvinson. The conservation area is a popular camping destination and is equipped with showers, toilets, laundry, playground and picnic areas. The Millennium Trails wind along portions of Morrough Creek and are a great way to further explore the area. Call (519) 847-5357 for more information.

Albion Hills Conservation Area (Maps 26/G4, 27/A4)
⬚ ⬚ ⬚ ⬚ ⬚ ⬚ ⬚ ⬚ ⬚

Albion Hills Conservation Area was the first conservation area established in Ontario. The natural area is well known by recreationists as a trail destination park. Mountain bikers will find over 27 km (16.8 mi) of trails, including some of Ontario's best technical trails. Hiking is also a popular activity and in the winter the trails convert into a fabulous cross-country trail system. Other activities visitors can enjoy include fishing, paddling, picnicking and swimming at the parks beach area. Campers will find 230 campsites complete with showers and laundry facilities. This conservation area can be accessed via Queen Street (County Road 50), near Cedar Mills. For more information call (800) 838-9921 or for camping reservations call (416) 667-6295.

Allan Park Conservation Area (Map 24/F1) ⬚ ⬚ ⬚ ⬚

In addition to over 10 km (12 mi) of trails that are used for both hiking and cross-country skiing, the day-use area offers picnicking and a stocked trout pond. The area makes a great location for a peaceful, fun day in the outdoors and can be reached off the Concession 2 Side Road east of near Hanover.

Archie Coulter Conservation Area (Map 7/D1) ⬚ ⬚ ⬚

This 54 ha (134 ac) natural area is home to 4 km (2.5 mi) of interconnected trails that bisect the Carolinian forest. There is an observation tower and many places for a tranquil picnic. In winter, cross-country skiers use the trail system. The conservation area is located between St. Thomas and Aylmer, off Brouwers Road.

Backus Heritage Conservation Area (Map 8/F3)
⬚ ⬚ ⬚ ⬚ ⬚

The Backus Heritage Conservation Area is a popular retreat for history buffs. A 19th Century historic village has been restored and includes the Backhouse Mill, which was originally built in 1798. Visitors can explore the village or visit the nature centre. In addition to the village, there is plenty to do outdoors. Campers will find 165 campsites complete with showers, flush toilets and laundry facilities. There is a park pool, a stocked trout pond for anglers and over 12 km (7.5 mi) of wooded trails to explore. For more information on the conservation area and its many educational programs call (877) 990-9932.

Ball's Falls Heritage Conservation Area (Maps 16/G2, 17/A2)

Ball's Falls Heritage Area offers visitors a chance to step back in time by touring restored mid 19th Century buildings. Hikers have plenty to choose from including the Cataract and Bruce Trails, but most people come to see the scenic falls on Twenty Mile Creek. There is also a picnic area. There is a small fee to access the area.

Bannockburn Wildlife Area (Map 18/B3)

The Bannockburn Wildlife Area is a small tract of wild space that is home to a deciduous forest, marshland and white cedar stands. Visitors can hike along marked loop trails and may be lucky enough to spot a deer along the way. A picnic area and outhouse is available at the parking area, which can be accessed off the west side of Bannockburn Road east of Bayfield.

Beamer Memorial Conservation Area (Map 16/D1)

This conservation area is best known for the Lookout Trail, which leads up Grimsby Mountain. From the lookout platform, there are some fantastic views of Lake Ontario and the Niagara Escarpment. Picnic tables and toilets are also offered at the conservation area. To reach the area, take County Road 12 (Grimsby Road) south from the Queen Elizabeth Way at Grimsby.

Belfountain Conservation Area (Map 26/E7)

Set along a portion of the Niagara Escarpment northwest of the village of Erin, the highlight of the area is the suspension bridge over the West Credit River. The conservation area also offers a peaceful picnic area, the 1.5 km (0.9 mi) long Trimble Trail and fishing opportunities in the cool, clear river.

Belwood Lake Conservation Area (Maps 25/G7, 26/A6)

This man-made reservoir is formed by the damming of the Grand River near the town of Fergus. Although there are a series of properties along the shore of the reservoir, the main access to the conservation area is found at the Shand Dam off County Road 18. In addition to a picnic area, canoe rentals are available to better explore the lake. Fishing and swimming are also common in the lake. Hikers and bikers have plenty to choose from, including short shoreline trails or the long distance Elora Cataract Trail.

Big Bend Conservation Area (Map 6/A3)

The Big Bend Conservation Area lies along the northern shore of the Thames River east of Wardsville. Visitors will find 26 campsites set in a semi open setting, while swimming, paddling and fishing in Thames River are popular pastimes. Amenities at the conservation area include a day-use picnic area, a boat launch, washrooms and showers. Call (519) 354-7310 for more information.

Big 'O' Conservation Area (Map 2/B2)

This small conservation area is located in the village of Comber off Elizabeth Street. The area was established in 1992 through a local donation and is a fantastic destination for birdwatchers. Migrating birds visit the area each spring and fall, providing a great display. A short trail leads through a mix of poplar/maple bush and around a wetland area.

Binbrook Conservation Area (Maps 15/G3, 16/A3)

This large, 358 ha (885 ac) conservation area is home to the largest inland lake in the Niagara watershed, Lake Niapenco. Most visitors enjoy water-based activities, from the sandy beach and swimming area to fishing and boating/canoeing around the lake. There is also a picnic area and trails that loop around the lake. There is a small fee to access the conservation area, which is located south of the city of Hamilton.

Boyd Conservation Area (Map 27/D6)

The Boyd Conservation Area is located in Woodbridge and is accessible off Islington Road. The conservation area is a popular green space with hiking trails along the East Humber River as well as a picnic area. Group camping is offered to organized groups by calling (905) 851-0575.

Brant Conservation Area (Map 14/G2)

Found in the west side of the city of Brantford, the Brant Conservation Area offers camping opportunities amid a young forest setting. The Grand River is the predominant feature of the conservation area, and anglers, paddlers and people looking for a refreshing dip all take advantage of the easy access to the water. There is also a trail system to explore. For campsite information call (888) 376-2212.

Brucedale Conservation Area (Map 29/D4)

Set along the eastern shore of Lake Huron, the Brucedale Conservation Area is located south of the town of Port Elgin not far from Highway 21. The area was established in 1956 and was originally purchased to mainly provide a boat launch onto Lake Huron. Today, along with camping opportunities visitors can enjoy a day-use picnic area, swimming at the sandy beach, or a short hike through a treed setting. Other amenities at the 50 ha (123 ac) conservation area include flush toilets, showers and a playground. For campsite reservations call (519) 389-4516.

Bruce's Caves Conservation Area (Map 37/B7)

Hidden in the Niagara Escarpment is an important natural area that protects the Bruce's Caves. The caves were created thousands of years ago by wave erosion of the lake, which once extended to the cave area. Today, the Bruce Trail traverses through the northern border of this conservation area. The Bruce Cave Side Trail makes an interesting detour. Access to the picnic area can be found off Side Road 20 northeast of the settlement of Oxenden.

Bruce's Mill Conservation Area (Map 28/A4)

During the month of March, the Bruce's Mill Conservation Area is home to the Sugarbush Maple Syrup Festival. Curious visitors can watch old fashioned and modern maple syrup being produced and of course, taste plenty of maple treats. As summer approaches, the conservation area comes alive with visitors enjoying the many sports fields and the driving range. A series of trails traverse through the area and visitors can also enjoy the many picnic areas and picnic shelters at the park. Organized group camping is available. The conservation area is located north of Markham between the corner of Warden Avenue and Stouffville Road. Call (905) 877-5531 for more information.

Byng Island Conservation Area (Map 16/D6)

Byng Island is a favourite destination with boaters due to the easy access to the Grand River and nearby Lake Erie. The conservation area also offers a busy campground with showers and flush toilets. Outdoor activities offered at the conservation area include swimming in the public pool, picnicking, fishing and hiking/biking trails. While the area offers plenty of recreational opportunities, it also helps protect a thriving wetland. Boaters and paddlers can venture out onto the water to get a better view of its natural attributes. For campsite availability call (888) 376-2212.

C.M. Wilson Conservation Area (Map 5/B7)

Established in 1967, this 30 ha (74 ac) conservation area offers 100 campsites set in the Carolinian forest. With the convenience of showers and flush toilets, this campsite is a busy spot during the summer. Visitors can swim and relax on the beach or even rent a canoe to explore the man-made lake. A short trail system also winds through the forest and around a small pond. The conservation area is located southeast of the city of Chatham off Fargo Road. Campsite reservations and additional information are available by calling (519) 354-7310.

Cedar Creek and Beach (Map 1/F6)

Both the Cedar Creek and Cedar Beach Conservation Areas are located west of the town of Kingsville. Cedar Creek is one of the most important natural areas in the region and is home to a variety of wildlife including bald eagles, deer and waterfowl. A tiny conservation area protects a portion of the creek, which is best explored by canoe. Cedar Beach is a popular summer destination providing a nice picnic area.

Chippawa Creek Conservation Area (Map 16/F5)

Chippawa Creek is one of two conservation areas in the Niagara Conservation Authority that offers camping. The popular campground offers 156 sites (reservations are recommended) while day-trippers can enjoy the picnic area and nature trails. Fishing, canoeing and swimming are other activities that visitors can enjoy. During winter, cross-country skiers and snowshoers use the trails. The conservation area lies next to Dils Lake and can be reached via County Road 45 west of Welland. For more info or reservations call (905) 386-6387.

Christie Conservation Area (Map 21/E7)

The large, 336 ha (830 ac) reserve that encircles Christie Lake reservoir is a fantastic destination to escape to nature. Outdoor activities that are popular at the area include hiking over 10 km (12 mi) of trails, paddling on Christie Lake and swimming at the sandy beach area. If you don't have a canoe, paddleboats and canoes are available for rent during the summer months. Fishing enthusiasts will certainly enjoy testing their luck in one of the conservation area's nine stocked trout ponds. Playgrounds, picnic shelters and tables round out the amenities offered at the park. The conservation area is accessible off the south side of Highway 5 west of Hamilton.

Clinton Conservation Area (Map 18/D2)

The site of a former pig farm and slaughterhouse, the Clinton Conservation Area has been transformed into an outdoor recreation area complete with picnic tables as well as hiking and fishing opportunities. The conservation area is located southeast of the village of Clinton off the south side of Highway 8.

Coldstream Conservation Area (Map 12/D4)

This small conservation area is located along the shore of the Sydenham River northwest of London. The area is accessible via the Quaker Line off Ilderton Road (County Road 16). Camping is limited to groups, but there is a picnic area, playground and hiking trails available for day-use. For more information on the conservation area and its camping opportunities call (519) 245-3710.

Comfort Maple Conservation Area (Map 17/A4)

The main attraction to this conservation area is the ninety-foot high sugar maple tree. The maple tree is over five hundred years old

and is the oldest living sugar maple in Canada. The parking area to the conservation area can be found off Balfour Street northwest of Fonthill.

Confederation Park (Map 16/B1)

Confederation Park is a popular summer destination that lies along the shore of Lake Ontario just east of Hamilton Harbour. The park is home to a sandy beach where visitors can hike, bike or even inline skate along the park's paved breezeway. One of the highlights of the park is Wild Waterworks, which is a fun water park. Cool off in the wave pool or at any of the other wet and fun water rides. For more information on this park and the facilities available call (800) 555-8775.

Contestogo Lake Conservation Area (Map 20/A1)

Contestogo Lake is a favourite summer destination with locals and travellers. In addition to a campground with showers and laundry, there is a picnic area and even canoe rentals. Hiking enthusiasts can explore a few hiking trails available at the park, while paddlers will enjoy travelling around Contestogo Lake. Swimming is also a popular attraction at the lake during the summer months. The conservation area is located northwest of the city of Waterloo via the 3rd Line or County Road 11. For more information on camping and other features call (888) 376-2212.

Crawford Lake Conservation Area (Map 21/F4)

Crawford Lake is a small but deep lake that is home to a fragile natural environment. A boardwalk along the lakeshore provides a better view of the lake environment and makes up part of the 15 km (9.3 mi) trail system. Hikers, and in winter cross-country skiers, can enjoy exploring the Niagara Escarpment and a portion of the Bruce Trail. Amenities at the conservation area include a picnic area, visitor centre, café and gift shop. The park lies southwest of Milton off the Guelph Line (County Road 1).

Dalewood Conservation Area (Maps 7/B1, 13/A7)

This large 283 ha (700 ac) conservation area can be found north of St. Thomas via Dalewood Road. The conservation area is home to a good sized campground that is situated near the park reservoir. The reservoir provides some fishing opportunities while a number of hiking trails wind through the area and around the reservoir. Along with showers and toilets, the campground is equipped with a pool, which is a busy spot during the summer months. Call (519) 631-1009 for campsite and additional information.

Deer Creek Conservation Area (Map 8/D2)

The Deer Creek Conservation Area is 121 ha (300 ac) in size and found on the east side of a man-made reservoir. The campground offers 40 sites set in the Carolinian forest and the reservoir is a busy spot in the summer. Visitors can enjoy a sandy beach area, swimming, paddling and fishing. Other amenities that are offered at the conservation area are canoe rentals, picnic areas, playground and showers. To reach the park, follow County Road 59 southeast of Tillsonburg. For camping reservations and more information call (877) 990-9934.

Denny's Dam Conservation Area (Map 29/G2)

Denny's Dam is situated along the Saugeen River east of Southampton. The conservation area is a very popular fishing destination since the dam is a large holding area for migrating rainbow trout and salmon in the spring and fall. The small picnic area also provides access for paddlers testing the river.

Devonwood Conservation Area (Map 1/C2)

The Devonwood Conservation Area is located in the southern end of the city of Windsor off Cabana Road. The wooded area is home to a 4 km (2.5 mi) trail system as well as a picnic area.

Dundas Valley Conservation Areas (Map 15/E1)

The Dundas Valley is comprised of three small conservation areas creating one of the largest protected forest tracts in the region at 1,200 ha (2,964 ac). At the Dundas Valley Trail Centre you can pick up a more detailed trail map to help you explore the 40 km (25 mi) of multi-use trails. The trails pass through dense Carolinian type forest and are open to hiking, biking, cross-country skiing and snowshoeing. Visitors to the valley can also visit the historical Griffin House and the Hermitage Ruins. Both sites are remnants of the 19th Century and offer visitors the opportunity to learn more about the local history. For more information on the Dundas Valley Conservation Area call (905) 627-1233.

Durham Conservation Area (Map 30/G7)

Over 200 campsites set in a mature cedar forest are available at the Durham Conservation Area. The park is located along the Saugeen River east of the town of Durham and is home to the picturesque McGowan Falls. Visitors can explore the hiking/cross-country ski trails, take a dip in the river or enjoy a picnic. For more camping information call (519) 364-1255.

Dutton/Dunwich Conservation Area (Map 6/B2)

Set along the Thames River south of Glencoe, the Dutton/Dunwich Conservation Area is used mainly for access onto the Thames River. Both paddlers and anglers can explore the river. The conservation area can be reached off Coyne Road southeast of Glencoe.

E.M. Warwick Conservation Area (Map 6/D4)

This 14 ha (35 ac) conservation area was established in 1974 and is used mainly as a day-use area. Picnic tables and a shelter are available next to the beach on Lake Erie. There is also an observation tower that can be found on the short nature trail. Camping is restricted to organized groups and reservations must be made prior to arrival by calling (519) 354-7310.

Edenvale Conservation Area (Map 32/G3)

The Edenvale Conservation Area is a small preserve on the shore of the Nottawasaga River that can be found off of Highway 26 at Edenvale. Most visitors take advantage of the picnic tables but organized groups and users of the Nottawasaga River Canoe Route can camp in the area. Call (705) 424-1479 for more information.

Elora Gorge and Elora Quarry Conservation Areas (Map 20/F1)

Over the years, the Elora Gorge has become one of the more popular destinations around the Kitchener/Waterloo region. Campers will find 550 campsites, complete with showers, flush toilets and laundry. There are also picnic areas and a small (1 ha/2.5 ac) lake to take a dip in on hot summer days. Hiking trails have been established in and around the park and are a great way to get some outdoor exercise. Perhaps one of the biggest features offered at the gorge is the opportunity to fish in the Grand River. The river provides some of the best fishing opportunities in Ontario. Campsite reservations are highly recommended and can be made by calling (866) 668-2267. Additional swimming opportunities also exist at the Elora Quarry Conservation Area found north of the Elora Gorge off County Road 18.

Eugenia Falls Conservation Area (Map 31/D5)

The main attraction to this conservation area is the fabulous Eugenia Falls found along the Beaver River. The falls cascade over a high cliff along the Niagara Escarpment falling some 30 m (98 ft) into a deep gorge. The conservation area offers picnic tables, outhouses and a short trail to the falls. The parking area can be found off the west side of County Road 13, north of the town of Flesherton.

Falls Reserve Conservation Area (Map 23/B7)

The 93 ha (230 ac) Falls Reserve is located east of the town of Goderich off the south side of County Road 31 (Londesboro Road). The Maitland River provides a scenic backdrop for the park and a number of hiking/cross-country ski trails are found in the area. The river provides decent fishing opportunities or you can always try your luck at the bass and trout pond. Campers will find 185 campsites, many with electrical hook ups, washrooms, showers and a snack bar. Day-trippers can have fun at the horseshoe pits, picnic areas, and playground. Campsite reservations are recommended and can be made by calling (877) FAL-LSCA.

Fanshawe Conservation Area (Map 13/A4)

The Fanshawe Conservation Area is the most popular conservation area in the Upper Thames Conservation Authority. The park is well known for its 650 treed campsites that are all within walking distance of Fanshawe Lake. The lake is a great place for a swim on hot summer days or to explore by canoe or kayak. There are also a series of trails around the lake. Educational and interpretive programs are offered throughout the year and there are picnic areas and a large pool to enjoy. The conservation area is found northeast of the city of London. For campsite reservations or for more information call (866) ONT-CAMP.

Feversham Gorge Conservation Area (Map 31/G5)

East of Eugenia Lake, the Beaver River passes through the Feversham Gorge creating one of the most fascinating natural areas in the region. Along the 1.5 km (0.9 mi) hiking trail, visitors will pass through a dense forest to the edge of a 24 m (80 ft) high gorge. The access area to the conservation area can be found south of the village of Feversham off the west side of County Road 2. Picnic tables and outhouses are available at the parking area.

Fifty Point Conservation Area (Map 16/D1)

This recreation based conservation area is located along the shore of Lake Ontario between Hamilton and Grimsby. The conservation area has a popular beach, picnic area, playgrounds, a stocked fishing pond, soccer field and baseball diamond for visitors to enjoy. 47 seasonal campsites are available at the park, but they are in high demand throughout the year. The conservation area also offers a full service marina, which is equipped with a double boat launch and offers mooring for 312 boats. For more information and camping availability call (888) 319-4722.

Glencairn Conservation Area (Map 32/E5)

This small conservation area encompasses a portion of the Mad River in the village of Glencairn. Set amid beautiful stands of large cedar trees, the area offers picnic facilities as well as fishing and canoeing opportunities. The Ganaraska Trail is also found nearby.

Glen Haffy Conservation Area (Map 26/F4)

Visitors to Glen Haffy can enjoy some of the best trout fishing in Southwestern Ontario. The area is home to a trout hatchery, which provides trout for stocking in its four ponds as well as for other conservation areas. Along with fishing, several nature trails as well as the Bruce Trail travel through the conservation area. Other features at the park include picnic areas, a visitor centre and organized group camping. The conservation area is located east of Orangeville off Airport Road (County Road 7), south of Highway 9. More information can be obtained by calling (905) 584-2922.

Guelph Lake Conservation Area (Map 21/A2)

Located due north of the city of Guelph, the Guelph Lake Conservation Area is a popular summer destination. The conservation area encompasses much of Guelph Lake and has a good sized campground available throughout the spring to fall season. Paddling and fishing opportunities abound, while swimming is also a big attraction during the summer. For campsite reservations and information call (888) 376-2212.

Haldimand Conservation Area (Map 9/F1)

Haldimand Conservation Area lies along the northern shore of Lake Erie east of Port Dover. 235 campsites are available at the conservation area with the majority of the sites offering electrical hook-ups. Some of the outdoor activities visitors can enjoy include hiking, picnicking and swimming in Lake Erie. Showers, flush toilets laundry and a playground round out the amenities at the park. Call (877) 990-9938 for more information or campsite reservations.

Hay Creek Conservation Area (Map 9/A1)

This small conservation area surrounds a small pond encircled by a Carolinian forest. A short hiking trail traverses through the forest and provides access to Hay Creek where fishing opportunities exist. During the winter, the trail makes a decent cross-country ski route.

Headquarters Conservation Area (Map 24/D1)

As the name implies, this area is the actual headquarters to the Saugeen Conservation Authority. Visitors can learn more about the natural world at the education centre or pick up some souvenirs at the Wilderness Gift Shop. There are also a number of trails available for hiking and cross-country skiing, as well as a picnic area. The conservation area is located south of Hanover and is accessible via County Road 10.

Heart Lake Conservation Area (Map 27/A7)

This conservation area is a green space located close to Metro Toronto that is quite busy during the summer months. The lake provides fishing for stocked trout as well as swimming and paddling opportunities. If you don't have your own canoe, rentals are available. Hiking and cross-country skiing trails traverse through the area and there are picnic sites to pass the day away. Group camping is offered to organized groups such as scouts and other youth groups. Call (905) 846-2494 for more information.

Hibou Conservation Area (Map 34/E3)

The main attraction to the Hibou Conservation Area is its fantastic beach area. The conservation area lies along the east shore of Owen Sound and swimming and other water sports are readily enjoyed at the park during the summer. Other activities available at the park include a few established hiking trails as well as picnicking near the lakeshore.

C.J. McEwen and Highland Glen Conservation Areas (Map 11/A3)

These two small parks are located along the shore of Lake Huron west of the town of Forest. The conservation areas are each home to a sandy beach and picnic shelter, making them a popular spot during the hot summer months.

Hillman Marsh Conservation Area (Map 2/C6)

The Hillman Marsh is an important wetland area that is a favourite bird watching destination. Hundreds of birds can be viewed here during the spring and fall migration period. A 4.5 km (2.8 mi) trail has been established to help visitors get a closer view of the marsh. Facilities available at the conservation area include a sandy beach, picnic area, washrooms and nature centre. The Hillman Marsh is located between the towns of Wheatley and Leamington.

Hilton Falls Conservation Area (Map 21/F3)

The Hilton Falls is a beautiful waterfall along the Sixteen Mile Creek. Hiking/ski trails traverse through the forest cover to the site of the falls, which are quite spectacular when frozen in the winter. The conservation area is also home to one of the best mountain biking trails in the region, rounding out over 21 km (13 mi) of trails that are available. A picnic area and toilets are the main facilities available at this conservation area, which is found via County Road 9 west of Milton.

Holiday Beach Conservation Area (Map 1/B6)

Holiday Beach has long been a favourite summer stopover with locals and travellers alike. The conservation area lies along the north shore of Lake Erie, south of the town of Amherstburg. Facilities offered at the park include: a sandy beach area, 90 treed campsites, a picnic area, showers, laundry and fishing at the stocked trout pond. Hiking enthusiasts can explore two hiking trails available at the park. The conservation area has also been designated an important global bird area and is a popular bird watching location during the spring and fall migration period. In September, the conservation area is home to the Festival of Hawks, which includes workshops and wild hawk releases. For more information on camping and other features call (519) 736-3772.

Indian Falls Conservation Area (Map 34/D3)

The Indian Falls Conservation Area is located north of Owen Sound off County Road 1. The sports fields at the conservation area are well used throughout the summer, although the area is also home to a challenging and interesting hiking trail. The trail treks along a portion of the Indian Creek to the scenic Indian Falls. The horseshoe shaped falls drop approximately 15 m (49 ft).

Inglis Falls Conservation Area (Map 34/E5)

The predominant feature of the park is indeed the Inglis Falls, which cascade 18 m (59 ft) over the escarpment. The remains of a gristmill built in 1845 can be spotted below the falls and during the spring and fall, the river comes alive with spawning trout and salmon. Visitors to the area can witness this amazing event as the fish struggle to make their way to their spawning grounds. Trail users will find the Bruce Trail and a few adjoining trails to explore. Other amenities available at the conservation area are an information centre, picnic areas and a small downhill ski hill. For more information call (519) 376-3076.

Island Lake Conservation Area (Map 26/D4)

This 332ha (820ac) conservation area was established in 1970 after the construction of two water control dams along the Credit River were completed. The man-made reservoir is known as both Orangeville Reservoir and Island Lake. Visitors to the area can enjoy fishing, paddling, hiking, picnicking and swimming. Canoe and rowboat rentals are available throughout the summer. In the winter, the trails are groomed for cross-country skiing and ice fishing huts are available for rent. For more information or ice hut reservations call (905) 670-1615.

Izzy's Conservation Area (Map 14/G6)

Izzy's Conservation Area provides access to three small lakes known as Waterford Ponds. The lakes offer good fishing opportunities and are ideal for swimming, boating and paddling. If you don't have a boat, rentals are available. Along with a full service campground visitors can enjoy the picnic area. The conservation area is located north of Simcoe off the east side of Highway 24. Call (519) 443-4702 for more information.

Joany's Woods Conservation Area (Map 11/F2)

A fantastic series of trails traverse through the mixed forest of Joany's Woods and along the Ausable River. An interpretive guide is available to help hikers learn a little more about the natural environment of the area. The conservation area lies east of the village of Thedford.

John R. Park Conservation Area (Map 1/E6)

Originally built in 1842, the J.R. Park Homestead has been restored to its 19th Century charm. The homestead includes ten buildings such as a smoke house, ice house, forge and barns. You can learn more about the history of the area at the visitor centre. Outdoor activities include a trail down along Fox Creek as well as a waterfront boardwalk. The conservation area is open all year and admission fees apply. For more information call (519) 738-2029.

Kelso/Glen Eden Conservation Areas (Map 21/F4)

Motorists that speed along Highway 401 near Milton probably don't even notice Kelso Lake. That is too bad. After all, the crystal blue lake is a focal point to these two conservation areas and is a great spot for summer swimming, paddling and even wind surfing. If you don't have a canoe or kayak, the conservation area offers rentals. Mountain bikers can explore the 15 km (9.3 mi) of challenging trails, while hikers can travel a portion of the Bruce Trail. Plenty of picnic tables are available as well as washrooms and a visitor centre. In the winter, the area turns into a popular downhill ski area with over ten downhill runs available. For more information call (905) 878-5011.

Kopegaron Woods Conservation Area (Map 2/C5)

Kopegaron Woods is made up of a lush Carolinian forest that is home to many interesting trees such as dogwood, sassafras, sycamore and black cherry. A scenic boardwalk trail traverses through the dense wooded area. The 19 ha (47 ac) conservation area lies southwest of the town of Wheatley and is accessible via the Talbot Trail (County Road 34). Look for the parking/picnic area off the south side of the road.

Kortright Centre for Conservation (Map 27/D6)

The Kortright Centre is a fantastic place to take the family throughout the year. The centre offers educational programs and displays on the natural world including renewable energy. During the spring, the Sugarbush Maple Syrup Festival provides an intricate look at how maple syrup is made and there are always plenty of sweet treats available. The centre also has over 15 km (9.3 mi) of trails available for hiking or cross-country skiing. The centre can be found north of Woodbridge off Major Mackenzie Drive. For more information please call (905) 832-2289.

Lake Whittaker Conservation Area (Map 13/E6)

Lake Whittaker is located southeast of the city of London off Whittaker Road. The lake is the focal point of this conservation area and provides swimming, fishing and paddling opportunities. Visitors can also swim in the pool or hike along one of the forested trails. A good sized campground is available throughout the summer months and is equipped with showers, picnic areas and flush toilets. For more information on camping and park events call (519) 269-3592.

Laurel Creek Conservation Area (Map 20/C4)

The Laurel Creek Conservation Area is best known for its many cross-country ski trails that wind through the park-like setting. The trails are also utilized by hikers in the summer and are a great way to escape the city and get outdoors. Located in the west end of Waterloo, the conservation area is a busy summer camping destination. The campground is a full service park complete with showers. Visitors can also enjoy swimming and picnicking at this interurban conservation area. Call (888) 376-2212 for campsite reservations or more information.

Lighthouse Conservation Area (Map 2/D1)

Located at the mouth of the Thames River on Lake St. Clair, this small conservation area is merely 1 ha (2.5 ac) in size. However, it is home to one of the oldest original lighthouses in Ontario. The original lighthouse was constructed in the early 1800's but it was destroyed during the infamous War of 1812. The lighthouse was reconstructed in 1818 and has provided a beacon for boaters along the Thames River and Lake St. Clair ever since. The conservation area provides a small picnic area along with boat access to the canal.

Little Lake Conservation Area (Map 14/E5)

Set along the shores of Little Lake, this conservation area offers 45 campsites. Showers, flush toilets and picnic areas help make this park a comfortable place to visit. A small boat launch ramp provides access to the lake, while the beach is a favourite spot during hot summer days. There is also a short nature trail that leads past a wetland area. The conservation area can be accessed off County Road 19 northeast of Tillsonburg. Campsite reservations can be made by calling (877) 990-9935.

Long Beach Conservation Area (Map 16/G7)

Located along the northern shore of Lake Erie, this conservation area can be reached via Lakeshore Road (County Road 3) west of Port Colborne. The conservation area is one of two areas in the Niagara Conservation Authority that offers camping. There are 275 campsites available along with a sandy beach area, boat launch, playground, sports fields and a day-use picnic area. This is a busy campground during the summer and reservation should be made prior to arrival by calling (905) 899-3462.

Longwoods Road Conservation Area (Map 12/D7)

Take a step back into the past at the Ska-Nah-Doht Iroquoian Village and museum found at the Longwoods Road Conservation Area. Visitors can walk through a reconstructed native village that is dated back over 1,000 years ago. Explore the longhouses and other native structures and then visit the museum to see real native artefacts that have been recovered from the area. Educational presentations and displays teach of the simpler life that was prevalent well before European settlers arrived. Visitors can also get out and hike the over 6 km (3.6 mi) of hiking/skiing trails, which wind through the nearby Carolinian forest. Other amenities available at the conservation area are a day-use picnic area, suspension bridge and a gift shop. Group camping is offered to organized youth groups. The conservation area can be found southeast of London via Longwoods Road from Highway 402. For more information please call (519) 264-2420.

Lorne C. Henderson Conservation Area (Map 10/G6)

Set along Buttermilk Creek, this conservation area is a great place to escape for the weekend. Hike the nature trails along the creek and ponds or simply relax by the public pool. Campsites are available along with showers, flush toilets and a playground. The conservation area is located west of the town of Petrolia and is accessible via the Petrolia Line (County Road 4). Call (519) 882-2280 for more information.

Luther Marsh Conservation Area (Map 25/F4)

Luther Marsh is the largest wetland area in southwestern Ontario and is home to hundreds of bird and animal species. The marsh is a favourite paddling destination in the region as paddlers can literally spend hours exploring the area. Be sure to bring along your camera, as the marsh abounds in wildlife such as heron, waterfowl and songbirds.

The area also has a well established hiking and biking trail system that spans around the exterior of the marsh. During the winter, the hiking trails are often used for cross-county skiing. The marsh is located west of Orangeville and is accessible off Sideroad 21-22. There are a number of picnic tables available as well as canoe access points.

McBeath Conservation Area (Map 30/A6)

The McBeath Conservation Area is a water accessible only camping area located along the Saugeen River west of the village of Paisley. The area is home to about 30 treed campsites that are a popular stop over with paddlers on the river. Other facilities available at the area include a beach, picnic tables, outhouses and garbage/recycling bins.

McGeachy Pond (Map 3/E2)

Located within minutes of Rondeau Provincial Park, McGeachy Pond sees thousands of migrating birds in the spring and fall periods. Picnic tables are available at the entrance area and there is a viewing platform for bird watchers.

Minesing Swamp (Map 32/G4)

The Minesing Swamp is renowned as a diverse area with unique features that are rarely found in any other parts of the world. The swamp is actually made up of a variety of wetland habitats such as marsh, bog and fen and covers 6,000 ha (14,820 ac). Unique to the wetland are walleye that spawn on vegetation instead of gravel. The swamp is an excellent area for bird watching. In addition to the fifth largest blue heron colony in the province, there are over 200 species of birds present at various times of year.

The best way to explore the Minesing is by canoe. From the water, you can get immersed in the flooded forests of the swamp and find the solitude that can only be experienced by boat. There are also trails that travel along the Nottawasaga River and into the Hackberry Levee Forest. These trails can be used for hiking or in winter for cross-country skiing or snowshoeing.

Morrison Dam Conservation Area (Map 18/E6)

East of the village of Exeter, the Morrison Dam Conservation Area is accessible via the Morrison Line. The reservoir is the focal point of the conservation area and provides fishing opportunities for stocked trout. Hiking trails meander along the south side of the reservoir and Ausable River. Cross-country skiers and snowshoers also use the trails during the winter. Picnic shelters and outhouses are available at the parking/access area.

Mount Nemo Conservation Area (Map 21/G5)

This small conservation area encompasses a portion of the Niagara Escarpment and is located north of Burlington off the Guelph Line. The area provides access to the Bruce Trail and the Brock Harris Lookout. The lookout provides a spectacular panoramic view of the region including downtown Toronto. Picnic facilities are also available at the park.

Mountsberg Wildlife Centre (Map 21/D4)

Found just south of Highway 401, the Wildlife Centre is the highlight of this conservation area. Visitors can get a close up look at birds of prey, elk and bison or take part in the special events that are held throughout the year. There is also plenty to do outside in the area. Paddling and fishing is popular on the 200 ha (494 ac) reservoir and there are over 16 km (9.9 mi) of hiking/biking or ski trails. Picnic areas and waterfowl observation towers offer a different perspective to the area.

Mud Lake Conservation Area (Map 17/B6)

This 46 ha (114 ac) conservation area lies along the west side of the Welland Canal and protects a portion of the wetland and forest area around Mud Lake. Nature trails are the main attraction to the park, although bird watching and fishing are also popular activities. Access to the conservation area is via Elm Street north of Port Colborne. Look for a parking area off the east side of the road.

Naftel's Creek Conservation Area (Map 18/A1)

Set along Naftel's Creek south of the town of Goderich, this conservation area is accessible off the east side of Highway 21. The conservation area helps protect a mature cedar swamp, which can be extensively explored via the trail system. The trail system is a mutli-use system used by hikers in the summer and cross-country skiers/snowshoers during the winter.

New Lowell Conservation Area (Map 32/E4)

Developed mainly for a seasonal campground, this area can be accessed off of Glencairn Road or County Road 9 outside the town of New Lowell. The site offers close to 100 full service campsites as well as two beach areas and a covered picnic site that can be reserved for group use. The conservation area also encompasses a large reservoir, created from the damming of Coates Creek, where swimming, canoeing and some fishing is available. A small trail through the area provides opportunities for a short hike and cross-country skiing or snowshoeing in winter. Call (705) 424-1479 for more information.

Norfolk Conservation Area (Map 9/A1)

Norfolk is a recreation based conservation area located along the shore of Lake Erie west of Port Dover. The conservation area has a beach, picnic area, playground, and sports fields for visitors to enjoy. 164 seasonal campsites are available at the park, with most of the sites equipped with electricity. Other amenities at the conservation area include showers, laundry and change houses. For more information and camping availability call (877) 990-9937.

Nottawasaga Bluffs Conservation Area (Map 32/B5)

Protecting a section of the Niagara Escarpment, the Nottawasaga Bluffs is a scenic area with little development. The 37 ha (91 ac) conservation area is mainly a trail destination that includes a section of the Bruce Trail. There are picnic tables and for added adventure, there are many small caves that can be explored along the escarpment. The conservation area can be accessed off of County Road 62, west of the town of Creemore.

Parkhill Conservation Area (Map 12/A2)

The Parkhill Reservoir is the main feature of this conservation area. The reservoir was created in 1969 through dam construction along Parkhill Creek. Today the conservation area surrounds much of the reservoir and provides many recreational opportunities such as hiking, picnicking and bird watching. Swimming at the beach area, paddling and fishing are all popular pastimes on the reservoir. A campground is also available. The conservation area is located just outside of the town of Parkhill, northeast of London. For more information call (519) 235-2610.

Petun Conservation Area (Map 32/A3)

The 41 ha (101 ac) conservation area is located southeast of Collingwood, just north of the Pretty River Valley Provincial Park off Concession Road 2. The Bruce Trail travels through the area providing access to a portion of the beautiful Niagara Escarpment. From the trail a few scenic viewpoints can be found.

Pinehurst Lake Conservation Area (Map 20/G7)

Set amid a mature Carolinian forest, Pinehurst Lake is a busy summer destination. The conservation area offers a full service campground, picnic areas, extensive hiking trails and a fabulous beach area. The conservation area is found south of Cambridge and reservations are recommended for camping. Call (888) 376-2212 for more information.

Pittock Conservation Area (Map 14/A1)

The Pittock Conservation Area is home to over 250 campsites that are all set within walking distance of Pittock Reservoir. There is canoe and boat access to the reservoir, which is also a popular sailing and fishing destination. While visitors can relax by the pool, they can also soak up some rays at the sandy beach on the reservoir. Educational and interpretive programs are offered throughout the year and there are picnic areas found around the park. You can find the Pittock Conservation Area northeast of Woodstock off County Road 4. For campsite reservations or more information call (866) ONT-CAMP.

Pottawatomi Conservation Area (Map 34/C4)

West of the city of Owen Sound, the Pottawatomi Conservation Area can be accessed via the Derby-Sarawak Townline or Highway 6. The highlight of the area is the scenic Jones Falls, which can be reached by a short trail from the Highway 6 parking area. The falls cascade over 12 m (39 ft) in a tiered fashion and are worth a photo. The Bruce Trail traverses through the park passing by a few impressive viewpoints. Visitors can also hike or ski the established trail west of the Bruce Trail.

Rattlesnake Point Conservation Area (Map 21/G4)

Rattlesnake Point offers over 10 km (12 mi) of fantastic trails that wind along the Niagara Escarpment and link up with the Bruce Trail. The trail system passes by some of the most scenic viewpoints along the escarpment. A picnic area is available at the park, which can be found off the Appleby Line west of Milton. Group camping is also available, although reservations must be made prior to arrival. Call (905) 878-1147.

Rattray Marsh Conservation Area (Map 22/D4)

Established in 1975, the Rattray Marsh is located in the outskirts of Mississauga on Lake Ontario. The marsh is home to hundreds of birds and mammals and is a highly valued natural resource amid the urban development. A waterfront trail passes through the lively marshland, while there are a number of self-guided nature trails that wind their way through the wetland on a mix of boardwalks and natural paths. Be sure to bring along your camera, as there is plenty to capture on film.

Rockwood Conservation Area (Map 21/C2)

The Rockwood Conservation Area is best known for the old mill ruins that lie along the Eramosa River. The park is also the sight of some dramatic limestone cliffs set along the Niagara Escarpment. In addition to an established trail system, the area is also home to a popular, full service campground. The nearby millpond gives visitors a chance to picnic and swim on hot summer days. Call (888) 376-2212 for campsite reservations or more information.

Rock Glen Conservation Area (Map 11/F3)

This scenic conservation area lies along the west side of Ausable River just north of the village of Arkona. Hiking trails travel through the Carolinian forest setting and along the river to a lookout over the Rock Glen Falls. Visitors can also venture down to the base of the falls to search for fossils. Other facilities available at the conservation area are picnic areas and a museum where a fine display of fossils is on display.

Rogers Reservoir Conservation Area (Map 27/F1)

This 39 ha (96 ac) conservation area is an urban outdoor hideaway located north of the city of Newmarket between Green Lane and Concession Road 2. The reservoir and surrounding marshland is a part of the Holland River system and provides good opportunities for bird watching and marginal fishing. There are also two small, easy trails on either side of the reservoir that can be used for hiking or biking. In addition to picnic facilities, the conservation area offers group camping by reservation only. Call (905) 895-1281 for more information.

Rouge Park (Map 28/D6)

Rouge Park is over 4,700 ha (11,600 ac) in size making it the largest interurban park in North America. It has been designed as an interurban wild area and is not developed. Several rustic trail systems allow visitors to escape the rigors of urban life. For more information on this unique park and its outdoor opportunities call (416) 287-6843.

Saugeen Bluffs Conservation Area (Map 29/G4)

This 100 ha (247 ac) area lies along the east shore of the Saugeen River south of Port Elgin. 200 campsites along with amenities such as showers, flush toilets, laundry, playground and a picnic area are offered at the park. A few short trails trek through the sugar bush setting and fishing and paddling opportunities exist on the Saugeen River. Canoe and kayak rentals are available at the park. For campsite reservations call (519) 364-1255.

Scanlon Creek Conservation Area (Map 27/E1)

Located northeast of Bradford, this conservation area is home to a man-made reservoir where visitors can enjoy swimming, picnicking and paddling. Other amenities available include a nature and education centre as well as a sugar shack where maple syrup is produced during the spring. A well established trail system also traverses through the park. For more information call (905) 895-1281.

Shade's Mills Conservation Area (Map 21/A6)

Shade's Mills is as much a winter destination as a summer destination. During the snowy months, the park offers a fantastic array of cross-country ski trails. In the summer, the large reservoir is the focal point of the park as visitors can enjoy swimming, fishing and paddling. The conservation area is open for day-use only and has a number of picnic areas for visitors to use.

Sharon Creek Conservation Area (Map 12/E7)

The Sharon Creek Conservation Area is situated on the Sharon Creek Reservoir southwest of London. The conservation area provides a picnic area, a few hiking trails, fishing, paddling and swimming opportunities. Camping for organized groups such as scouts or girl guides is available with prior reservations. For more information call (519) 354-7310.

Shetland Conservation Area (Map 5/D2)

Set along the Sydenham River west of Newbury, the Shetland Conservation Area is mainly used as a day-use picnic area, although it also offers organized group camping. For more information on group camping opportunities call (519) 245-3710.

Spencer Gorge/Webster's Falls Conservation Area (Map 21/F7)

Located in Dundas off Harvest Road, which can be picked up off Brock Road, this conservation area is home to one of the most spectacular views along the Niagara Escarpment. Visitors often marvel at the sight of the Webster's and Tew's Falls. Tew's Falls is the larger of the series as it drops 41 m (135 ft) and is only slightly shorter than the more famous Niagara Falls.

Spirit Rock Conservation Area (Maps 36/G7, 37/A7)

Visitors to the Spirit Rock Conservation Area will enjoy fabulous views from atop the Niagara Escarpment. The Bruce Trail travels through the area, and there is a short trail system that loops around the remains of the McNeill estate, originally constructed in 1881. From along the Bruce Trail, hikers can view Spirit Rock in the east side of the park. The rock was named such after the mythological native story about a broken hearted lover that leapt off the rock to her death below. To reach the conservation area, head north from Wiarton along Highway 6 and look for the access road off the east side of the highway about 2km (1.2mi) from town.

Springwater Conservation Area (Map 7/D1)

With over 260 campsites, 182 with electrical hook ups, Springwater Conservation Area is a popular camping destination during the summer months. A large pond with a small sandy beach and swimming area forms the hub of the area. The pond is a good spot for kids to fish and canoe and paddleboat rentals are available. There is also 8 km (5 mi) of trails, a playground and picnic areas. Day access fees apply for trail use and picnic areas. This 150 ha (370 ac) area is accessible off County Road 35 southwest of the town of Aylmer. It is recommended to call (519) 773-9037 prior to arrival if you plan to camp at the park.

St. Johns Conservation Area (Map 17/B4)

Located north of Fonthill, this 28 ha (69 ac) park is home to a stocked trout pond and nature trails. The pond is a favourite kid's attraction and the nature trails traverse through the park and along a boardwalk near the pond.

Stevensville Conservation Area (Map 17/E6)

Visitors to this conservation area can enjoy fishing in Black Creek, picnicking and hiking. The park is located near the village of Stevensville, west of Fort Erie.

Stoney Island Conservation Area (Map 29/B6)

Set along the eastern shore of Lake Huron north of Kincardine, there is a picnic area along with over 8 km (5 mi) of multi-use trails. The trails meander through the conservation area and are maintained by the Kincardine Cross-Country Ski Club. A warm up hut and a snowshoeing only trail help make this a popular winter destination.

Strathroy Conservation Area (Map 12/B5)

Found just north of the town of Strathroy, this conservation area lies along Sydenham River. The area offers 3 km (1.9 mi) of hiking trails that traverse through a scenic floodplain forest. There is also a picnic area for visitors.

Terra Cotta Conservation Area (Map 26/F7)

This scenic conservation area is home to several trails including the Bruce Trail and access to the Caledon Trailway. In addition to hiking, the trails are popular winter destinations for cross-country skiers and snowshoers. There is also a picnic area set near the parks' ponds and organized group camping is available for youth groups. Call (905) 877-9650 for more information.

Tremblay Beach Conservation Area (Map 2/C1)

The Tremblay Beach Conservation Area is located east of Belle River and lies along the southern shore of Lake St. Clair. The area is 30 ha (70 ac) in size and helps protect one of the last marshes left in Essex County on Lake St. Clair. The main attractions to the area are the fabulous sandy beach and bird watching opportunities.

Two Creeks Conservation Area (Map 2/D4)

Located north of the town of Wheatley, the Two Creeks Conservation Area can be accessed via Wheatley Road (County Road 1). The conservation area is an important migration stopover spot for a variety of birds throughout the spring and fall. Hiking trails have been established through the park to provide bird watching and nature appreciation opportunities. Picnic tables are also available for day-use along the creek.

Valens Conservation Area (Map 21/C6)

Valens Conservation Area is a favourite camping destination for people in the Guelph and Hamilton areas. There are 200 campsites, 60 with electrical hook ups, as well as showers and laundry facilities. The sandy beach and picnic area are great places to be on hot days, while anglers and paddlers are often out on around the 76 ha (188 ac) lake. There is also a nice trail system that provides easy hiking and, in winter, groomed cross-country ski trails and snowshoe routes. The conservation area is located east of Galt and can be reached via the Old Beverly Road (County Road 97). For more information on camping and other features call (519) 736-3772.

Wainfleet Bog Nature Reserve (Map 17/A6)

The Wainfleet Bog is the largest protected tract managed by the Niagara Conservation Authority. At 801 ha (1,980 ac) in size, the bog is an important wilderness in the region and offers outdoor enthusiasts a picnic area and nature trails.

Wainfleet Wetlands Conservation Area (Map 17/A7)

Protecting a large 181 ha (447 ac) tract of wetland habitat, the Wainfleet Wetlands Conservation Area has limited facilities available for visitors. Fishing opportunities exist at the area.

Warwick Conservation Area (Map 11/D5)

Located minutes off the north side of Highway 402 near the village of Warwick, this conservation area offers treed campsites, a picnic area and a swimming pool. A short hiking trail helps visitors explore the area. Other amenities available include flush toilets, showers, laundry facilities and a playground for the kids. For more information call (519) 849-6770.

Wawanosh Park & Valley Conservation Areas (Map 23/E6)

Northwest of the village of Blyth, the **Wawanosh Park Conservation Area** can be accessed off Nature Centre Road. The park lies along the Maitland River and is a superb spot to enjoy nature. In addition to a small seasonal campground situated in stands of white cedar, there are two spring fed ponds that are stocked with trout. The ponds are a favourite with younger anglers. Other amenities include short hiking trails, a day use picnic shelter, a playground and swimming. Call (877) FAL-LSCA for more information.

The nearby **Wawanosh Valley Conservation Area** also offers hiking trails that double as cross-country ski and snowshoe trails in the winter. This conservation area also offers educational programs for organized groups throughout the year. For more information on the programs available please call (519) 523-4788.

Wawanosh Wetlands (10/C3)

The Wawanosh Wetlands is an important wetland area that is located east of the city of Sarnia. The wetland can be seen from Highway 402, although it is accessible via The Blackwell Sideroad north of the highway. The wetland is home to a variety of birds and is a good bird watching destination. Facilities available at the wetland are a scenic trail around the wetland and a picnic shelter.

Westfield Heritage Village (Map 21/C7)

Westfield Heritage Village is a 147 ha (363 ac) conservation area that is home to 33 refurbished historical buildings. Visitors can walk around the 19th Century village and learn more about the people that helped establish our country. The conservation area also boasts two trail systems around the village. The trails are open year round for hiking and, in winter, skiing. Educational programs are also offered throughout the year. For more information call (519) 621-8851.

Westminster Ponds Natural Area (Map 13/A5)

Set in the heart of the city of London, this natural area is designated as a very important wetland area. A series of natural path and boardwalk trails wind through the wetland and are a favourite with bird watchers.

Wildwood Conservation Area (Maps 13/C1, 19/C7)

The Wildwood Conservation Area is well developed area located south of Stratford via Highway 7. The conservation area offers 450 treed campsites that are all set within walking distance of the man-made Wildwood Lake. The lake has a sandy beach area and is a popular spot for sailing, paddling and other water sports. There is also a large swimming pool for visitors to enjoy. Over 3 km (1.9 mi) of hiking/cross-country ski trails are available and visitors can also enjoy the many picnic areas around the park. Educational and interpretive programs are also offered throughout the year. For campsite reservations or more information call (866) ONT-CAMP.

Woodend Conservation Area (Map 17/D2)

Hiking is one of the main attractions to this conservation area. Visitors to the area can explore remains of a United Empire Loyalist homestead and limestone kiln as they trek through this wooded area of the Niagara Escarpment. The conservation area is located Southwest of St.Catherines, not far off the Queen Elizabeth Highway.

Multi-Use Trails

(Hiking, biking, ATV's and much more)

There is no other region in Ontario that can rival the sheer number and size of the trails found in Southwestern Ontario. From the world renowned Bruce Trail to the hundreds of conservation areas and park trails, there is literally a lifetime of hiking possibilities. Add in a good variety of trails found in the cities and the hundreds of kilometres of abandoned rail lines and you will surely see, feel and hear all that this dynamic part of the province has to offer. Hikers, bikers, horseback riders and even ATV users all take advantage of this incredible trail network.

In the winter many of these routes come alive with other trail users. In fact, next to hiking, cross-country skiing is the most popular trail activity in the region. There are many well established cross-country trail systems throughout the area and snowshoeing has increased in popularity over the past few years. Snowmobiling is quite popular in the northern portion of the region. Snowmobiles can be found on much of the unmaintained backroads during winter and in some places snowmobiles even replace vehicles as the main method of transportation. There is a maintained network of trails in the region that are administered by the Ontario Federation of Snowmobile Clubs. To travel on these systems, however, trail permits must be obtained before hand.

We must note that it is very difficult to mark all of the trails on the maps, especially the city trails. For this reason, each description includes road access to help you find the trailhead. You may also notice that there are literally hundreds of side trails branching from the Bruce Trail. We could only describe a few of the more popular alternatives. If we have missed a trail you think is worth noting, please let us know.

In the following reference section, we have rated the trails according to their difficulty:

Easy: The route is well marked and involves very little uphill or downhill travel. The terrain is generally easy to traverse and is not marred by natural obstacles. These trails are ideal for inexperienced users.

Moderate: The trail could entail some strenuous climbs and may not be marked. The terrain could be challenging due to obstacles such as fallen trees or sharp corners. Be prepared, as these trails can challenge even experienced users.

Difficult: These routes are very rarely marked and involve challenging climbs or descents on numerous occasions. Orienteering skills may be required to maintain tracking the trail. The routes are usually rustic with fallen trees or grown in sections.

All distances are for round trips unless otherwise noted.

Day use or overnight use passes must be purchased and displayed on your dashboard for use of all facilities and trails within National Parks, Provincial Parks and many Conservation Areas.

A.W. Campbell Conservation Area Trail (Map 11/F7) 🚶 ⛷ 🎿

This conservation area offers two easy, connected loop trails. They can be combined to make a 3.3 km (2.0 mi) hike. The trail travels over a combination of natural path and boardwalk areas, while taking you through a mix of meadow, floodplain and deciduous forest settings. This conservation area can be found off the south side of Shiloh Road near the town of Alvinson. There is a gatehouse where visitors are required to pay a small fee for day-use of the trails. A detailed map of the conservation area is also available at the gatehouse.

Alliston Area Trails (Maps 25 & 32) 🚶 🚴

Riverdale Park Trail (Map 32/G7)

In the town of Alliston a short trail can be found between King Street North and Church Street North. The trail is an easy route that is about 1.5 km (0.9 mi) in length and travels along the scenic Boyne River. The route follows the river between the two roads and through a portion of town before entering Riverdale Park. For a longer route, the trail can be followed further west past King Street to Earle Rowe Provincial Park.

Spring Creek Trail (Map 26/G1)

This 2 km (1.2 mi) easy loop trail begins at the Spring Creek Peace Park off the south side of Albert Street East. The trail heads east along Albert Street then loops southwest. The second half of the route travels along the trickling Spring Creek back towards the park and playing fields.

Altona Forest Trail (Map 28/D6) 🚶 🎿

Located in the city of Pickering, the Altona Forest can be accessed via County Road 27 north of Highway 401. The forest offers 2 km (1.2 mi) of trails suitable for hiking or cross-country skiing. The forest terrain includes some open space and is a great spot to escape the rush of city life.

Apps' Mill Conservation Area Trail (Map 14/G2) 🚶

The Apps' Mill Trail is an easy 3.6 km (2.2 mi) loop that follows Whitemans Creek most of the way. The route traverses through dense forest cover and past some very old maple and beech trees. Along the trail, hikers will also pass by a wetland area and the Oxbow Pond. This conservation area is located just west of the city of Brantford off the north side of Robinson Road, which is found west of Highway 24.

Avon Trail (Maps 13/C1, 19/E6, 20/B4) 🚶 🎿 ⛷ 🏕

The Avon Trail links the Thames Valley Trail in the west to the Grand Valley Trail in the east. Beginning from the town of St. Mary's, the trail passes the south end of Wildwood Lake before entering the open field areas that dominate the landscape. Forested sections, road travel and a number of creative landowners help add to the diversity along the route. North of Wildwood Lake, the trail passes by the east end of Stratford before heading east to Waterloo. The connection with the Grand Trail is found near the suburb of Conestogo north of Waterloo. The Avon Trail is approximately 100 km (62 mi) one-way from St. Mary's to Conestogo. The trail is generally easy to travel, although there are a few more difficult areas, especially if you attempt large portions of trail all at once. For a trail guide or more information contact the Avon Trail on the web at www.avontrail.ca

Ausable Trail (Map 11/F3) 🚶 🎣 🏕

The Ausable Trail is a scenic route that follows the shore of the Ausable River from the Rock Glen Conservation Area north to Joany's Woods Conservation Area. The trail is approximately 9 km (5.6 mi) in length and is a great way to get an intimate view of the river.

Bangor Marsh Management Unit Trails (Map 35/A4) 🚶 🏕

East of the small village of Rockford, the parking area for the Bangor Management unit is located off the north side of County Road 18. From the parking area, the trails meander across a mix of boardwalks, pathways and old roadbeds. In total, the trail system is about 4 km (2.5 mi) in length and passes through a mix of forest area, wetland and field. Generally, the trail that skirts the marsh and lowland area is regarded as easy, while there is also a trail that climbs atop the Niagara Escarpment providing great picturesque views. Additional amenities available at the Bangor Marsh Trail include a section of educational plaques along the boardwalk section and a lookout tower over the marsh.

Bannockburn Trail (Map 18/C3) 🚶 🎿

The Bannockburn Trail is actually within the Bannockburn Provincial Wildlife Area. The wildlife area is home to a variety of natural areas including wetlands and white cedar stands. From the parking area on Bannockburn Line the trail heads south over the Bannockburn River before linking up with the main loop. The loop skirts the perimeter of the wildlife area along a mix of wood chip, natural and boardwalk paths. Cross-country skiing is available during the winter months, although the trails are not always track set. There is a small fee for using the trail in order to maintain the easy 1 km (0.6 mi) loop.

Barrow Bay Loop Trail (Map 36/G2)

At the corner of Scenic Caves Road and Rush Cove Road, there is a small parking area and the trailhead for the Barrow Bay Loop. The route begins by following the Rush Cove Road north through a mature maple and birch mix forest. The trail soon opens up to the shoreline of Barrow Bay as it winds towards the Barrow Bay Escarpment. At this point the trail leads down the escarpment and follows the shoreline west for about 1.5 km (0.9 mi) through large boulders and other rocky footing. To return, you can follow the same route back or you can scramble towards the top of the escarpment and follow the escarpment back to the main trail. Regardless, the shoreline portion of this route is by far the most challenging portion of the hike and is regarded as difficult. The remaining portion of this 8.5 km (5.3 mi) route is generally easy.

Bartley Smith Greenway Trails (Map 27/F6)

Located in the North York community of Vaughan, the Bartley Smith Greenway Trail system is divided into two separate sections. The southern section of the trail begins near Steeles Avenue West and treks north along the West Don River Valley. The moderate trail is made up of a gravel surface and travels through a mix of green space and urban development. From Steeles Avenue West, the trail travels underneath Highway 407 north for approximately 6 km (3.7 mi) one-way.

The northern section of the trail picks up from just north of Major Mackenzie Drive West (County Road 25) and spans north to Teston Road. A return hike along this easy portion of the greenway trail is approximately 6 km (3.7 mi) in length. It passes by the magnificent Langstaff Eco Park, a former industrial wasteland that has been transformed into a fantastic wetland area. In fact, the wetland is known as one of the largest reconstructed wetlands in Ontario and home to waterfowl and small mammals such as beavers.

Bayview Escarpment Nature Reserve Trail (Map 35/B2)

To reach the Bayfield Escarpment Trail, follow Highway 26 west from the town of Meaford to the St.Vincent –Sydenham Townline and head north. The parking area for the trail is located off the east side of the road about 4.5 km north of the highway. This easy to moderate 7 km (4.3 mi) trail follows an old road through the nature reserve. The trail treks through some wooded sections and is suitable for hiking and biking during the summer and snowshoeing or cross-country skiing during the winter.

Big Bend Conservation Area Trails (Map 6/A3)

The parking area off Walnut Grove, just past the picnic area provides access to this easy 1 km (0.6 mi) trail. The route travels north past a fishing pond before it veers east to a Purple Martin house and the return trip back. The conservation area is found off Big Bend Road south of Glencoe.

Big Creek National Wildlife Area Trail (Map 8/F4)

Set along the northern shore of Lake Erie, the Big Creek National Wildlife area is a fascinating natural place to visit and has been designated as a World Biosphere Reserve site. The trail travels atop a dyke used to control water levels in the marsh ecosystem. The route is an easy 2 km (1.2 mi) loop featuring a lookout platform that provides the opportunity to view a wide range of wildlife including reptiles, waterfowl and small mammals. To be more specific, the reptiles include the rare leopard frog and eastern fox snakes, while interesting birds such as terns and American bitterns can be spotted at times. Bald

eagles and during the spring tundra swans can also be seen at times. A portion of the trail system is closed from September 15th to May 15th in order to limit disturbing wildlife in the area.

Blyth Brook Community Greenway Trail (Map 23/E7)

The main parking and access area for this trail is located in the town of Blyth off County Road 4 near Blyth Brook. This parking area is actually in the middle of the trail system. To access the western end of the trail, you can find the trailhead off the north side of Gypsy Lane near the local community centre and arena. From Gypsy Lane, the trail heads west, eventually veering north towards the abandoned rail line and a recent tree planting site. Eventually, the trail heads east along the railbed over County Road 4 and ends around the old Grand Truck Railway stone arch bridge.

Boyd Conservation Area (Map 27/D6)

In the city of Vaughn, the Boyd Conservation Area can be reached via Islington Avenue just south of Rutherford Road. The conservation area is home to several interconnected trails that are suitable for hiking during the summer and cross-country skiing during the winter. The trails make up about 6 km (3.7 mi) of easy routes and trek through the varied geography of the area.

Bronte Creek Provincial Park Trail (Map 22/A5)

Located in the north end of Burlington, Bronte Creek Provincial Park offers trails for hikers and bikers to experience. The three trails are set in separate areas. The northern and southern trails provide views of the Bronte Creek and pass a few lookout areas. The mid park trail is a maze of connected routes, with one route passing by a small pond. Day-use fees apply for non-camping visitors to the park.

Bruce's Mill Conservation Area Trail (Map 28/A4)

West of Stouffville, Bruce's Mill Conservation Area can be found off the south side of Stouffville Road between Kennedy Road and Warden Avenue. The conservation area is a fantastic place to visit and there is a number of interesting nature oriented events, including the ever

popular Sugarbush Maple Syrup Festival that can be enjoyed during the year. The trail system is comprised of approximately 10.5 km (6.5 mi) of easy interconnected loop routes through the mix of forest cover and field spaces. The trails are a great way to burn off excess calories after visiting the sugar shack where maple syrup is produced. During winter cross-country skiers frequent the trails.

Bruce National Park Trails (Maps 38, 39) ▲ 🚶 ⬤ 🏕

While destination hikers often enter the Bruce National Park on the Bruce Trail, there are several trails that have been established in other parts of the park.

Cyprus Lake Trail (38/G4)

The Cyprus Lake Trail is an easy 5 km (3.1 mi) loop that circles the scenic lake. It is accessible from several locations in the campground.

Half Way Log Dump Trail (Map 39/A4)

For backcountry camping enthusiasts, the Half Way Log Dump makes a fine overnight destination. The trail begins from the parking area on the Emmett Lake Road and leads to the Bruce Trail. Hikers then follow the rugged trail east along the scenic escarpment to the High Dump interior camping area. From the camping area, you can either return to Emmett Lake or continue south to the Crane Lake Road. A second vehicle would allow you to complete a moderate 14 km (8.7 mi) one-way trip. The campsite is about the halfway point of the route.

Marr Lake-Georgian Trail (Map 38/G4)

Beginning from the parking area at the north end of the Cyprus Lake, the Marr Lake Trail travels northwest to the southern shore of Marr Lake. The trail skirts the lake before heading north towards the edge of the escarpment. The route then follows the escarpment providing several fantastic views of the Georgian Bay. The trail eventually links up with what is known as the Georgian Trail, which heads south back to Cyprus Lake. Including the Georgian Trail, this route is an easy 3 km (1.9 mi) loop.

Singing Sands Trail (Map 38/F5)

The trail to Dorcas Bay is known as the Singing Sands Trail. The easy 3 km (1.9 mi) loop follows an old road from the picnic area on Dorcas Bay Road. The trail leads west past some rare Alvar plant life and wetland areas to the sand dunes, after which the trail is named. Alvar is usually only found in parts of Estonia and Sweden and can endure some of the harshest of climates. \

Bruce Trail (Maps 15-17, 21, 26, 30-32, 34-39) ▲ 🚶 🏕

Established in 1967, the Bruce Trail is the longest and oldest recreational hiking trail in Canada. It is also considered one of the best long distance hiking trails in North America, if not the world. From the Niagara River to Tobermory, the trail spans 800 km (497 mi). Combined with the many side trails along the way, the Bruce Trail is Ontario's greatest hiking destination and a must experience in Southwestern Ontario.

The trail follows the Niagara Escarpment most of the way providing hundreds of picturesque views along the way. Some sections can be easy and even follow the side of roads, while other portions are quite a challenge as the trail climbs up the escarpment and skirts along steep cliff edges. The natural beauty of the area, when combined with the many attractions along the route, does not go unnoticed. Over 400,000 hikers enjoy the Bruce Trail each year.

While following the trail on our maps, you will notice numerous offshoot side trails marked. These trails often lead to interesting natural features or other attractions and are well worth the detour if time permits. Below we have divided the Bruce Trail into sections according to where the trail appears on our maps. The sections have been organized according to the direction the trail travels across our maps, which is east to west and south to north. Hence, the trail begins on Map 17 and travels west onto Map 16 and so on. For a very detailed description and maps, be sure to bring along a copy of the Bruce Trail Guide. Call (800) 665-4453 for more information.

Map 17

The trail begins north of Niagara Falls at Queenston Heights Park near the Canada/United States border. The trail starts its long journey by heading west through a mix of urban and rural areas before reaching Silent Hills Provincial Park. The park is a popular spot for trail users and is home to several interesting and challenging side trails. From Silent Hills Provincial Park the trail continues west along the escarpment to Balls Falls Conservation Area.

Map 16

The Balls Falls Conservation Area is a good access area for day-trippers along the Bruce Trail. Heading west, the trail passes over the escarpment and climbs up Grimsby Mountain. The route continues west along the edge of the escarpment all the way to the southern end of Hamilton. In this section, the trail climbs up and down the escarpment and can be a bit more challenging for unseasoned hikers.

Map 15

Through Hamilton, the route follows the escarpment into the densely wooded Dundas Valley. Much of the valley is protected by the local conservation authority and has a number of established side trails for hikers to explore. There are also a number of amenities available in the conservation areas including the Dundas Valley Trail Centre. The Bruce heads north out of the valley towards the Spencer Gorge.

Map 21

The Spencer Gorge Conservation Area is where visitors can hike along the top of the deep gorge and view two beautiful waterfalls. The trail follows a few roads as it leaves the conservation area and eventually escapes into forest cover as it heads off road towards Mount Nemo Conservation Area. Enjoy the views before continuing northwest along a number of side roads leading to the Crawford Lake Conservation Area. This conservation area, offers visitors the opportunity to climb around and into the Nassagaweya Canyon.

As the trail heads north, it passes through the Keslo Conservation Area and eventually under Highway 401. Shortly after the highway, the trail climbs again to the top of the escarpment and continues its journey northward. From Highway 401, the trail travels through some forest cover all the way past Highway 7 to the Terra Cotta Conservation Area. A popular side trail located near Terra Cotta is the Credit Valley Footpath. This path travels southeast from the Bruce Trail along the Credit River to Georgetown.

Map 26

Travelling north from Terra Cotta, the Bruce Trail takes a detour towards the Forks of the Credit Provincial Park. At the park, there is a deep gorge that almost makes you feel like you are hiking in the mountains of Western Canada. The trail eventually turns back out of the park and continues north crossing the Little Credit River before reaching the village of Caledon East. From here, the route continues north to the Albion Hills Conservation Area, where overnight camping is available.

Shortly after reaching the Palgrave Conservation Area, the route veers west travelling over a number of forested and open hills to the Glen Haffy Conservation Area. Overnight camping is offered at Glen Haffy, which is located near the village of Mono Mills. The Bruce Trail continues northeast along a mix of side roads and trail eventually reaching Mono Cliffs Provincial Park. Mono Cliffs is a non operating park that has a few interesting side trails and tremendous views in the north end of the park. Just north of Mono Cliffs, the trail travels through Boyne Valley Provincial Park where more countryside views are offered.

Map 32

Continuing north from the Boyne Valley, the Bruce Trail soon passes by the Eden Shelter. The shelter is an open face structure suitable for up to eight people and is a great place to spend the night. North of the shelter, the trail travels past the Nottawasaga Bluffs Conservation area and through Devil's Glen Provincial Park. Camping is available at both the conservation area and park, although the provincial park is no longer maintained. The approach to Devil's Glen is quite unique as the trail descends into a deep valley then climbs to the top providing a superb view of the valley.

From Devil's Glen, the trail continues north through Nottawasaga Lookout Provincial Nature Reserve and the Pretty River Provincial Park before reaching the Petun Conservation Area. Near the conservation area the trail passes by the highest point on the trail at 540 m (1,772 ft). Camping is available at the conservation area.

Maps 31 & 35

A very scenic portion of the trail begins west of Petun along Blue Mountain. The views of the Georgian Bay are breathtaking. From the mountain the trail heads southwest to the picturesque Beaver Valley. The Beaver Valley Lookout is a natural highlight of the trail, after which the Bruce veers north along the other side of the valley. Heading north, the trail travels past the Beaver Valley shelter and eventually crosses County Road 7 where the route heads west. Travelling west, the trail passes by many open field areas and past the Ambrose and Bighead Campsites.

You may notice that this section of the Bruce Trail is covered on two maps. The maps covering the Bruce Peninsula (Maps 34-39) are at a larger scale than the southern maps. This allows us to show more detail on the remarkable part of the province.

Maps 34 & 30

The Bruce Trail travels northwest from the Bighead Campsite to Owen Sound. In Owen Sound camping is also available at Harrison Park on the south side of the city. The trail continues along the West Rocks providing nice views of the city and surrounding area before passing through the Pottawatomi Conservation Area. At this point, the route begins traveling north along the Bruce Peninsula. The route follows roads for a short distance before veering into the woods along blazed trails. Eventually, the route passes by Bass Lake before crossing County Road 1.

Map 37

Continuing along the Bruce Peninsula, the trail passes atop Skinner's Bluff east of the town of Wiarton. Along the Bluff, there are nice views of Colpoy's Bay. The Bruce then descends into Wiarton where it follows the waterfront. Camping is available at the Blue Water Beach Park in Wiarton. As the trail heads north, enjoy the views to the south of Skinner's Bluff before disappearing into the forest. This section is a little more challenging as it skirts the edge of the escarpment over to Malcolm Bluff and eventually Jones Bluff. Jones Bluff offers panoramic views of the Georgian Bay and area. If these views are not enough, nearby Sydney Bluff should be a rewarding destination. The trail finally descends to the peaceful shores of Hope Bay.

Map 36

The easy waterside section is short lived as the Bruce Trail once again climbs atop the escarpment. Following the bluffs along the northwest shore of Hope Bay, hikers are once again presented with some fabulous views. The rustic shoreline with Sydney Bluffs in the distance are definitely picture worthy. The trail soon heads west into deeper forest cover before breaking out along the shore of the Lion's Head Provincial Nature Reserve. The trail follows the scenic bluff around Lion's Head before descending into the village of Lion's Head. The village is a good place to pick up supplies and to rest at one of the campsites. The trail continues north along Whippoorwill Bay through a combination of forests and scenic shoreline bluffs overlooking the Georgian Bay. The trail also passes the lakeside Reed's Dump Campsite on the way to Smokey Head White Bluff Nature Reserve.

Map 39

The Bruce Trail continues its pattern of forest cover, bluffs and shoreline travel, as it makes its way north to Dyer's Bay. This part of the trail is wilderness travel at its best. Eventually the Bruce makes it to the Dyer's Bay Road crossing, where the trail heads inward towards the Bruce Peninsula National Park. At this point, the trail follows a few side roads and enters the park along the Crane Lake Road. Once inside the park, the route becomes even more secluded. The trail passes by Upper Andrew and Moore Lakes before breaking out onto the rugged shoreline of the Georgian Bay. The High Dump interior park campsite is found at this point and makes a nice stopover. The next several kilometres of trail follows the serene shore of the Bruce Peninsula.

Map 38

The last stretch of the Bruce Trail begins from the Storm Haven Campsite, a national park interior camping area. The trail follows the wild Georgian Bay shoreline offering fantastic views along the way. The terrain in this area is a combination of steep forested slopes and rocky shoreline and will challenge most hikers. The trail continues through the park and at long last ends at the small lakeside village of Tobermory, some 800 km (497 mi) away from Niagara Falls.

Cabot Head Trail (Map 39/D4) 🚶 🚻

Located along the eastern shore of the Wingfield Basin, the Cabot Head Trail is one of the hidden highlights of the Bruce Peninsula. From Dyer's Bay Road, follow the Cabot Head Road north along the scenic Lake Huron shoreline to the 'Y' in the road. The parking area and trailhead is located just past the junction. It is an easy 1 km (0.6 mi) route that follows the road north to the Cabot Head Lighthouse. The lighthouse is over 100 years old and is still manned by volunteers. In addition to a small museum explaining the history of this part of the Bruce Peninsula, the lighthouse also offers a breathtaking view from the top. On a clear day Flowerpot Island and Cape Croker are visible. From the lighthouse, the trail continues north to Wingfield Point and returns via a shore trail along the Wingfield Basin. In the basin, the wreck of the steamship Gargantua remains.

Caledon Trailway (Maps 26/F7-G4) 🚶 🚲 🐎 🚻

The Caledon Trailway travels between the settlements of Terra Cotta and Palgrave and is part of the Bruce Trail system. The trail spans 35 km (22 mi) along an easy slope of an abandoned CN railway line. The railway line was built in the mid 1870's and greatly aided in the growth of trade in the region. In 1989, the railway was designated as a recreational trail. Beginning at Terra Cotta, the route follows the Credit River for a good distance before reaching Inglewood. The route then travels northeast, paralleling the Little Credit River to the village of Caledon East. From Caledon East, the route continues northeast crossing the Humber River before entering the village of Palgrave. The geography of the Caledon Trailway is very pleasing as the route passes by a mix of farm fields and hardwood stands. A variety of birds and other wildlife can be viewed along the trail including larger mammals such as deer, fox and coyotes.

Cambridge to Paris Trail (Maps 20/G6-14/G1) 🚶 🚲 🐎 🚻

In the town of Cambridge, the trailhead for Cambridge to Paris Rail Trail is located near the junction of Concession Street (County Road

aeronautical charts topo maps topo maps street maps globes
www.pathfindermaps.ca
1-888-447-4745
PATHFINDER MAPS
5-10511 Hwy 7
Carleton Place ON K7C 3P2
gps by magellan nautical charts

97) and East River Road (Highway 24). A parking area is located off the west side of East River Road along with washrooms and trail signage. The trail spans approximately 19 km (11.8 mi) one-way and follows the old railbed adjacent to the Grand River. In several areas along the route, you will be rewarded with great views of the historic river. At the 9 km (5.6 mi) point, the trail passes through the village of Glen Morris, where you will pass another parking/access area to the trail. The trail ends 10 km (6.2 mi) south of Glen Morris at a parking/access area at the town of Paris where the route meets East River Road.

Cape Croker Indian Park Trail (Map 37/A4) 👤 🚶

The scenic Cape Croker Trail is found at Cape Croker Indian Park north of the town of Wiarton. From County Road 9, follow the Hope Bay Road east along Hope Bay and Sydney Bay, eventually reaching the park. The moderate 8 km (5 mi) loop begins by traversing along a boardwalk before winding its way up towards steep limestone cliffs overlooking Sydney Bay and the Melville Sound. Atop the cliffs a camera would come in handy, as the view from the cliffs is fabulous. The trail skirts along the cliffs before heading back down towards the parking area. The park is set near the sacred native land of the first nation Chippewas of Nawash.

Centennial Park Trail (Map 27/E3) 👤 🎿

West of Aurora, this trail is accessible off Jane Street (County Road 55), just north of the 16th Side Road. There is a small parking area off the east side of Jane Street that provides access to the trailhead. This 1.5-2 km trail system is comprised of three connected loop trails. During the summer the trails are quite easy to navigate on foot; however, during the winter the trails vary from easy to difficult for cross-country skiers.

Charles Whitney Trail (Map 20/G5) 👤 🚶

Located in the north end of Cambridge, the Charles Whitney Trail can be found in Riverside Park. The park entrance is located off King Street along the east side of the Speed River. The trail follows the north shore of the river before eventually following a boardwalk over a wetland area. The wetland is home to countless birds and small mammals. In all, the trail is an easy 4 km (2.5 mi) hike.

Christie Conservation Area Trails (Map 21/E7) 👤 🚶

The Christie Conservation Area is located just east of Hamilton off the south side of Highway 5, west of Brock Road (County Road 504). Visitors will enjoy the over 9 km (5.6 mi) of easy trails that circle the Christie Reservoir. The main features of the trails include the 9 m (30 ft) high dam and the more secluded wilderness section of the route.

Chrysler Canada Greenway Trail (Map 1/B1-G6) 👤 🚴 🐎 🎿

The birth of the Chrysler Canada Greenway Trail began in 1995 with the purchase of an abandoned rail line by the Essex Region Conservation Authority. The greenway trail is now part of the Trans Canada Trail and travels from Kingsville north to Oldcastle, south of Windsor. The trail is a 42 km (26 mi) one-way multi use route suitable for hiking, biking and horseback riding (in sections). During the winter cross-country skiing is possible. Below are descriptions of the complete route broken down into sections. Note all distances below are for one-way travel.

Colasanti's to Kingsville

Beginning at the popular tourist attraction east of Kingsville, the section from Colasanti's Tropical Gardens to Kingsville is an easy 6.3 km (3.9 mi). From Colasanti's, the trail travels south along Peterson Road before cutting southwest towards Kingsville. The route crosses the Graham Side Road and Highway 18 before heading into Kingsville. This portion of the trail ends at the Kingsville Train Station, which was erected in 1889 and is designated under the Ontario Heritage Act as architecturally and historically significant.

Kingsville to Harrow

From the Kingsville Train Station the greenway trail parallels County Road 20 all the way west to the town of Harrow. Along this easy 15.5 km (9.6 mi) section of the trail, you will pass by several farms, including Schwab Farms, about half way between the two towns. A parking area, picnic table and toilets are available at the farm. This portion of the trail ends at the Trans Canada Trail kiosk in the town of Harrow. At the kiosk you will find picnic tables and a parking area.

Harrow to Oldcastle

The 21 km (13 mi) stretch between Harrow and Oldcastle is the longest stretch of the trail without an official rest stop area. Although the grade of the trail is easy, this portion of the trail is regarded as moderate in difficulty if it is attempted in its entirety. From Harrow, the trail veers north as it heads towards the city of Windsor. The route passes along the scenic farming countryside and is a pleasant hike or bike. About 5 km (3 mi) south of Oldcastle there is a small parking area for access to the trail system.

Clark Wright Conservation Area Trails (Map 12/A6) 👤 🎿 ⛷️

An easy 1.9 km (1.2 mi) collection of interconnecting loops lead through the wooded area of this conservation area. The route passes over a small creek, past some wetland and meadow areas, making this a great spot for a day in the outdoors. In addition to hiking, the trail system is becoming more popular with snowshoers and cross-country skiers during winter. The conservation area is found south of Strathroy off Walkers Drive.

Clinton Conservation Area Trail (Map 18/D2) 👤 🚴 🎿

The Clinton Conservation Area is located south of the town of Clinton off the east side of Highway 8. A small parking area is located at the area complete with a picnic shelter, playground and washrooms. The trail consists of two interconnected loops creating an easy 2 km (1.2 mi) trail. The route traverses along the peaceful Bayfield River and through a mature forest. The trail is used primarily by hikers, however bikers and in winter cross-country skiing enthusiasts can explore the area.

Clubine Forest Tract Trail (Map 28/C2) 👤

North of Claremont, the Clubine Forest Tract is accessible via the 4th Concession Road. The tract offers hikers the opportunity to explore an easy 2 km trail through the reclaimed forest.

Coldstream Conservation Area Trails (Map 12/D4) 👤 🚶 🎿 ⛷️

The Coldstream Conservation Area Trail system is split up into two separate trails. The **Cedar Walk** is an easy 0.9 km (0.6 mi) route along a boardwalk through a part of the rare cedar swamp. Visitors will enjoy an intimate view of the swamp and its local wildlife. The **Gravel Pit Trail** is regarded as easy to moderate in difficulty and spans 2.3 km (1.4 mi) past an old gravel pit and through a floodplain forest. Over the years the pit has slowly been reclaimed by nature and combined with the forest areas, making for a great place for nature appreciation and bird watching. Both trails can be used for cross-country skiing and snowshoeing; however, the gravel pit tour is not the preferred ski route at this conservation area. The conservation area and trails can be accessed from Ilderton Road (County Road 16), the Quaker Line and off Coldstream Road.

Crawford Lake Conservation Area Trails (Map 21/F4) 👤 🚶 📖

Southwest of Milton, the Crawford Lake Conservation Area is accessible from Guelph Line south of Highway 401. Steeles Avenue is the access road to the area, which branches off the east side of Guelph Line. There is a fee to access any of the five interesting trails:

Crawford Lake Trail

This easy 1.4 km (0.9 mi) trail circles the majestic Crawford Lake. The lake is home to a fragile aquatic ecosystem, which visitors can learn more about from educational plaques along the trail.

Escarpment Trail

The Escarpment Trail is an easy 2.6 km (1.6 mi) loop that travels through a mature forest stand that opens up at a scenic lookout. From the lookout, hikers can take in the Nassagaweya Canyon and the vast countryside around it.

Nassagaweya Trail

As the longest trail in the conservation area, this route spans just over 5 km (3.1 mi) and is regarded as moderate in difficulty. The trail passes through forest cover before descending into the Limestone Creek Valley. The trail then ascends the escarpment and heads east to the picturesque Rattlesnake Point.

Pine Ridge Trail

The easy 2 km (1.2 mi) Pine Ridge Trail loops from the visitor centre to the edge of the escarpment.

Woodland Trail

The Woodland Trail is an easy 2.7 km (1.7 mi) loop that heads south through some mature forest cover and links up with the Bruce Trail for a short period before heading back to the visitor centre.

Culham Trail (Map 22/C3-A1) 🚶 🚲

Once completed, this long distance trail will stretch from Erindale Park in Mississauga north all the way to the city of Brampton. The trail is planned to travel along the Credit River Valley, through mature tree stands and past many wetland areas. The route will also be passing by remnants of original settlement in the area, including old homestead ruins, dams, orchards and mills. Large portions of the trail are currently complete. For more detailed information on the trail contact the Mississauga Parks and Rec at (905) 896-5384.

Dagmar Mountain Bike Centre (Map 28/E3) 🚲 ⛷ ❄

Dagmar Mountain was originally established as an alpine and cross-country ski centre, although over the years has developed into a great place for mountain bikers. The centre is home to over 20 km (12.4 mi) of moderate trails that traverse through a mainly wooded setting. There are some technical sections that will challenge even the best riders. The centre is located north of Ajax, not far off County Road 23 (Lake Ridge Road). For more information on hours and fees call (905) 649-2002.

Dofasco Trail (Map 16/B1) 🚶 🚲 ❄

The Dofasco Trail was built with support from a number of local Hamilton area companies and organizations that included the Conservation Foundation, the City of Hamilton and Dofasco Inc. The trail can be accessed from the Devil's Punchbowl Conservation Area to the east of County Road 20 or 87 Acres Park. The trail essentially travels between the two parks totalling 11.5 km (7.1 mi) one-way. From the Devil's Punch Bowl Conservation Area, this moderate trail travels east through a mix of open field and tree areas for about 5 km (3.1 mi) before entering the Vinemount South Swamp (as of printing of this book the Vineland Swamp portion of the trail was not complete and a road detour was available). The swamp is teaming with life and is one of the largest natural areas in the Hamilton area. From the swamp, the trail proceeds east towards 87 Acres Park.

Devil's Monument Trail (Map 39/D6) 🚶 ❄

The Devil's Monument Trail is a moderate 4 km (2.5 mi) loop that begins by hiking east along a portion of the Bruce Trail to the edge of the escarpment. From the cliff, a fantastic view of Dyer's Bay and Lake Huron can be taken in. The trail then follows the cliff south to a view of Devil's Monument (or Devil's Pulpit), which is a 14 m (44 ft) high rock stack that was once an arch that has been eroded by the wave

action of Lake Huron. From the monument, a shortcut can be taken to the west side of the loop, otherwise, proceed south along the trail to Borchardt Road where the route begins its loop back to the parking area. To reach this trail, follow Highway 6 north from Wiarton to Dyer's Bay Road and head east. After the southern facing turn on Dyer's Bay Road look for Britain Lake Road. About 1.5 km (0.9 mi) down Britain Lake Road there is a small parking area off the west side at the trailhead.

Doon Heritage Trail (Map 20/F5) 🚶 ❄

The Doon Heritage Trail is a leisurely stroll through a historic pioneer village. Along this 3 km (1.9 mi) walk, visitors will be immersed in an early 20th Century town site complete with an old railway station, grocery and covered bridge. For hours of operation and more information call (519) 748-1914. The heritage town and trail can be reached by following Homer Watson Boulevard south from Highway 401 to Huron Road. Take Huron Road east and look for the parking area off the north side of the road.

Dorchester Mill Pond Trail (Map 13/C5) 🚶 ⛷ ❄

The Dorchester Mill Pond was created in 1810 in order to create mill power for local mills. Today, the area around the pond is host to two picnic areas and the Mill Pond Trail. This easy 3.5 km (2.2 mi) route circles the pond, passing by two lookouts and across a newly constructed bridge that provides a close up view of the dam. While you cannot ski the trail during the winter, it is possible to travel the trail with snowshoes. Located in the west end of the town of Dorchester, there are four access/parking areas around the pond.

Dundas Valley Conservation Area Trails (Map 15/E1) 🚶 ❄

Set along the northwest corner of Ancaster, the Dundas Valley Conservation Area is an urban paradise. There are numerous access points, but the main entry is at the visitor centre off the east side of Governors Road (County Road 99). The conservation area is home to a collection of over 40 km (25 mi) of multi-use trails set amid a Carolinian forest and wetland environment. The trails range in difficulty from easy to moderate and can provide hundreds of hours of outdoor adventure. Some of the main features of the trails include the Niagara Escarpment, the Victorian Train Station reproduction (Visitor Centre) and simply the expanse of forest and wetlands to explore. For a small fee a detailed trail map can be purchased at the visitor centre.

Durham Regional Forest Tract Trails (28/D2)

The Durham Regional Forest Tract is a collection of municipal forest properties found south of Uxbridge. While each tract does host a trail system, the main forest tract can be reached via the 7th Concession Road south of Goodwood Road (County Road 21). As part of the Oak Ridges Moraine, the main forest tract was reforested with red and white pine over seventy years ago. Today, the big pines are a welcome rarity and make a great natural canopy for visitors to enjoy.

The trail system in the Durham Regional Forest Tract is estimated at over 20 km (12.4 mi) and is a multi use system suitable for hikers, bikers and horseback riders. Hikers will find most of the trails relatively easy with some moderately difficult sections. For mountain bikers the system varies greatly from easy to difficult, depending mainly on elevation gains. During the winter months, portions of the trails are used for cross-country skiing, although they are not groomed.

Earl Rowe Provincial Park Lookout Trail (Map 32/G7)

Located just northwest of the town of Alliston, Earle Rowe Provincial Park can be reached off the 7th Concession Road. There are a few short hiking trails available at the park, including the Lookout Trail. This is the most popular trail in the park and stretches less than 1 km in length as it loops from the main parking area back along the Boyne River. Along the trail a fantastic view of the river and countryside is available.

Eldred King Tract Trails (Map 28/A2)

Accessible east of Newmarket off Highway 48, the Eldred King Regional Forest Tract offers over 13 km (8.1 mi) of hiking/biking trails. The trails traverse along a collection of older roads and natural paths, and offer a maze of connected routes. Visitors to the system can enjoy the extensive forest cover, as well as views of the Black River.

Elgin Trail (Maps 6/G1-7/A2)

Stretching between Port Stanley on Lake Erie to Paynes Mills west of St. Thomas, the Elgin Trail travels 35 km (21.2 mi) one-way. There are several different access points to shorten this easy multi-use trail. The trail follows Kettle Creek most of the way to St. Thomas and then follows Dodd Creek most of the way between St. Thomas and Paynes Mills.

Elora Cataract Trailway (Maps 25/G7-26/E6)

Similar to many of Southwestern Ontario's great trails, the Elora Cataract Trail follows an old abandoned rail bed. The trail stretches 47 km (29 mi) one-way from the town of Fergus to the village of Cataract. Overall, the multi-use trail is regarded as easy in difficulty due to the flat grade of the route. From Fergus, the trail follows the old CP railbed north to the southern shore of Belwood Lake and through the Belwood Lake Conservation Area. The route continues east towards the village of Hillsburgh, past the northern reaches of the quaint town of Erin, before culminating at the Cataract Provincial Park.

Elora Gorge Trail (Map 20/F1)

Fantastic views of the Grand River and the Elora Gorge are found on a pair of trails. The longer trail is an easy 2.5 km (1.6 mi) loop that skirts the top of the 20+ m (66+ ft) high cliffs of the gorge. The trail crosses over a Grand River tributary and along the northern shore of the river. The other hike leads south for a 1.5 km (0.9 mi) return trip. The conservation area and trails are found off the west side of County

Road 21, south of the village of Elora.

Eugenia Falls Conservation Area Trail (Map 31/D5)

Located north of the town of Flesherton, the conservation area is found off the west side of County Road 13, about 3.5 km (2.2 mi) north of the junction with County Road 4. Although only 1 km in length, this trail is one of the gems of Southwestern Ontario. The easy trail traverses along the Cuckoo Valley through a mixed forest eventually meeting the climax of the hike, the Eugenia Falls. The Eugenia Falls is an impressive 30 m (98 ft) waterfall along the Beaver River. The trail can also be used for cross-country skiing during the winter months.

Eramosa River Trail (Map 21/B3)

In the heart of the city of Guelph, the Eramosa Trail can be accessed off the west side of Victoria Street just south of York Road. From the trailhead, it is a 4 km (2.5 mi) return hike along the northern shore of the Eramosa River. The trail passes through a maintained park like setting home to a number of big willow trees. The trail returns after reaching the confluence of the Eramosa and Speed Rivers.

F.W.R. Dickson Trail (Map 20/G7)

This trail is located in the F.W.R Dickson Wilderness Area, which is found off the north side of the Brant-Waterloo Road south of Cambridge. The wilderness area is comprised of a mix of forest and wetland habitat, the perfect ingredient for an interesting hike. The trail is an easy 2 km (1.2 mi) loop trail that travels north around a small pond and back.

Falls Reserve Conservation Area Trail (Map 23/A7)

This easy loop travels 3.2 km (2 mi) from the parking and picnic area down to the site of the Maitland River and the fantastic Benmiller Falls. From the falls, the trail parallels the river before reaching the conservation area boundary and then veering back to the parking area. For added adventure, the Maitland Trail, a long distance route, continues east and west from the conservation area. There is a small fee to use the conservation area's facilities, which are located southeast of Goderich. Follow County Road 31 (Londesboro Road) to the Falls Reserve Line, which travels south to the conservation area. Watch for poison ivy near the river area.

Fanshawe Conservation Area Trail (Map 13/A3)

The Fanshawe Conservation Area is a large conservation area that lies northeast of the city of London off Clarke Road. There are five trails to explore but during the months of April to October, there is a small access fee. During winter, ski rentals are available for those interested in cross-country skiing. Be sure to pick up a trail map at the front gate.

Perhaps the most popular trail and certainly the longest is the **Fanshawe Lake Trail**. This moderate 22 km (13.7 mi) route skirts the shoreline of the lake over a number of hilly areas and through a mixture of forests and meadows. This trail is popular with bikers. The other four trails range from 1.5 km (0.9 mi) to 4 km (2.5 mi) in length and are all easy to travel. The shorter trails generally travel through a combination of mixed forest areas and are accessible from the campground.

Flowerpot Island (Fathom Five Marine Park) Trails (Map 38/E2)

The only access to Flowerpot Island is by boat from Tobermory. Visitors can dock their own crafts along the east side of the island or take one of the many tour boats from Tobermory to the island. While a boat is the best way to view the island's famous flowerpot rock formations, a few of the formations can be seen from these trails.

Flowerpot Island Loop

From the docking area, the Flowerpot Island Loop is an easy 3 km (1.9 mi) trek through the forest and rocky terrain of Flowerpot Island. The route skirts along the eastern shore of the island passing by a natural cave and a few small flowerpot displays before terminating at the lighthouse and museum.

Marl Trail

Shortly along the Flowerpot Island Loop Trail, the Marl Trail branches south. The trail leads past the Marl Beds to the southern shore of the island. The Marl Beds are soft bottom ponds that were once a small cove on the islands. The trail returns back the same route completing an easy 1.2 km (0.7 mi) hike.

Fonthill to Thorold Rail Trail (Map 17/B4-C3) 🚶 🚲

This rail trail is not officially a recreation trail, although many locals have been using it for some time. The trail stretches approximately 10 km (6.2 mi) between the two towns making this a moderate 20 km (12.4 mi) return trip. One word of caution, however, there is some large holes and rocks along portions of this route, which could make biking a challenge to some users. Access can be found from several intersecting roads along the route.

Fort Erie Friendship Trail (Map 17/E7-G6) 🚶 🚲 👫

The Fort Erie Friendship Trail is a hiking/biking route that can be accessed from Gorham Road in Ridgeway or from Edgemere Road in Fort Erie. The paved trail closely follows the southern side of Dominion Road (County Road 1) providing views of Lake Erie along the way. The trail is an 18 km (11.2 mi) return trek and is regarded as easy due to the paved nature of the route.

Ganaraska Trail (Map 32/D4) ⛺ 🚶 🛶 🎿 👫

The Ganaraska trail is a long distance route extending from Port Hope along the banks of the Ganaraska River, to Midland and eventually Glen Huron where the trail connects with the Bruce Trail. In this book we only cover the southern portion of the trail from just north of Wasaga Beach to Glen Huron. The trail traverses through a great variety of different natural areas including rolling farmland, the pre-Cambrian Shield, the shores of the Georgian Bay, and the Niagara Escarpment. The route varies in difficulty depending on the area and the distance you wish to travel. Camping is not permitted along private land but there are various parks, conservation areas, and private campgrounds to overnight at. In winter, the trail is great for cross-country skiing or snowshoeing. If you are planning an extended outing it is advised that you pick up the detailed Ganaraska Trail Guide to aid in your trip preparations and to help support the trail maintenance.

George G. Newton Nature Reserve Trail (Map 18/A1) 🚶 👫

The George G. Newton Nature Preserve is a 40 hectare land tract that was once the site of a thriving farm. The farm is now owned by the Federation of Ontario Naturalists and is being reverted back to a more natural state. A moderate 1.3 km (0.8 mi) loop trail travels through old orchards and past mature pine trees. The route begins by passing by the remnants of an old building before passing a small pond. Shortly after the pond, there is a side trail that can be followed south to the site of a small stream and an old dam where a sawmill was once located. The side trail is an additional 1.2 km (0.7 mi) through a mainly white cedar forest. The small parking area to the nature reserve and trailhead is located off the south side of Kitchigami Road just past Porter's Hill Line north of Bayfield.

George Richardson Park Trail (Map 27/G1) 🚶

George Richardson Park in Newmarket is accessible from the Bayview Parkway, north of Davis Drive. The park is home to an easy 3.2 km (2 mi) trail that skirts both sides of the Holland River floodplain. From the east side of the river, hikers can link up with the Mabel Davis Conservation Area trail found to the south.

Georgian Trail (Maps 31/D1-32/B2, 35/F3) 🚶 🚲 🛶 🎿 👫

The Georgian Trail is a fantastic route that stretches 32 km (19.9 mi) one-way between the towns of Meaford and Collingwood. The trail is accessible in over thirty areas, including off Highway 26 as well as in the towns of Meaford, Collingwood and Thornbury. The easy, well maintained route is made up of hard packed stones and has few inclines to negotiate. Along the trail travellers are offered great views of the beautiful Georgian Bay as well as Blue Mountain and will find other points of interest such as trestle bridges, sandy beach areas, Craigleith Provincial Park and the Thornbury Fish Lock. Both hikers and bikers can enjoy this trail during the summer months, while cross-country skiers and snowshoeing advocates utilize parts of the route during the winter months.

Glassford Arboretum Trail (Map 22/B1) 🚶

Just south of Brampton, the Glassford Arboretum Trail can be found at Meadowvale Park, between Highway 407 and Highway 401. The park is accessible off the Old Derry Road, which can be reached via Creditview Road. The Arboretum Trail is a popular local hiking trail in a research area for native plant re-establishment.

Goderich Millennium Trail (Map 23/A7) 🚶 👫

In the northern end of the town of Goderich the parking area to this trail is off the northwest side of Highway 21, just north of the crossing of the Maitland River. From the parking area the trail heads west in a moderate 1 km (0.6 mi) loop. The scenic trail begins by following the river, then heads back towards the parking area.

Goderich to Auburn Trail (Map 23/B7) 🚶 🚲 🛶 🏍 🎿

Beginning in the town of Goderich on shore of the Maitland River, this old railbed heads east to the settlement of Auburn. The easy trail is approximately 13 km (8.1 mi) in length but can be continued east past Auburn. If you do continue, please respect private property and do not trespass. For added adventure, you can loop back to the trailhead along the Maitland Trail (see below).

Goderich Waterfront Trail (Map 23/A7) 🚶 👫

This boardwalk trail passes along the picturesque Lake Huron shoreline and past three fabulous sandy beaches. Along with the beaches, visitors can also enjoy the many sheltered picnic areas. The trailhead is located at the main beach at the Lake Huron waterfront, which is found off West Street south of the town square or from Wellington Street. The 3 km (19 mi) route travels east to Rotary Cove, an alternate access point.

Goodwood Forest and Secord Forest Tract Trails (Map 28/C3) 🚶 🛶

Northwest of Claremont, visitors can find the Goodwood Forest Tract off the west side of 3rd Concession Road, while the Secord Tract lies further north off the east side of the 3rd Concession Road. The Goodwood Forest Tract is slightly longer and more difficult covering 3 km (1.9 mi). The Secord Tract is home to an easy to moderate 2 km (1.2 mi) route. Well suited for hikers, both trails can also be used by cross-country skiers in the winter.

Gordon Glaves Memorial Pathway (Map 15/A2) 🚶 🚲

The Gordon Glaves Memorial Pathway was established in 1993 and is an extension to the S.C. Johnson Trail and the Hamilton to Brantford Rail Trail. The 12.5 km (7.8 mi) pathway winds its way through the southern end of Brantford from the Wilkes Dam east to the trailhead of the Hamilton to Brantford Rail Trail. The easy pathway begins by winding its way along the eastern shore of the Grand River. At the 1.5 km (0.6 mi) mark, you will pass by the main parking and access area to the pathway at Waterworks Park. At the 6 km (3.7 mi) point you will find Earl Haig Park and access to a side trail. The offshoot trail travels south of Colborne Street and links up with the main trail some 8 km (5 mi) later. Continuing along the main path, the route passes by the Mohawk Chapel, a Six Nation First Nation historic site. Just east of the chapel, the path passes by the Kanata Iroquois Village, an interesting local attraction. Eventually the trail meets the rail trail parking area where another adventure can begin.

Grand Bend Rotary Nature Trail (Map 10 inset) 🚶 🚴

Beginning in the town of Grand Bend the Rotary Nature Trail travels south to the entrance of the Pinery Provincial Park. The easy trail covers 9 km (5.6 mi) one-way as it parallels the Ausable River and Highway 21. The trailhead can be found at the Ontario Street Bridge over the Ausable River.

Grand Trunk Rail Line Trail (Map 20/G6) 🚶 🚴 🏇

The Grand Trunk Rail Line Trail is located in the heart of Cambridge and can be accessed from River Bluffs Park, which lies off the east side of George Street. This former rail line route is now a great interurban hiking trail that parallels the Grand River north towards Fountain Street. Hikers will enjoy the view of the river in several areas as well as a portion of the route next to some fabulous limestone bluffs. The trail is an easy 12 km (7.5 mi) return hike.

Grand Valley Trail (Maps 16/C7-26/D6) ⛰ 🚶 🚵 🏇

The Grand Valley Trail is a fantastic long distance trail that begins near the shore of Lake Erie at Rock Point Provincial Park. From the park, the trail spans some 250 km (155 mi) one-way north all the way to the town of Alton south of Orangeville. The Grand Valley Trail is quite similar to the Bruce Trail in its makeup. The trail traverses along a combination of side roads and blazed trails for an easy to moderate route as long as you limit the distance you travel in any given day. Portions of the Grand Valley Trail do follow other existing trails, such as the Elora Cataract Trail, but for the most part, the route follows its own path.

The trail parallels the Grand River most of the way providing scenic views of the river and countryside in several areas. The unique trail also passes through the urban centres of Brantford and Kitchener as well as several small parks and conservation areas. If you plan to hike the trail from end to end, camping is limited to a few nearby conservation areas. For the most part you will also have to arrange alternate accommodations with either a motel, hotel or bed and breakfast.

Greenwood Conservation Area Trail (Map 28/E5) 🚶 🎿

North of the town of Ajax, the Greenwood Conservation Area can be reached by Westney Road (County Road 31). The conservation area helps protect a portion of the Duffins Creek and is a fantastic place to enjoy the great outdoors along the easy 2 km (1.6 mi) hiking trail. The trail doubles as a moderate cross-country ski trail during the winter as it follows Duffins Creek most of the way.

Guelph Lake Nature Centre Trail (Map 21/A2) 🚶

The Guelph Lake Nature Centre and Trail is found north of town on Conservation Road, which is found off Victoria Road. There is a trailhead off the south side of the road just past the Guelph Lake Dam. The trail is an easy 1.5 km (0.9 mi) loop trail that takes you through a cedar forest to the banks of the Speed River.

Guelph Radial Trail (Map 21/B3) 🚶 🚴 🏇 (Aug/06)

The trailhead to the Guelph Radial Trail lies off the east side of Watson Road South (County Road 41) just south of Stone Road. The popular recreational trail follows the north shore of the Eramosa River for about 5 km (3.1 mi). It is an easy route that provides good views of the river. It is possible to continue east, eventually connecting with the Bruce Trail at the Limestone Conservation Area.

Hamilton to Brantford Rail Trail (Maps 15/A1-21/G1) 🚶 🚴 🏇 📷 🏇

The Hamilton to Brantford Rail Trail was Canada's first off-road interurban trail. It was established in 1996 and offers an easy 32 km (20 mi) one-way route. The trail has been split up into three separate sections for easier interpretation below:

Hamilton to Dundas Valley CA

The trailhead for this route can be found off Ewen Road in the west end of the city of Hamilton. There is a parking area at the trailhead as well as signage marking the beginning of the trail. The section from Hamilton to the Dundas Valley Conservation Area is 5.5 km (3.4 mi) in length and passes through Sanctuary Park along the way.

Dundas Valley CA to Jerseyville

At the Dundas Valley Conservation Area visitors can enjoy various activities such as interpretive hikes, educational programs and an historic trail display. From the conservation area, the Rail Trail climbs up a marginal grade to Summit, which offers a nice view of the Summit Muskeg Preserve. From Summit, the route passes by a small parking area near the Highway 52 crossing before continuing west to Jerseyville. The total distance of this section is approximately 13 km (8.1 mi).

Jerseyville to Brantford

In the small village of Jerseyville, visitors can find the parking area and access point to the trail in the west side of the village off Jerseyville Road. From Jerseyville it is an easy 13.5 km (8.4 mi) to the Brantford access area. Along this stretch of the trail the route passes under Highway 403 and past the site of the 1986 landslide that decommissioned the rail line.

Hamilton Harbour Front Trail (Maps 21/G7) 🚶 🏇

You can find this trail along the northern harbour waterfront beginning at Bayfront Park. The 6.8 km (4.2 mi) trail travels west underneath York Boulevard and Highway 403 to Princess Point. The highlights of this easy hike include the Desjardins Canal and a floating walkway. The trail also provides a connection to the Lake Ontario Waterfront Trail.

Hanlon Creek Trail (Map 21/A3) 🚶 🏇

In the city of Guelph, this trail begins across from the Stone Road Mall at the intersection of Stone Road and Scottsdale Drive. The trail follows the south side of Stone Road for a few hundred metres before heading south towards University Village Park. The route hikes through University Park then over Ironwood Road and into the forested Hanlon Creek Park. As the trail continues south, it eventually travels through Preservation Park where visitors can view a magnificent century old Eastern hemlock. The route returns along the same path and is an easy 3 km (1.9 mi) hike.

Hanover Community Trail (Maps 24/D1-30/D7) 🚶 🚴 🎿 ⛷

Hanover is a small Southwestern Ontario farming community that is a great place to visit. At one time, the community relied heavily on its many railway connections to transport goods to and from the community. Today, similar to many Ontario communities, many rail lines have become obsolete, leaving a perfect foundation for trail development. Access to the trail system can be found from several areas around the town, however Hanover Park is generally the main access to the network. Currently, there is about 11 km (6.8 mi) of easy trails that have been developed along the charming Saugeen River. The multi-use trail offers a peaceful environment for a hike or bike ride or cross-country ski or snowshoe in winter.

Hardwood Hill Management Unit Trail (Map 23/G3) 🚶 🎿 ⛷

West of the small village of Teeswater, this area lies near the corner of the County Road 6 and Side Road 25 South. The management unit is home to an easy 1.2 km (0.7 mi) trail that winds its way through a mix of hardwood highlands and hemlock filled lowlands. The area is used primarily by hikers, although cross-country skiing and snowshoeing is slowly picking up in popularity.

Hay Swamp Trails (Map 18/C6) 🚶 🚴 🎿

The Hay Swamp is a large, provincially significant wetland that is a unique mix of wetland and mixed forest areas. To access the trail areas, follow County Road 83 (Dashwood Road) west from Exeter and look for trailheads off the north side of the road. The trails follow old logging roads that are slowly returning to a more natural state. There are over 10 km (6.2 mi) of interconnecting routes; some are becoming overgrown, but the majority are easy to travel and in quite good shape. There are very few trail markers along the trails and it is possible to get turned around in this system, but difficult to get lost. Donations to the Ausable Bayfield Conservation Area are always welcome for use of this outdoor area.

Headquarters Conservation Area Trails (Map 24/D1) 🧍 🎿

South of the town of Hanover, you can find the Headquarters Conservation Area by following County Road 10 to Concession Road 18. Head east on Concession 18 and look for the conservation area off the north side of the road. The trail system is made up of a 4.6 km (2.9 mi) loop that has a number of connected side trails. Travellers will experience hardwood forests, a cedar bog and pass by a cool spring fed stream. The trails are also quite popular during the winter with local cross-country skiers.

Heber Down Conservation Area Trail (Map 28/F4) 📷 🧍 🎿

Visitors to the conservation area can experience the beauty of this natural area on any of its three trails. The **Springbanks Trail** and the **Devil's Den Trail** are 2 km (1.2 mi) and 1 km (0.6 mi) in length respectively, and are both easy self guided interpretive trails. Trail users can also branch out along a more extensive 10 km (6.2 mi) route that further explores the area. The 10 km (6.2 mi) trail system is also used for cross-country skiing during the winter. Hikers will find the trail generally easy to travel, although skiers should expect anything from easy to difficult along this route. The Heber Down Conservation Area lies north of the town of Whitby off Coronation Road. Trail guides can be picked up from the main gatehouse at the conservation area from late spring to early fall. A small fee is required for use of the trail system.

Hilton Falls Conservation Area Trails (Map 21/F3) 🧍 🚴

Just west of the town of Milton, the Hilton Falls Conservation Area can be reached via Campbellville Road (County Road 9). The conservation area is home to a large collection of trails, which together span over 16 km (9.9 mi). The trails are all interconnected and trek through forests and open areas as well as around the Hilton Falls Reservoir to the sight of the Hilton Falls. The falls are quite scenic as the Sixteen Mile Creek cascades over a rock cut down into a small pool. The Bruce Trail can also be accessed from a connector trail within the conservation area.

Hollage Tract Trail (Map 28/A2) 🧍 🚵 🚴

The Hollage Tract is a regional forest tract that can be found east of Newmarket off Highway 48, just south of Vivian Road. Parking is available at the forest headquarters found off the highway. The tract has over 3 km (1.9 mi) of easy trails that head east through the lush Vivian Creek Valley to the Ninth Line Road. The mixture of pine trees includes some large white pine trees.

Holland River Trail (Map 27/F1) 🧍 🚵 🎿 🏂

The Holland River Trail is accessible from the west side of the 2nd Concession Road north of Newmarket near the Rogers Reservoir Conservation Area. The trail is an easy 3 km (1.9 mi) loop trail that begins by paralleling the Holland River then loops back through a variety of terrain. Travellers will pass through mixed forest cover, open field and wetland environments before returning to the trailhead. The trail is well marked with gravel and woodchips and doubles as a popular cross-country skiing and snowshoeing location during the winter.

Holland River Valley Trail (Map 27/F3) 🧍 🚵

In the town of Aurora, the Holland Valley Trail travels north to south along the East Branch of the Holland River. There are several access points to the trail, including the Aurora Leisure Complex, the town hall, Lambert Wilson Park and Sheppard's Bush Conservation Area.

The route can also be picked up from the Vandorf Side Road and St. John's Side Road, the southern and northern access areas to the respective route. The easy 4 km (2.5 mi) one-way trail is made up of hard packed gravel as it passes through a mix of forest cover, wetland and open fields.

Hullett Provincial Wildlife Area Trail (Map 18/D1) 🧍 🚴

This important wildlife area is located northeast of the town of Clinton. There are a few access points available to the area, but the main access is found off the east side of Wildlife Lane, which branches off Highway 8 east of Clinton. The parking area is off the east side of the road north of Hydro Line Road. The wildlife area has a number of interesting natural features such as century old maple trees and is the home of the endangered Sandhill Crane. There are over 10 km (6.2 mi) of easy trails to explore. From wetland habitat to dense forest cover, these trails provide a variety of different environments to experience. From many areas along the trails, hikers can spot small mammals such as foxes or coyotes as well as birds such as the hawks and waterfowl. Water access in this wildlife area is restricted from May 15th to August 1st in order to limit disturbance to wildlife.

Humber Valley Heritage Trail (Map 27/D6) 🧍 🚵 🚴

Located near the town of Kleinburg, the Humber Valley Heritage Trail follows the historic paths of natives, who once followed this route known as the Toronto Carrying Place Trail. It is an easy to moderate 3.5 km (2.2 mi) one-way route that stretches from Major Mackenzie Drive West north to Stegman's Mill Road. There are three main parking areas for the trail. Bindertwine Park, which is found off Stegman's Mill Road, provides access in the north end. The McMichael Art Gallery and William T. Foster Woods both lie off Islington Avenue and provide access to the middle and southern portions of the trail respectively. The trail traverses through the Humber River Valley through some mixed forest and field areas, providing fine views of the river in many areas. Future plans may see the trail extend north to link up with the Trans Canada Trail and to extend south all the way to Lake Ontario.

Huntington Trail (Map 27/G6) 🚶

The Huntington Trail lies between Leslie Street and Bayview Avenue just below Highway 407 in North York. The trail is best accessed from Huntington Park and is an easy 4 km (2.5 mi) return trip. The trail is a fantastic urban trek that traverses through surprisingly dense forest cover in several sections.

Island Lake Conservation Area Trails (Map 26/D4) 🚶

The Island Lake Conservation Area can be found just northeast of the town of Orangeville. The conservation area is set along the quaint shores of the Orangeville Reservoir, also known as Island Lake. There are four great trails available for visitors to enjoy:

Old Meadow Trail

This easy 1.5 km (0.9 mi) trail loops from the parking area through a number of fields and meadows. The open spaces are under the slow process of natural succession and you can witness some in the early stages while others have established a small forest.

Plantation Trail

The Plantation Trail is an easy 1 km (0.6 mi) hike that loops through an open field area, and a nut tree plantation.

Shoreline Trail

The Shoreline Trail is another easy 1 km (0.6 mi) trail that travels from the northern parking area to the shore of the reservoir. The route then follows the reservoir as it heads east, eventually looping back to the Old Meadow Trail and parking area.

Sugar Bush Trail

Although the longest trail in the conservation area, the Sugarbush Trail is a short 2 km (1.2 mi) hike. The easy trail starts on the Old Meadow Trail before heading south across a number of rolling fields to a maple tree tract. The route continues through the bush before eventually linking up with the Old Meadow Trail once again to return to the parking area.

Joany's Woods Trail (Map 11/F2) 🚶 ⛷ 🎿 🏕

Joany's Woods is a Wildlife Management Area that is maintained by the Ausable Bayfield Conservation Area. To find the site look for Boot Hill Road east of Thedford. The **Lookout Trail** is the easier of the two trails in the woods. It is an easy 3.2 km (2 mi) loop from the parking area through the quiet woods and past a few wetland areas. The **Tulip Tree Trail** is moderate in difficulty and spans 4.4 km (2.7 mi) over some challenging slopes through the majestic Carolinian forest and along portions of the Ausable River. A conservation region pass is required for use of the trail system. Passes can be purchased from the Ausable Bayfield Conservation Region. Call (519) 235-2610 for more information.

John E. Pearce Provincial Park Trail (Map 6/E4) 🚶 🏕

South of Wallacetown, you can find John E. Pearce Provincial Park along the shore of Lake Erie. The park is designated as day-use only and is a popular attraction for travellers looking for a summer picnic spot. A short (under 0.5 km long), easy trail leads along the cliffs in the southern end of the park. The trail provides spectacular views of Lake Erie below.

Kelso/Glen Eden Conservation Area Trails (Map 21/F3) 🚶 🚴 🏕

To the west of Milton, the Keslo/Glen Conservation Area is home to some of the best multi-use trails in the area. Over 10 km (6.2 mi) of interconnected trails are located within the conservation area with some geared to mountain bikers and others catering to hikers. Some of the highlights of the trail system include fabulous escarpment lookouts, old farm ruins and lime kiln ruins.

Keppel Rail Trail (Map 34/B3) 🚶 🚴 🐎 ⛷ 🎿 🛷

The Keppel Rail Trail follows the old rail line between the settlements of Benallen, Shallow Lake and the village of Park Head. At Benallen

the trail can be found off County Road 17, while in Shallow Lake, the trail crosses Highway 6. In Park Head, the trail is accessible off County Road 10 or Park Hill Road. The easy route stretches 12.8 km (7.9 mi) one-way and passes by a mix of terrain including wetland areas, forest stands, field and urban areas. The trail is regarded as a multi use trail system and is suitable for hikers, bikers and horseback riders during the summer. Motorized vehicles are not permitted on the trail except for snowmobiling during the winter. Cross-country skiers and snowshoers also utilize the trail in the less remote areas.

King City Trail (Map 27/E4) 🚶 ⛷

North of King City, you can find this 5 km (3.2 mi) trail by following Keele Street North (County Road 6). Look for the trail just after the crossing with Dennison Street. The trail travels from east to west along the Humber River, crossing Keele Street almost in the middle of the route.

Kirk Cousins Wildlife Management Area Trails (Map 13/A6) 🚶 ⛷ 🎿 🏕

The Kirk Cousins Management Area has been designated as a provincially significant wetland and is a fantastic place for bird watching. Over 117 different bird species have been identified including many rare and threatened species. Inside the wildlife area is a collection of interconnecting loops and side trails totalling about 5 km (3.1 mi). They skirt the A'Nowaghi Forest Ponds and offer two viewing platforms. The native translation of "A'Nowaghi" is "place of turtles", which the ponds truly are. To reach the management area, follow Wellington Road south from Highway 401 in London to Scotland Drive. Head east along Scotland Drive and look for the parking area off the north side of the road. Access is restricted to conservation authority pass holders. Passes can be purchased at the Kettle Creek Conservation Authority. Call (519) 631-1270 for more information.

Kitchener Trails (Map 20/E5) 🚶 🚴 🏕

Homer Watson Park Trail

Homer Watson Park is located in southern Kitchener off Wabanaki Drive east of Homer Watson Boulevard. This easy 2.9 km (1.8 mi) one-way hike leads through the park to a lookout over the Grand River. From the lookout the trail heads south along the river passing through an old forest home to some of the oldest beech and maple trees in the region.

Iron Horse Trail

The Iron Horse Trail is set in the heart of the city and can be reached from Borden Street in the south or from Allen Street in the north at the city of Waterloo boundary. Both Allen Street and Borden Street are accessible from the west side of King Street East. The trail follows a portion of the old Grand River Railway, which was constructed in the early 1900's. The easy 5 km (3 mi) one-way route is suitable for both hikers and bikers as it travels through a mix of residential, business and park settings.

Monarch Woods Trails

Located in the southwest end of the city of Kitchener, the Monarch Woods Trails are accessible off the Fischer-Hallman Road just north of Victoria Street. The main trails lie off the west side of the road and there is a short trail off the east side of the road that stretches southeast to Victoria Street. The main trails are a mix of easy, connected routes that travel through a park setting and around the Henry Sturm Creek. The highlight of the trail network is the mature forest and a regenerated monarch feeding area. In total there are about 2.5 km (1.6 mi) of trails that span through this woodlot.

Pioneer Tower Trail

The Pioneer Tower Trail is accessible via King Street East along the southern shore of the Grand River. The easy 8 km (5 mi) return hike follows the southern shore of the river all the way to a historical lookout tower. The tower was constructed in the early 1800's at the site of one of the first farms established in the county.

Steckle Woods Trail

The Steckle Woods is located in the southern end of the city and is accessible off the west side of Homer Watson Boulevard just south of Bleams Road. From the parking area, approximately 4 km (2.5 mi) of easy interconnected trails dissect the lush woodlot. The best time to visit the trails is in the month of May when wildflowers in the woods are in full bloom.

Tilt's Bush Trail

Tilt's Bush is an urban forest area found in the southern portion of Kitchener. The forest is located just west of Homer Watson Boulevard and can be accessed via Biehn Drive, Black Walnut Drive or Bechtel Drive. The forest is home to a collection of approximately 2 km (1.2 mi) of easy trails along Stratsburg Creek.

Kolapore Uplands Trails (Map 31/F4) 🚶 🚲 🏕

The Kolapore Uplands Trail system is located in the Kolapore Demonstration Forest. To find the demonstration forest, follow County Road 2 south from the town of Thornbury. The parking/access area for the forest is located off the west side of the road just north of the corner with the Osprey-Collingwood Road. The demonstration forest and surrounding area hosts a collection of approximately 60 km (37.3 mi) of interconnected trails. The trails are used extensively by skiers during the winter and by hikers and bikers during the summer months. Trails range from easy to moderate as they traverse through mixed forests and past some wetland and field areas.

Klopp Woodland Trail (Map 18/B5) 🚶 🚲

The Klopp Commemorative Woods is a part of one of Southwestern Ontario's largest wetland and forested areas, the Hay Swamp. The scenery around this area is truly magnificent and offers a nice change to the farmland that dominates the region. At the time of the writing of this book, the trail system was yet to be completed, although there are plans to develop a short loop trail. Currently, there is a series of walking paths through an established garden and meadow area that are ideal for an evening walk. The planned use of the trail is to include biking and cross-country skiing. Donations are always welcome to help build and maintain the trails. The area is located just east of the small town of Zurich off the north side of County Road 84 (Zurich-Hensall Road). Look for the Klopp Commemorative Woods Sign off the side of the road.

Komoka Provincial Park Trail (Map 12/E5) 🚶 🚲 🐎 🏕 🎿 👣

Komoka Provincial Park is a non operating provincial park that lies to the west of the city of London off County Road 3 (Gideon Drive). This Thames Valley park is home to four interconnecting trails; The **White, Yellow, Blue** and **Orange Trails** combine to make up an 11.5 km (7.1 mi) network. The White Trail is the longest in the mix as it traverses 4.5 km (2.8 mi) over some moderately difficult areas and along portions of the Thames River. The other three trails all provide some views of the river and are much easier to travel. The White Trail is for hikers only, while the other three trails are frequented by hikers, bikers and horseback riders in the summer and cross-country skiers or snowshoers during the winter.

Kortright Centre for Conservation Trail (Map 27/D6) 🚶 🏛

The Kortright Centre for Conservation is a fabulous 324 ha (800 ac) preserved area complete with forest cover, meadowlands and wetland habitats. The centre can be reached via Pine Valley Drive north of Rutherford Road and offers over 15 km (9.3 mi) of trails for visitors to enjoy. The trail system is made up of a number of connected loops, and at certain times, the centre also offers interpretive programs such as wildflower hikes and bird feeding. For more information on the centre and its scheduled events call the Toronto Region Conservation Authority at (416) 661-6600.

Lafarge Trail (Map 21/E7-C5) 🚶 🚲 👣

The Lafarge Trail was developed as a hiking/biking route and is a 22 km (13.7 mi) one-way trip from north to south. Along the moderate route travellers will pass along the scenic Niagara Escarpment, past the Christie Conservation Area Reservoir and through two important local wetland areas. The route is made up of off-road trail as well as road sections. Although the roads are not heavily travelled, always be aware of oncoming traffic. Access to the north is available off Gore Road at the Puslinch Wetlands Reserve. From the reserve it is 4 km (2.5 mi) east to the trailhead. To access the southern end of the route, parking is available at the Christie Conservation Area off Highway 5 or further south off Old Highway 99 at Middletown Road.

Lake Whittaker Conservation Area Trail (Map 13/E6) 🚶 🏕 🐟 ♿

Southeast of London, you can find this conservation area off Whittaker Lane, which leads north from County Road 37. A conservation pass is required to enter the area, which can be picked up at the gate during summer months or from the Kettle Creek Conservation Authority, (519) 631-1270. The Lake Whitaker Trails are a collection of three connected trails that lead around the lake and past several interesting wetland areas. Portions of the system also pass through older tree plantations as well as sugar bush areas. Two of the trails are 2.5 km (1.6 mi) in length while the shortest of the three is just over 1.5 km (0.9 mi). By the summer of 2003 the Ivan Row Trail, which will be wheelchair accessible, is scheduled to be completed.

Longwoods Road Conservation Area Trails (Map 12/D7) 🚶 🏕 🐟 👣 ♿

Within the conservation area there are a number of different parking/access areas to the trails. The trails are a collection of about 6.5 km (4 mi) of generally easy interconnected routes. There are a number of areas that are made of boardwalk and are wheelchair accessible, including the sections along Mill Stream and the west side of the pond. Viewing birds and smaller mammals is a popular activity along this stretch. The conservation area is found west of London off County Road 2 (Longwoods Road). There is a small admission fee into the conservation area and snowshoe rentals are available at certain times of the winter. For more information on costs and times the gate is open, call (519) 354-7310.

Lorne C. Henderson Conservation Area Trail (Map 10/E7) 🚶 👣

Located west of the town of Petrolia, the Lorne C. Henderson Conservation Area can be reached off the south side of Petrolia Line (County Road 4). The conservation area is well known as a bird watching haven as hundreds of different species frequent the area at various times of the year. A 5 km (3.1 mi) series of trails travel through the conservation area winding through open fields, pond areas and forest.

Lucan Conservation Area Trail (Map 12/D2) 🚶 🐟

This small conservation area offers an easy 1 km (0.6 mi) hike through a magnificent tract of older hardwood trees. The trail also travels downhill

FEDERAL PUBLICATIONS INC.

• Maps on paper & CD ROM
• Topographic Maps
• Road Maps
• Atlases

• Nautical Charts
• Aeronautical Charts
• Touring & Recreational Guidebooks

165 University Ave. Toronto
(416) 860-1611   1-888-433-3782
www.fedpubs.com

to the site of a spring fed water hole on the Ausable River. This is a popular fishing and swimming spot. At the village of Lucan, head west along William Street for about 4 km (2.5 mi) and look for the service road to the conservation area off the north side of the road.

Luther Marsh Conservation Area Trails (Map 25/F4)

The Luther Marsh is one of the largest wetland areas in Southwestern Ontario and is located northwest of the town of Grand Valley. To find the wildlife area, follow Concession Road 8-9 and turn north along Side Road 21-22. There are four trails for visitors to explore:

Bootlegger Trail

The Bootlegger Trail follows old roads, circling the marsh. The trail is the best way to explore and experience this diverse and vast wetland as it provides intimate views of the marsh. The 14 km (8.7 mi) return trail is regarded as easy to travel by bike, although hikers may find the length challenging. Two viewing platforms along the northeast portion of the marsh help visitors get a better view of the marsh.

Harrier Trail

The Harrier Trail is a 1 km (0.6 mi) side trail accessible off the northwest portion of the Bootlegger Trail.

Mallard Pond Trail

This easy 2 km (1.2 mi) loop travels around a wetland area that is often full of waterfowl.

Shoreline Trail

The Shoreline Trail is accessible from the main parking area and is an easy 2 km (1.2 mi) hike along the northeast shore of the marsh. Along the trail visitors will be rewarded with nice views of the marsh and its surroundings.

Lynde Shores Conservation Area Trail (Map 28/F6)

Located along the Whitby shore of Lake Ontario, the Lynde Shores Conservation Area is home to two provincially significant wetlands. An easy 2.5 km (1.6 mi) hiking trail travels around the wetlands, providing good views of this dynamic natural environment. There are viewing platforms, ideal for bird watching along the way. Dogs are not permitted at this environmentally sensitive area.

Lynn Valley Trail (Map 9/B1 to 15/A7)

The Lynn Valley Trail is another Southern Ontario rail trail that travels between the towns of Port Dover and Simcoe. This rail line was constructed in the late 1800's and was an integral part of development of the area. Parking areas are available at the four access points which are found in Port Dover off Queen Street, off St. John's Road (County Road 3), off Lynn Valley Road and in Simcoe off the east side of Highway 24. The trail is an 8 km (5 mi) one-way trip making for an easy to moderate hike or an easy bike ride. Along the trail travellers will pass through open fields and Carolinian forest areas.

Mabel Davis Conservation Area Trail (Map 27/F2)

This small conservation area lies in the heart of the town of Newmarket. Access to the area is available from Davis Drive or the Bayview Parkway. A return hike along the Mabel Davis Trail can stretch up to 3 km (1.9 mi) in length, although there are a few short cuts along the way. The easy trail travels through forests of Sugar Maple, Basswood, Willow and the rare Black Cherry as well as along the old Holland River lock system.

MacGregor Point Provincial Park Trails (Map 29/D3)

MacGregor Point Provincial Park is located just south of Port Elgin off Highway 21. The park is home to four exciting trails:

Ducks Unlimited Trail

This easy 3.5 km (2.2 mi) trail route features a rehabilitated wetland habitat that thrives with wildlife. The trail circles the wetland and passes by a viewing tower, which provides for a great view of the wetland area. From the tower, dozens of bird species and other mammals can be viewed.

Huron Fringe Trail

This boardwalk stretches along the Lake Huron shoreline providing splendid views of a wetland environment. The hike covers 1.2 km (0.7 mi) and is wheelchair accessible. Informative plaques are set out along the way to further enhance your trail experience.

Lake Ridge Trail

The Lake Ridge Trail is an easy 4 km (2.5 mi) loop through an old abandoned farming area, which includes mature apple trees and stone fence rows. The highlight of the route is the active beaver pond, which supports a diverse natural environment.

Old Shore Road Trail

Set along an old road, this trail is a favourite of bikers visiting the park. The easy 6 km (3.7 mi) route follows a portion of the original settlers route in the region. Other features of the trail include the fantastic views of Lake Huron and wetland habitats.

Maitland Scenic Cemetery Trails (Map 23/A7)

Even though the title of this trail seems eerie, it is really a hidden outdoor gem in the Goderich region. The trail is found by taking Highway 8 southeast from Goderich approximately 2 km (1.2 mi) from the junction with Highway 21. The entry gate lies off the north side of the highway and parking is available just inside the entrance or at the north end of the cemetery. The two trails available are the Entry Gate Trail and the Look Out Loop.

The **Entry Gate Side Trail** is an easy 1.3 km (0.8 mi) loop trail that winds its way through a hardwood forest. The off road section of the trail is the bulk of the excitement as it twists north, eventually meeting the main cemetery access road. Following the roadway south back to the access area completes the loop. The **Look Out Loop** begins from the northern parking area and travels north to the Pipers Dam, the site of a spectacular cliff. From the cliff, the Maitland River flows majestically below. The loop trail follows a good portion of the river and is completed in 2 km (1.2 mi). Be sure to respect private property along these trails.

Maitland Trail (Maps 18/B1, 23/A7-C7)

The Maitland Trail is another long distance trail that stretches from the town of Goderich to the village of Auburn. The trail is around 37 km (23 mi) in length one-way and is moderate in difficulty due to the distance involved and the steep sections with tricky footing. The route follows along the northern shore of the Maitland River most of the way providing many picturesque photo opportunities. There are several access points to this route with the primary parking/access areas found near the Goderich airport and near the main beach area. For added adventure, you can loop back to the trailhead along the Goderich to Auburn Trail (see above).

Maitland Woods Trail (Map 23/A7)

The Maitland Woods is located in the southeast end of Goderich. To find the trail take Huckins Street east off Highway 21. At the end of Huckins Street there is a parking area and trailhead access to the middle of the system. An alternate access is available by taking Suncoast Drive east off Highway 21. Suncoast Drive accesses the northern end of the trail system, although there is no parking area. A parking area lies off Parsons Court southeast off Suncoast Drive. The trail system is made up of three easy loops. The main loop trail is 3 km (1.9 mi) in length with the potential to shorten the trip into 1.5 km (0.9 mi) and 0.5 km (0.3 mi) loops. The route passes through a variety of flora and fauna, as well as past a few wetland areas. No pets are permitted on this trail.

Maple Keys Sugar Bush Trail (Map 24/C7)

West of the small town of Listowel, this conservation area lies off Maple Keys Line. Up until the past few years, this area was the home to maple syrup production. Today the area offers two hiking trails. The popular

A Hiker's Guide *to* Ontario's Walking Trails.

Hike Ontario is a non-profit organization which represents the interests of walkers and hikers in the province. We are the primary source of hiking information in Ontario. Membership is open to individuals at no charge. Trail associations and clubs should inquire about our affordable services. Contact us for details on the benefits of membership.

Use Hike Ontario to discover trails right in your backyard!

hike ontario
experience it...one step at a time

info@hikeontario.com
www.hikeontario.com

Loop Trail is a short 0.8 km (0.5 mi) loop, while the Plantation Trail is an easy 2 km (1.2 mi) hike. Both trails are ideal for hiking or skiing during the winter months and take the traveller through some mature stands of maple trees and a few plantation areas.

Marthaville Habitat Management Area Trail (Map 10/E6) 🚶

You can find the Marthaville Habitat Management Area northwest of the town of Petrolia via Petrolia Line (County Road 4). The area is an old gravel pit that is slowly being regenerated into a natural area. The easy 3 km (1.9 mi) loop trail passes by rehabilitated wetland, prairie grass and forest area.

Massie Trail (Map 34/G5) 🚶 🚲 ⛷

The Massie Trail is located southeast of the town of Owen Sound and is used primarily in the winter as a cross-country ski trail. However, the 10 km trail is becoming more popular with bikers and hikers. The route traverses through mixed forest including some fine mature pine stands. Bikers will find the route to be generally easy; however, some hikers may find the hilly terrain moderate in difficulty in areas. The parking area for the trail system is found off the west side of the 6th Concession Road, south of County Road 18.

Merritt (Welland Canals Parkway) Trail (Map 17/C1 to C6) 🚶 🚲 👣

The Merritt Trail is an off road hiking and biking trail that stretches from St. Catharines south to Port Colborne. The trail is also known as the Welland Canals Parkway Trail since it follows the waterway for most of its 45 km (27.9 mi) route. The trail is generally easy to traverse and is well marked with yellow blazes throughout its entirety. Access can be made at a number of areas along the way.

Mill Pond Park Trail (Map 27/F5) 🚶 🚲

Located in the Toronto suburb of Richmond Hill, Mill Pond Park is a valued outdoor space amid urban development. The main access to the park is from Mill Street, which is picked up from Bathhurst or Trench Street. The park's focal point is the Mill Pond, which was created in the mid 1830's by the damming of the Don River. The dam was the source of a vital supply of power for the local sawmill. Visitors can enjoy the 1.5 km (0.9 mi) collection of easy, paved trails.

Millennium Trail (Map 17/D3) 🚶 🚲

In the southwest corner of Niagara Falls, this paved trail runs north to south along the Ontario Power Corporation Canal. The trail is accessible from a few areas, although McLeod Road at the route's southern end and Lundy's Lane in the north are the main access points. The trail is an easy 4 km (2.5 mi) return hike or bike and is a great way to get some exercise in the heart of Niagara Falls.

Milne Dam Conservation Park Trail (Map 28/B5) 🚶 👣

The Milne Dam Conservation Park is located in the city of Markham and is accessible off the east side of McCowan Road just north of Highway 407. Plenty of parking is available at the park as well as a few picnic tables for visitors to enjoy. The hiking trail is made up of a few connecting loops that span approximately 2 km (1.2 mi) in length. The route is known as a good bird viewing area as the trail passes through forest cover, a field and a wetland area. A small fee is required to park a vehicle at the park during the summer months.

Mono Cliffs Provincial Park Trail (Map 26/D2) 🚶 👣 🚻

Mono Cliffs Provincial Park is a day-use park that lies north of Orangeville. The park can be reached off Mono Centre Road (County Road 8). The Bruce Trail passes through this park and over the years other side trails have been established. Currently there are two established side trails, which are both accessible from the parking area. You can either head northeast along the easy 3 km (1.9 mi) loop or northwest along the 4.5 km (2.8 mi) loop. The shorter loop takes you atop an isolated portion of the escarpment providing breathtaking views of the surrounding countryside along the entire route. The second loop follows the Bruce Trail and the valley bottom to the site of Jacob's Ladder. Jacob's Ladder is a set of wooden stairs that climbs to the top of the escarpment providing a view of a magnificent crevice along the way. Along the stairs, visitors will also find educational signage on the natural wonders of the area. The trail then returns south along the top of the escarpment some 43 m (141 ft) above the valley floor.

Moore Habitat Management Area Trails (Map 4/G1) 🚶 🚲

The Moore Habitat Management Area is located just west of the settlement of Cromar off the north side of Springs Line Road. Visitors to the management area will find 4 km (2.5 mi) of trails that travel through this diverse area. Along the trail, hikers and bikers will enjoy trekking through floodplain forest tracts, grass prairies, and upland forests.

Morrison Dam Conservation Area Trail (Map 18/E6) 🚶 ⛷

Just east of the town of Exeter, you can find the Morrison Dam Conservation Area located off the east side of the Morrison Line south from County Road 83. Parking, along with a picnic area and washrooms, are found near the trailhead. The area boasts a moderate 5 km (3.1 mi) loop that follows the shores of the Ausable River. A small fee is required for use of the trail.

Mountsberg Conservation Area Trails (Map 21/D4) 🚶 👣

West of the town of Milton, the Mountsberg Conservation Area lies just south of Highway 401 off Concession Road 14. A small fee is required to access five trails for visitors to explore:

Lakeshore Lookout Trail

Beginning from the visitor centre, the Lakeshore Lookout Trail heads north along the northern shore of the Mountsberg Reservoir. The route passes through a wetland area before reaching the mid point of the route where a lookout platform is available. The route then loops back completing an easy 5.5 km (3.4 mi) hike.

Nature Trivia Trail

This is the shortest and easiest trail in the conservation area at 1 km (0.6 mi) in length. The trail helps educate hikers on the natural wonders of the conservation area.

Pioneer Creek Trail

The Pioneer Creek trail is the longest trail in the conservation area, spanning over 6.5 km (4 mi). The moderate route passes through wetland habitat, crosses Pioneer Creek and features the remnants of a lime kiln from the mid 1800's.

Raptor Centre Trail

This fascinating trail is a 1.6 km (1 mi) loop through the renowned Raptor Centre. The centre holds wild birds of prey such as red tailed hawks and owls. All of these birds have been injured or sick at one point and are being rehabilitated at the centre with the hopes of releasing them back into the wild.

Sugar Bush Loop Trail

The Sugar Bush Trail is an easy 1.5 km (0.9 mi) loop that passes by a wetland area and the west side of a small pond.

Mount Nemo Conservation Area Trails (Map 21/G5)

On clear days, the view from Mount Nemo can be impressive. The area is home to a 4.9 km (3 mi) set of loop trails, which stretch from the parking area east to a ridge along the Niagara Escarpment. The conservation area is located north of Hamilton via Colling Road, which is found off Guelph Line (County Road 1). A small fee is required to access the area.

Naftel's Creek Conservation Area Trail (Map 18/A1)

Between the towns of Goderich and Bayfield, the Naftel's Creek Conservation Area lies off the east side of Highway 21. There is a parking area just off the highway, which acts as the trailhead. The trail traverses in a 3.2 km (2 mi) moderately difficult loop through a mix of conifer tree stands and wetland areas. In the wetlands, hikers will appreciate the boardwalks to prevent ecological damage and keep their feet dry. Three side trails are linked to the main trail and are ideal for extending your hike. Watch for poison ivy near wetland areas.

New Hamburg Trail (Map 20/A6)

The New Hamburg Trail's eastern access lies off the north side of Highway 7/8 near the eastern shore of the Nith River. The western access is from the W.J. Scott Conservation Area in the village of New Hamburg. This easy 12 km (7.5 mi) return route travels from Highway 7/8 and along the southern shore of the Nith River to the village of New Hamburg. Settled in the early 1800's, New Hamburg is home to many century homes and buildings, making this an interesting destination for history buffs. The highlight of the trail is the heritage waterwheel, the largest operating waterwheel in North America, along the Nith River.

Niagara River Recreational Trail (Map 17 E1 to G6)

Visitors to the Niagara Region can access this long distance trail from several areas as it stretches from Niagara on the Lake south to Fort Erie. The trail parallels the Niagara River for over 56 km (35 mi) providing fantastic views of the river and the city of Niagara Falls. The trail is paved, which makes it suitable for a variety of users including bikers and rollerbladers.

Nokiidaa Trail (Map 27)

At the time of printing this book, the Nokiidaa Trail system was yet to be completed; however, several potions of the route were in place. The word 'Nokiidaa' is an Ojibway word meaning to 'walk together' and the trail does just that. It joins a network of established trails in the area. The system is planned to stretch from Aurora north past Holland Landing and eventually from the Oak Ridges Trail north to Lake Simcoe. For more information on route progress or updates, check online at www.backroadmapbooks.com or call the town of Aurora parks department at (905) 727-3123.

North Tract Trails (Map 28/A1)

The north regional forest tract is located south of Mount Albert off the west side of Highway 48 just north of Vivian Road. The tract is the second largest York regional forest tract and offers over 10 km (6.2 mi) of easy to moderate trails for visitors to enjoy. The forest was actually farmland during the late 1800's but it was reforested between 1925 and 1945 and now boasts mature stands of a variety of trees.

Oak Ridges Trail (Maps 27/A3 to 28/G2)

The Oak Ridges Moraine has grown in public awareness over the past few years due to the development of this important area. The moraine is a height of land that stretches from east to west north of Toronto that forms the headwaters for many rivers and streams flowing both south and north. The moraine is also an important habitat area for local wildlife and is seen by many as the last line of development for the urban sprawl of Metro Toronto.

The Oak Ridges Trail was developed to help preserve portions of the moraine and to help create awareness of this beautiful area. The long distance hiking trail extends over 200 km (124 mi) one-way and is a great way to experience the wilderness despite the proximity of Metro Toronto. The trail is comprised of a mix of side roads and blazed trails, with more and more trail sections being established annually. The route varies in difficulty from easy to moderate, although if you do choose to travel long distances in any one outing, the trail can be quite challenging. The hilliness of the moraine provides both a challenge to hikers and several nice viewpoints. For a more detailed description of the Oak Ridges Trail it is recommended to pick up a copy of the Oak Ridges Trail Guidebook by calling (877) 319-0285 or visiting www.orta.on.ca.

Ojibway Prairie Trial (Map 1/A2)

The Ojibway Prairie Trail can be found at the Ojibway Prairie Provincial Nature Reserve near the west end of Windsor. The reserve can be accessed off the south side of Titcombe Road east of Matchette Road and offers under 3 km (1.9 mi) of trails. Set amid a prairie grass environment, the trails offer a chance to see many unique plants. For more education on this once vast Southern Ontario ecosystem you can visit the nearby Ojibway Nature Centre.

Oliphant Fen Trail (Map 36/E7)

The Oliphant Fen Trail is found just north of the village of Oliphant by following Shore Road north from the village. The trail lies along the west side of the road and there is a small parking area at the access point. The trail was developed by local naturalists and is an easy 0.3 km (0.2 mi) boardwalk trail suitable for wheelchair use. The boardwalk traverses through the fen providing views of various flora and fauna, including wildflowers, throughout the spring to fall months. Visitors will also enjoy the many educational interpretive plaques that are stationed along the route.

Owen Sound Trails (Map 34/E3)

In the city of Owen Sound there are a number of urban walkways and trails to enjoy, one of the more popular and established trails in the city is the **Harbour Walkway**. The walkway begins from the visitor centre near Kelso Beach and travels east along the harbour front all the way past the Owen Sound Community Centre. The easy trail is a 12 km (7.5 mi) return trip and provides an intimate view of Owen

Sound. Both biking and hiking is a regular feature of the walkway. For more information on other interurban walks in Owen Sound call (888) 675-5555.

Paisley Trail (Map 29/G5) 🚶 🚵

This easy 6 km trail travels along the dykes of the Saugeen River. The route begins just outside the town of Paisley and traverses through some forest cover and past fields before entering the town. In town, the route passes by several historic buildings including the Paisley Town Hall. Although the trail can be reached from a number of different areas in and around town, the main access/parking area is found at Rotary Park.

Parkhill Conservation Area Trail (Map 12/A2) 🚶 🚵 , ◹ 🏕

The Parkhill Conservation Area is a large conservation area at over 800ha (1,976acres). It is located just outside of the village of Parkhill off County Road 7 (Elginfield Road). A series of connected trails allow you to explore 8 km (5 mi) of trails. In addition to following Parkhill Creek and its tributaries, visitors will be rewarded with views of wetland habitat as well as mature Carolinian forest areas. During the spring, this is a fantastic area for wildflower viewing, while all season long a variety of birds can be viewed. The trails are mainly utilized by hikers; however, ATV's and motor bikes are permitted on portions of the trails. A special permit must be obtained to enter the conservation area trails with off-road motorized vehicles, while a small admission fee is required by all users. For more information call the Ausable Bayfield Conservation Authority at (519) 235-2610.

Penetangore Path (Map 29/B7) 🚶 📄 🏕

In the town of Kincardine, the Penetangore Path is an easy 4 km (2.5 mi) hike located along the shore of Lake Huron. Parking is available at Kincardine Harbour and the trail begins at the Kincardine Lighthouse and Museum. A portion of the path is made up of a boardwalk and there are a number of interpretive plaques along the boardwalk that describe local shipwrecks found in Lake Huron not far from the harbour. The trail then follows the North Penetangore River east through the town and eventually to the Geddes Property Environmental Park.

Perch Creek Habitat Management Area Trails (Map 10/D6) 🚶 🏕

Found just outside of Sarnia, the Perch Creek Habitat Management Area Trail is accessible off the west side off Waubuno Road. Home to over 5 km (3.1 mi) of hiking trails, the management area protects upland forest, wetland and floodplain forest areas. The trail system is regarded as easy, although footing can be tricky in a few areas along the trail.

Petticoat Creek Conservation Area Trail (Map 28/D6) 🚶 🏊

In the southern end of Pickering, this conservation area can be reached via Whites Road south of Highway 401. The conservation area lies along the shore of Lake Ontario and provides an easy 1 km (0.6 mi) trail for visitors to enjoy. The trail is well marked and is surfaced with wood chips throughout much of its length. During the winter, the trail double as a short cross-country ski route when snowfall permits. A small fee is required for access to the conservation area.

Petrel Point Trail (Map 36/E6) 🚶 🏕

North of the settlement of Red Bay you can find the Petrel Point Trail by taking Huron Road to Petrei Point Road. The trail is made up of a boardwalk along both sides of the road. The easy 0.3 (0.2 mi) route passes through a cedar forest and into a local fen environment. In late spring and early summer the main attraction to this boardwalk is wild orchids.

Petrolia Discovery Trail (Map 11/A6) 🚶 🏕

Located in the town of Petrolia, this easy 2 km (1.2 mi) collection of loops can be accessed from the Bridgeview Conservation Area. The trail system traverses through the conservation area along Bear Creek and through a Carolinian Forest. Visitors can explore the remnants of a 19th century oil discovery en route. Further educational information on the history of oil discovery in Petrolia can also be found at the historic outdoor museum, Petrolia Discovery.

Pinehurst Lake Conservation Area Trails (Map 20/G7) 🚶 🏊

Located at the Pinehurst Lake Conservation Area, this trail system is accessible by following County Road 75 south from Cambridge. Look for the conservation area signage off the east side of the road just south of Glen Morris Road. The trail system is quite extensive and over 10 km (6.2 mi) of routes can be hiked during the summer or skied in the winter. In general, the trails are easy to hike and can be shortened or lengthened depending on the distance you desire. A small fee is required to access the conservation area.

Pinery Provincial Park Trails (Maps 10 inset, 11/E1) 🚶 🚵 🏊 🎿

Pinery Provincial Park is located just south of the town of Grand Bend via Highway 21 and is home to a large collection of multi-use trails. Hikers can explore the one of ten hiking trails with the shortest being a mere 1 km in length. Along with the many hiking trails, there is also a 10 km (6.2 mi) biking trail available. During the winter, most of the trails are groomed or track set for cross-country skiing, and a few trails are also suitable for snowshoeing.

Point Clark Trails (Map 23/A2) 🚶 🚵

In and around the town of Point Clark are four fantastic hiking trails. The Attawondaron Nature Trail, Clark Creek Floodplain Trail, the Deer Run Nature Trail and the Tuscarora Road Nature Trail. Each trail offers a different natural perspective and are all easy to hike. Collectively, the trails span approximately 3 km (1.9 mi) and are accessible from several different points around town. For more information on the trails call the township at (519) 395-2909.

Point Farms Provincial Park Trail (Map 23/A6) 🚶 🚵 🏊 🎿

Just north of the town of Goderich off the west side of Highway 21 you can find Point Farms Provincial Park. The park can be quite busy during the summer months; however, there is always room for using the trail systems. A small day-use fee is required to use the trails; however, you can also access the park's great beach area. There are three easy hiking trails offered at the park totalling 6 km (3.7 mi) in length. The trails also are used in the winter for ungroomed cross-country skiing or snowshoeing.

Point Pelee National Park Trails (Map 2/C7) 🚶 🚵 🏊 🏕 🎿

Point Pelee National Park is a popular destination for its bird watching, beach area and recreation trails. The park is home to seven trails including the renowned Marsh Boardwalk Trail. In total there is approximately 11.5 km (7.1 mi) of trails available to explore with much of the trails designated for hiking only. Both hikers and bikers can utilize the Centennial Trail. The Marsh Boardwalk Trail is a unique 1 km long boardwalk that juts out into the heart of a marsh. Along

the boardwalk visitors are offered an intimate view of the wetland environment without getting their feet wet.

Porritt Tract Trail (Map 28/A3) 🚶 🚴

East of Newmarket, the Porritt Regional Forest Tract is located north of Aurora Road (County Road 15) off Kennedy Road north (County Road 3). Parking is available off the west side of Kennedy Road at the trailhead. The trail traverses through a mix of original forest and mature plantations covering a return distance of approximately 3 km (1.9 mi). There are a few side trails to lengthen or shorten your journey.

Port Franks Trail System (Map 11/E1) 🚶 🚴 ⛺

This trail system is located in the Port Franks Wetland and Forested Dunes Area. The natural area lies between the Ausable River and Lake Huron and is home to a variety of ecosystems. The easy trails form an 11 km (6.8 mi) collection of routes, which include a short loop trail through the Karner Blue Butterfly Area.

Purple Woods Conservation Area Trail (Map 28/G2) 🚶 🎿

Home of the local spring Maple Syrup Festival, the Purple Woods Conservation Area makes a great destination throughout the year. The conservation area is located south of Port Perry off Simcoe Street (County Road 2). Visitors can enjoy the 4 km (2.5 mi) return trek, experiencing the serenity of nature along the easy trail. Cross-country skiing is permitted along the trail during the winter, although the trail is not groomed.

Queen Street Property Park Trail (Map 27/G2) 🚶 🚴 rollerblade

The Queen Street Park is located between Davis Drive and Queen Street in the town of Newmarket. The park is home to one of Canada's first concrete bridges, which was constructed in 1909. A short 1 km (0.6 mi) trail travels along the west side of the Holland River culminating at the historic bridge. The trail is paved.

Rattray Marsh Conservation Area (Map 22/D4) 🚶 ⛺

Set near the Lake Ontario shoreline in northern Oakville, the Rattray Marsh Conservation Area is home to an easy 3.5 km (2.2 mi) hiking trail. The trail spans through the wetland expanse of the Rattray Marsh providing plenty of opportunities to view wildlife such as waterfowl and small mammals.

Rattlesnake Point Trails (Map 21/G4) 🚶 ⛺

West of Milton, Rattlesnake Point Conservation Area is located just off the Appleby Line (County Road 8). There are three trails to explore: the Rabbits Run Trail, the Vista Adventure Trail and the Buffalo Crag Trail. In total, it is possible to hike over 5.5 km (3.4 mi) through the conservation area. The trail system is set atop the Niagara Escarpment, with both the Vista Adventure and the Buffalo Crag Trails providing breathtaking canyon views from the cliff side. A nominal fee is required to access the area.

Red Hill Valley Recreational Trail (Map 16/A1) 🚶 ⛺

This urban trail is a moderate 14 km (8.7 mi) return route that has a number of alternate access points to help shorten the route. The trail stretches from Lake Ontario at Confederation Park southwest along the Red Hill Creek Valley to the Albion and Buttermilk Falls. Travellers will be amazed at the amount of natural areas that this valley offers, despite the fact it is found in the heart of Hamilton. In the south, the main parking areas are located off Mountain Brow Boulevard above the Albion and Buttermilk Falls.

Rock Glen Conservation Area Trail (Map 11/F3) 🚶 🚴 ⛺

There are many points of interest in this conservation area. The museum is home to deposits of Devonian Era Fossils and Native artifacts, while the trail system highlights the scenic Rock Glen Falls. The 1.5 km (0.9 mi) of trails travel through the Carolinian forest cover to the lookout on the Ausable River. The conservation area is found north of the village of Akrona via Rock Glen Road.

Rock Point Provincial Park (Map 16/E7) 🚶 ⛺

This Southern Ontario park is quite popular throughout the year and offers over 4 km (2.5 mi) of hiking trails for visitors to explore. The scenic trails follow the Lake Erie shoreline and lead through mature tree stands. Rock Point Provincial Park is south of the town of Dunnville along the northern shore of Lake Erie.

Rockwood Lake Conservation Area Trail (Map 21/C2) 🚶 ⛺

This conservation area is home to over 5 km (3.1 mi) of trails cutting through the forest cover and along portions of the Eramosa River. The main feature of the trail system is its glacial potholes. The potholes are up to 20 m (45 ft) deep and were carved out of the landscape thousands of years ago with the retreat of glaciers. To reach the conservation area follow Highway 7 (York Road) northeast from Guelph. The conservation area lies off the southeast side of the road just before the highway reaches the village of Rockwood.

Roger's Reservoir Conservation Area Trail (Map 27/F1) 🚶 🚴 🎿

This small conservation area is accessible off the 2nd Concession Road, north of Newmarket. The conservation area lies along the Holland River and is home to an easy 4.5 km (2.8 mi) trail system that follows the river. The trail passes through mixed forest cover and during the summer, wildflowers are a highlight of the route.

Rondeau Provincial Park Trails (Map 3/F1) 🚶 🚴 🔋 ⛺

Found on a gorgeous peninsula of Lake Erie, the Rondeau Provincial Park can be accessed via the Kent Bridge Road (County Road 15). The park offers five recreational trails for visitors to explore:

Black Oak Trail

This easy 1.5 km (0.9 mi) loop trail lies in the northeast end of the park. Hikers along the route will find mature stands of pine and oak trees.

March Trail

If you are looking to view some wildlife, the easy to moderate 15 km (9.3 mi) Marsh Trail has plenty to offer. The trail is suitable for both hikers and bikers as it travels through an expansive marsh area full of wildlife, such as herons, waterfowl and turtles.

South Point Trail

Set amid the more secluded southern portion of the park, the South Point Trail is suitable for both hikers and bikers. The trail is an easy to moderate 8 km (5 mi) route that reaches the southernmost tip of land. Along the shoreline some superb sights of Lake Erie can be found.

Spicebush Trail

Along the Spicebush Trail hikers can educate themselves about the ecology of the southern hardwood forest. The easy trail is approximately 1.6 km (1 mi) in length and is accessible in the northern end of the park.

Tulip Tree Trail

Accessible from the southeast end of the park, this short trail traverses along a boardwalk through a lush woodland area. Hikers will enjoy this easy 1.5 km (0.9 mi) loop.

Rouge Park Trails (Map 28/D6) 🚶 🐎 🎿

The Rouge Park is one of North America's largest urban parks and is an excellent place to get outdoors and get some exercise. The park is located between Pickering and Scarborough and offers a few trail alternatives:

Orchard Trail

This easy trail is a 3.2 km (2 mi) return hike from Twyn Rivers Drive to Beare Road and back. The route travels through a regenerated forest setting where it is possible to spot the odd deer on occasion. Near Twyn Rivers Drive, the remnants of Maxwell's Mill can be seen. The Mill was one of the first mills in the 1800's that used the Rouge River for power during early pioneering.

Riverside Trail

The Riverside Trail is an easy 5.4 km (3.4 mi) trail that stretches from Twyn Rivers Drive south to the Glen Rouge Campground near Highway 2. The trail traverses along portions of the Rouge River and through mixed forest much of its distance.

Vista Trail

From Twyn Rivers Drive, the Vista Trail heads north through a mixed forest along what was once a part of a historic native portage to Lake Simcoe. The moderate route traverses a ridge most of the way and is a 3 km (1.9 mi) return hike.

Royal Botanical Gardens Trails (Map 21/G7)

Royal Botanical Gardens is the home of the Bruce Trail headquarters. In addition to venturing on this famous long distance hike, there are over 8 km (5 mi) of trails for day trippers. The main trail is known as the **Captain Cootes Trail**. It leads along the shore of Lake Ontario to the lookout at Bull's Point before linking up with the **Grey Doe Trail**. The Grey Doe Trail is unique, due to the tree identification along the way. The two trails form a nice 3 km (1.9 mi) loop. To reach the gardens, follow Highway 6 to Plains Road West and head east. Plains Road West meets the Old Guelph Road, which is then followed south to Arboretum Road. Take the Arboretum Road west into the parking area. An admission fee is required to access the area.

S.C. Johnson Trail (Maps 13/G7, 14/A2)

The SC Johnson Trail was established in 1998 through the purchase of the old railbed by SC Johnson & Son Limited. The easy trail spans 11.5 km (7.1 mi) connecting the town of Paris and the city of Brantford. In Paris, the trailhead can be found at the crossing of the route over East River Road (Highway 24). Parking is available at the access area, which also doubles as an access to the Cambridge to Paris Rail Trail. At the 4 km (2.5 mi) mark, the route passes by another access and parking area to the trail off Powerline Road. The route then crosses over Highway 403 and follows Oak Park Road and Hardy Road before meandering into a more secluded setting. The trail ends at the Wilkes Dam, Brantford's water reservoir. A small parking area is available at the dam.

St. Catherine's City Trails (Map 17/B1-C2)

NS&T Rail Trail

In the heart of St. Catharines, the NS&T Rail line once was an integral part of the function of the city. Today, this portion of the abandoned line has become a highly used urban trail. Although the trail is not yet developed, the route is a good hike or bike from Lakeshore Road south to Roehampton Road. The trail is an easy 10 km (6.2 mi) return trip.

Participark Trail

Beginning along the west side of Twelve Mile Creek, the Participark Trail is accessible from below Rodman Hill or off Glendale Avenue. The trail is an easy 9 km (5.6 mi) hike that follows the shore of the creek. The route returns to the access area via the less developed eastern creek bank pathway.

Waterfront Trail

At the northern end of the city, trail users can access this fabulous trail linking Port Weller Harbour in the east with Port Dalhousie in the west. The route is an easy 15 km (9.3 mi) return trip and offers fabulous views of Lake Ontario along the way.

St. Clair River Trail (Maps 4/C3-10/A6)

The St. Clair River Trail remains a work in progress; however, the route is passable all the way from south of Port Lambton to just north past Corunna. The route is comprised of a mix of existing trail system and roadway spanning over 32 km (20 mi) one-way. Currently, the

portion of the trail south of Sombra Village and around Courtright is not complete. Hikers/bikers travelling through these portions are recommended to simply follow the St. Clair Parkway. The parkway is not a heavily used roadway and makes a decent alternative until the trail can be completed.

Travellers along the route will enjoy the mix of urban views and parkland but the highlight of the trail is the great views of the St. Clair River. The river is an important shipping waterway for both Canada and the United States. Although the terrain along most of the trail is easy to travel, if you plan on hiking or biking extended distances, the route should be regarded as moderate in difficulty.

Sarawak Rail Trail (Map 34/E3)

In the city of Owen Sound, the trailhead to the Sarawak Trail is located near Kelso Beach in the west side of the city off Range Road. The trail heads northwest along an old rail bed towards the settlement of Benallen covering 6 km (3.7 mi) one way. The easy trail slowly climbs the Niagara Escarpment and offers magnificent views of the surrounding countryside, including the Georgian Bay, at the higher elevations. It is a multi-use trail for hikers, bikers and horseback riders. In the winter, cross-country skiing is possible, however snowmobilers are the main users of the trail.

Sarnia Trails (Map 10)

Bluewater Trails (B4)

The Bluewater Trails travel along the Sarnia River and Lake Huron shoreline in the west end of Sarnia. Access to the trails is available from many areas near the waterfront, although the Sarnia Marina tends to be the most popular access point. Currently, hikers and bikers can travel from Campbell Street in the south end of the city all the way to the public beach area in the northwest end of the city. The route is approximately a 10 km (6.2 mi) one-way trek and offers intimate views of Sarnia and its shoreline areas. The trail system is still being developed.

Howard Watson Nature Trail (C4-E3)

Beginning from the east side of Sarnia, the Howard Watson Nature Trail travels north then east towards Camlachie. In Sarnia, the trail can be accessed from Exmouth Street and from several other roads along its entire length from there on. The trail is about 20 km (12.4 mi) in length one-way from start to finish and follows the old Grand Trunk Rail line, constructed in 1859. En route to Camlachie, the easy to moderate trail passes by urban areas, although it also passes through several mature tree stands and mixed wild areas. Both hikers and bikers will enjoy this long distance route.

Sauble Falls Provincial Park Trail (Map 33/E1) 🚶 🚴

Visitors can find Sauble Falls Provincial Park north of the town of Sauble Beach off County Road 13 (Sauble Falls Parkway). The small park is home to an easy 2.5 km (1.6 mi) loop trail. The route travels along the southern shore of the Sauble River passing several sand dunes to the view of Sauble Falls.

Saugeen Rail Trail (Map 29/F3) 🚶 🚴

The Saugeen Rail Trail follows an old CN Railway bed between the communities of Port Elgin and Southampton. The railbed was created in the mid 1800's as the railways pushed north from the southern Ontario ports. In 1995, the route was officially established as a recreation corridor for all to enjoy. The actual trail extends 6 km (3.7 mi) one-way between the communities; however, users have established a loop route that follows the scenic shoreline roads from Southampton back to Port Elgin. In Port Elgin, the trailhead can be found off River Street. The terrain is gentle and the route is easy to follow before its terminus at McNabb Street in Southhampton.

To continue along the loop back to Port Elgin, begin by following McNabb Street south to South Street. Take South Street west for a short while and veer south onto Lorraine Drive. Lorraine Drive eventually connects with North Shore Road as the route travels south along the beautiful Lake Huron shoreline to Port Elgin. Continue along North Shore Road and look for Market Street, which will take you east back to Highway 21. The parking area for the trail is a few hundred metres away to the north on River Street. There are several access points to this route, including additional parking areas at the 10th Concession Road crossing and in Southampton.

Saugeen River Trail (Map 24/B1) 🚶 🚴 ⛷ 🚶

The quiet town of Walkerton is home to the Saugeen River Trail. The trail is accessible from many points around town as it follows the dykes along the Saugeen River. The trail is about 5.5 km (3.4 mi) in length and is regarded as easy to travel. Several side loops branch from the main trail and join up with access points within town. Both bikers and hikers are welcome to travel the trail during summer months, while cross-country skiing and snowshoeing are popular during the winter.

Scout Tract Trail (Map 28/A2) 🚶 🚴

Located east of Newmarket, the Scout Regional Forest Tract is home to an easy 3 km (1.9 mi) loop trail. The trail is best suited to hikers, although bikers are known to frequent the trail on occasion. The trail begins by passing between two small ponds before looping through a mix of forest cover and open field. Access to the forest tract is off the south side of Vivian Road between Kennedy Road (County Road 3) and McCowan Road.

Seaton Hiking Trail (Map 28/D5) 🚶 ⛷

The Seaton Hiking Trail is located north of the city of Pickering and is accessible from several points, including County Road 4 (Taunton Road). The trail stretches from the 3rd Concession in the south all the way north to Highway 407. The route is a moderate 10 km (6.2 mi) one-way hike along the scenic West Duffin Valley.

Selkirk Provincial Park (Map 15/F7) 🚶 🚶

Selkirk Provincial Park is a popular camping destination during the summer months and is located northeast of Port Dover. The park

offers hiking enthusiasts the chance to explore the **Wheeler's Walk Trail**, a 2 km (1.2 mi) loop trail that provides a close view of the park's forests, meadow and main wetland area. The focal point of the route is a boardwalk over the Spring Creek, which further displays the wetland habitat.

Shade's Mills Conservation Area Trails (Map 21/A6) 🚶

In the east end of Cambridge, the Shade's Mill Conservation Area is accessible via Avenue Road. The conservation area offers over 14 km (8.7 mi) of connected trails to explore. The system begins by crossing a footbridge over Mill Creek and then enters a large tract of mixed forest. Some of the more prevalent trees in this forest include basswood, white ash and an assortment of pine trees. A small fee is required to access the conservation area.

Sharon Creek Conservation Area Trail (Map 12/E7) 🚶 🚴 ♿

This conservation area trail is an easy 1 km (0.6 mi) trail that traverses through the Elliot-Madill Memorial Forest. To extend your outing, you can also hike the many conservation area roads to various areas such as a tall grass prairie, a chestnut tree grove and a thriving wetland. Portions of the trail are wheelchair accessible. You can find the Sharon Creek Conservation Area southwest of the city of London off Springer Road.

Short Hills Provincial Park Trails (Map 17/A3) 🚶 🚴 🐎 🚶

Short Hills Provincial Park is a beautiful Niagara Escarpment park that is located south of St. Catherines. The park is home to a fine collection of trails that wind their way through the woods. Although there are multi-use trails available at the park that can be utilized by both hikers and bikers and in certain sections horseback riders, approximately 10.5 km (6.5 mi) of the trails are designated for hiking only. The hiking trails range in difficulty from an easy 1 km (0.6 mi) stroll to a difficult 4.6 km (2.9 mi) climb.

Simcoe Trail (Map 27/F1) 🚶

North of Holland Landing, visitors can find the Simcoe Trail off the Queensville Side Road or from the Holland Landing Conservation Area to the south. The Simcoe Trail travels between these two access points and is an easy 8 km (5 mi) return trip. Hikers will enjoy the abundance of mixed forest cover in this urban area.

Spencer Gorge Wilderness Area Trails (Map 21/F7) 🚶 🚶

The Spencer Gorge is a fascinating 'Y' shape formed by the creeks slowly eroding the Niagara Escarpment. The trail begins by passing Tews Falls, a scenic display in itself. From the falls, the trail can be followed either south or west. The west branch skirts along the escarpment climaxing at Webster's Falls. The southern route traverses along the eastern end of the escarpment eventually reaching Dundas Peak where you will be rewarded with a fantastic panoramic view of the gorge and countryside. In total, these two routes make up about 3 km (1.9 mi) of trail. For further adventure, other trails have been established along the western side of the gorge in the valley bottom. The trail system is located off Harvest Road. To reach Harvest Road, follow Highway 8 to Dundas and turn north onto Brock Road. Harvest Road is a few hundred metres north along Brock Road. Head east along Harvest Road and look for the signs to the trailhead.

Stapleton Tract Trail (Map 23/F4) 🚶 ⛷

Northwest of the town of Wingham, the Stapleton Tract Trail is located off South Kinloss Avenue. The trail is an easy to moderate 2.6 km (1.6 mi) trek along rolling terrain through wetlands and a series of mature hardwood trees.

Starkey Hill Trail (Map 21/C3) 🚶 🚴 🚶

East of the city of Guelph, the Starkey Hill Trail can be reached via the Akrell Road (County Road 37). The trailhead lies off the north side of the road east of the settlement of Akrell. From the trailhead this easy 3.5 km (2.2 mi) loop trail begins by travelling through a young forest and open field before heading into a mature forest. At about the mid point along the trail, there is a viewpoint. The spring and fall are better viewing times since foliage is at its lowest.

Stanley Trail (Map 18/B3) 🚶 🛶

This trail system has not been measured, although it is approximately 4 km (2.5 mi) in length. The route is easy to moderate in difficulty and traverses from an open field into a mixed forest area and back. The route offers wildlife viewing opportunities and is a great way to get some exercise. Hiking is the main use of the trail, and cross-country skiing is possible during the winter. To reach the trailhead, take County Road 3 (Mill Road) west from Varna and look for the trailhead off the north side of the road about 2 km down the road. Parking is available at the municipal complex.

Steve Bauer Trail (Map 17/B4) 🚶 🚲

This trail is named after one of Canada's most successful cyclists. The main access point to this Welland/Fonthill trail is from Quaker Road in Welland, although alternate access points do exist. From Quaker Road, the trail begins by following an old rail bed towards Fonthill. In Fonthill, the route travels along local streets for a few kilometres before changing back to an off road trail. The easy trail is a 12 km (7.5 mi) return trip that ends at Highway 20.

Strathroy Trails (Map 12/B5) 🚶 🛶 ⛷

There are two great trails available in the Strathroy area. The **Strathroy Conservation Area Trail** is an easy 2.8 km (1.7 mi) loop through a lowland floodplain forest and along portions of the Sydenham River providing good bird watching opportunities. The conservation area is located just outside of the village of Strathroy off Head Street.

West of the Strathroy Conservation Area, the **Strathroy River Walk** can be accessed from several different parking areas in the village. The river walk trail is an easy 5.5 km (3.4 mi) route that parallels the Sydenham River most of the way.

Stoney Island Conservation Area Trails (Map 29/B7) 🚶 🚲 🛶 ⛷

North of the town of Kincardine, you can find the conservation area off Concession 7, near Lake Huron. Visitors can enjoy the 8 km series of loop trails as they pass through a mix of mature hardwood, hemlock and cedar forests. Portions of the trails also provide some views of the massive Lake Huron. The trails are frequented by hikers and bikers during the summer, while cross-country skiers and the odd snowshoer will venture here in the winter.

Stouffville Town Trail (Map 28/B3) 🚶 🏃

The Stouffville Town Trail begins in the southern end of the town at Memorial Park and travels north all the way past the Stouffville Reservoir. Parking for the trail is available in several areas including at the town library or at Memorial Park off Park Street. The trail is an easy 8 km (5 mi) route that winds past several historic buildings before reaching the reservoir and the more rural portion of the route. At the reservoir, the trail continues around the water and into an Oak Ridges Moraine forest tract. The forest is a great place to enjoy the outdoors so close to an urban setting.

Sudden Forest Tract Trail (Map 20/G7) 🚶

The Sudden Forest Tract is located southwest of Cambridge off County Road 75 (Spragues Road) just south of Beke Road. Look for the parking area and trailhead off the east side of the road. From the trailhead, there are a number of interconnected trails that make up about 4 km (2.5 mi) of routes. The system passes through a mix of mature forest stands and wetlands, including a wetland boardwalk.

Terra Cotta Conservation Area Trail (Map 26/F7) 🚶 🚲 🛶

You can find the Terra Cotta Conservation Area north of Georgetown via the 10th Line Road. The conservation area is open year round, providing access to its 12 km (7.5 mi) trail system for hikers, bikers and cross-country skiing enthusiasts. The trail is generally easy to traverse for hikers and bikers, although cross-country skiers will find portions of the system moderate in difficulty.

Thames Valley Tail (Maps 6/G1, 12/F5, 13/A2) 🚶 🚲

The Thames Valley Trail is a 109 km (68 mi) link between the Elgin Trail in the south and the Avon Trail to the north. Beginning at the end of the Elgin Trail near Paynes Mills, the route heads north eventually meeting the Thames River at the Delaware Conservation Area southwest of London. The trail follows the Thames River northeast through London before following the North Thames River all the way to the town of St. Mary's. Along the route, there are also a number of side trails and different access points, especially in the city of London. The trail is regarded as easy in difficulty, but of course if large portions are tackled at any one time, the route can be quite a challenge. The trail passes by a wide variety of terrain from open fields to forest cover to wetland areas. While the majority of the route travels along public land, about 35% of the route does pass through private property; therefore, please respect private land and its owner's wishes. For a detailed guidebook or more information on the Thames Valley Trail call (519) 645-2845.

Tillsonburg Cycling Trail (Map 8/A2) 🚶 🚲 🛶 ⛷

The Tillsonburg Cycling Trail is a 22 km (13.7 mi) one-way route from Port Burwell Provincial Park to the town of Tillsonburg. The trail follows an abandoned rail line north from the park passing by the town of Staffordville along the way. The trail is easy to travel and can also be used by hikers, cross-country skiers and snowshoers.

Thornton Bales Conservation Area Trail (Map 27/E2) 🚶 🏃

West of Newmarket, the Thornton Bales Conservation Area can be found off the north side of the 19th Side Road. From the parking area there is an easy 1.5 km (0.9 mi) collection of loops that take you through the forest of maple and beech trees and up and over a number of hills. It is a bit more challenging than many of the trails in the area.

Tiger Dunlop Heritage Trail (Map 23/A7) 🚶 🚲 🏃

The Tiger Dunlop Heritage Trail is located in the northern portion of the town of Goderich. There are four access points scattered around town but the main access is found at the CPR Station at Goderich Harbour. From the station, the trail heads east towards the wooden structure of the Menesetung Bridge. The bridge crosses over the Maitland River and offers a nice view before the trail splits. The western section is a 1 km (0.6 mi) trek to the marina and back, while the trail heading east is a return 3 km route along the old railway bed to the Tiger Dunlop Tomb and Highway 21. At Highway 21, hikers can further their adventure by connecting to the Goderich to Auburn Rail Trail.

Toronto Area Trails (Maps 22, 27, 28) 🚶 🚴 👟

Despite its size, Toronto is a surprisingly scenic city that has done a great job developing their parks and trail systems. Along with the help of thousands of volunteers, urban trails like the Oakville Heritage Trails or the city's Discovery Walks are a fantastic way to get out of your house or car and onto a footpath. Fine destinations like the CNE waterfront or the Humber River Valley provide plenty to look at. For more information on urban hikes in the metro Toronto area contact the Toronto city parks department at (416) 392-1111.

Trimble Trail (Map 26/E6) 🚶 👟

The Trimble Trail is located at the Belfountain Conservation Area, which can be reached by following County Road 52 east from the town of Erin. The conservation area lies near the junction of County Road 52 (Bush Street) and County Road 1 (Mississauga Road). The trail is a side trail of the Bruce Trail and is an easy 3 km (1.8 mi) traverse along the steep slopes of the West Credit River Valley.

Turkey Point Provincial Park Trail (Map 9/A2) 🚶 👟

Turkey Point Provincial Park is located near the shore of Lake Erie off Turkey Point Road. There are two trails to explore:

Fin & Feather Trail

This easy route is less than 2 km (1.2 mi) in length and takes you from the park west to the nearby fish culture station.

Lookout Bluff Trail

The Lookout Bluff Trail is the more popular trail found within the park as it loops from the main park entrance road east towards the bluff. The easy 2.5 km (1.6 mi) trail travels through a mix of flora and fauna, including through forest cover eventually reaching the steep bluff. The route follows the bluff for a while, providing fantastic views of Lake Erie before returning back to the park entrance.

Unionville Valleylands Trails (Map 28/A5) 🚶

Located in Unionville, a suburb of Markham, the Valleylands Trails are accessible from a number of different locations. One of the main access points is from Main Street, just north of Highway 7. The easy trails are an intertwined collection of local park trails that stretch from Mildred Temple Park in the south all the way to Toogood Pond in the north. The system is made up of 7 km (4.3 mi) of trails and offer hikers a chance to enjoy the various parklands amid a highly developed area of Ontario.

Upper Canada Heritage Trail (Map 17/E1-E2) 🚶 🚴

Visitors to Niagara on the Lake can find the northern trailhead and parking area to this trail off York Road. The southern access is located off John Street near the intersection with King Street. The heritage trail is a 14 km (8.7 mi) long route that follows an abandoned rail line through Niagara on the Lake. Due to the distance involved, a return hike along the route can be rather challenging to complete.

Vandorf Park Trail (Map 27/G3) 🚶

East of the town of Aurora, follow Woodbine Avenue (County Road 8) north of the Vandorf Side Road to reach the Vandorf Park Trail. The parking/access area lies off the west side of Woodbine Avenue. Visitors to the park can enjoy hiking the easy 2 km (1.2 mi) loop that travels around the park, crossing the Holland River in sections. To extend your hike, the Oak Ridges Trail system can be picked up from the northeast or southwest ends of the park.

W. Darcy McKeough Conservation Area Trail (Map 4/E2) 🚶 🚴 👟

Located south of the village of Wilkesport, the McKeough Conservation Area is accessible via the Holt Line. Two trails can be found at this conservation area. The main trail is an easy 3 km (1.9 mi) route that traverses through a Carolinian forest that is heavily treed with rare blue ash. The second trail is a 14 km (8.7 mi) return hike along the W. Darcy Floodway. The trail has been replanted over the last decade making for a very scenic hike. From the conservation area, the trail travels west along the floodway all the way to the St. Clair River and back.

Walker Woods (West Forest Tract) Trail (Map 28/D2) 🚶 🎿

Walker Woods is located south of Uxbridge off the 7th Concession Road. The tract is the base for a 6 km (3.7 mi) trail system that is ideal for hiking during the summer or cross-country skiing in the winter. The trail is generally easy to traverse on foot, although there are a few hills and tricky sections that can make skiing a bit more challenging. All trails are well marked and make a great place to get some outdoor exercise.

Warwick Conservation Area Trail (Map 11/D5) 🚶 👟

In the village of Warwick, the conservation area offers visitors the opportunity to explore a provincially significant wetland habitat. The easy 2 km (1.2 mi) trail traverses through the wetland providing good views of rare wetland plants.

Waterfront Trail (Maps 16/B1-G1, 17/B1-E1, 21/G7, 22/A7-F1) 🚶 🚴 👟

This long distance trail will eventually create a fantastic trail around the infamous Golden Horseshoe of Lake Ontario. Currently, the trail is made up of a combination of secondary road routes and off road paths around Lake Ontario. Although all sections of the trail are yet to be connected, visitors will find many pieces ready for exploring.

The trail starts in Niagara-on-the-Lake in Paradise Grove Park and begins its trek west towards Hamilton. In Hamilton the main access point is Confederation Park. After crossing Hamilton Harbour to Burlington, the Burlington/Oakville Lakeshore sections provide splendid views of Lake Ontario. Perhaps the most popular portion of the trail is the Toronto Harbourfront and Beaches section. This portion of the trail follows the dynamic Toronto shoreline through several parks and past the scenic beach areas of the city. From Toronto, the route heads west (off our maps) past areas such as Pickering and Ajax en route towards the city of Trenton. For a more detailed guide of the route contact the Waterfront Regeneration Trust at (416) 314-9490.

Waterloo Trails (Map 20/D4) 🚶 🚴

Bechtel Park Trail

The Bechtel Park Trail can be reached in the northeast end of Waterloo near the corner of University Avenue East and Bridge Street. Parking is available off the west side of Bridge Street at the playground. From the playground this easy 4.5 km (2.8 mi) collection of interconnecting trails travel through a forest tract and down to Laurel Creek. Along this route you may be lucky to spot waterfowl, rabbits or even deer.

Twin Oak's Trail

In the northern portion of Waterloo, the Twin Oak's Trail can be accessed from Northfield Drive North or from Heasley Park off Parkside Drive. Northfield Drive is accessible off the west side of Highway 86. This trail is an easy 4 km (2.5 mi) return hike that follows Cedar Creek most of the way. During the spring, wildflowers can be viewed along this route.

Wawanosh Valley Conservation Area Trail (Map 23/D6) 🚶 👟

Hikers will enjoy the hemlock, red pine, and hardwood forest cover as they tackle this moderate 3 km (1.9 mi) loop. The trail heads north from the parking area, crossing Belgrave Creek before descending to the Maitland River and the return trip home. There are three offshoot trails that can be picked up along the way to shorten your loop. To find the conservation area, look for Nature Centre Road north of the village of Blyth. Watch for poison ivy near the Belgrave Creek and Maitland River.

Welland Canals Parkway (Map 17/C2) 🚶 🚲

Located in the east side of the city of St. Catharines, this easy 9 km (5.6 mi) paved trail is a great way to get some exercise and escape the city. The trail runs parallel to the Welland Canal from Lakeshore Road to Glendale Avenue. Both hikers and bikers can enjoy this scenic route as it skirts the east side of the city.

Wesley Brooks Conservation Area Trail (Map 27/F2) 🚶 🏕

Visitors can find the Wesley Brooks Conservation Area in the town of Newmarket via the Cane Parkway or Water Street. The conservation area is home to an easy 2 km (1.2 mi) loop trail that traverses along a paved route along a portion of the Holland River and around Fairy Lake. The southern sections of the trail travel through mature tree stands, while the Fairy Lake portion of the trail features the lake and its intricate wetland environment.

West Rocks Conservation Area Trails (Map 34/D4) 🚶 🏕

The access area to this set of trails is at the Inglis Falls Conservation Area found south of Owen Sound. To find the conservation area, follow 2nd Avenue East south and look for the access off the east side of the road just outside of town. The trail system is about 10 km (6.2 mi) in length and is regarded as moderate in difficulty. They interconnect with the Bruce Trail from the Inglis Falls Conservation Area north to the west side of Owen Sound. The route travels through a mix of open space and forest along the Niagara Escarpment, providing superb views of Owen Sound and the Georgian Bay.

Wheatley Provincial Park (Map 2/D5) 🚶 🏕

Located just south of the town of Wheatley, Wheatley Provincial Park is a very popular summer beach destination. Besides strolling along the 2 km (1.2 mi) long beach, park visitors can also venture out along the easy 2 km (1.2 mi) set of trails that meander through the park. One trail system loops along the Two Creek area, while the other travels between the beach and the group camping area.

Whitby Town Trails (Map 28/G5) 🚶 🚲

In the town of Whitby, visitors can access two interurban hiking trails. Each trail is wheelchair accessible and can be enjoyed by both hikers and bikers. The **Ash Creek Trail** is accessible from Bradley Drive as well as Garden Street and is 1.3 km (0.8 mi) in length. The **Scott Trail** can be accessed via Dundas Street and Manning Road and is 1 km (0.6 mi) in length.

Wildwood Conservation Area Trails (Maps 13/C1-19/D7) 🚶 ⛷

Located just east of the town of St. Mary's, the Wildwood Conservation Area is a great place to experience the outdoors. Two trail systems are available for visitors to enjoy:

Dr. R.S. Forest Trails

This collection of three trails offer about 6 km (3.7 mi) to explore. Each trail is marked by colour; the blue trail is 2 km/1.2 mi long, the green trail is 1 km/0.6 mi long and the red trail stretches 3 km/1.9 mi. The trails travel through a mix of forest cover and wetland area and are regarded as easy. Skiers will find portions of the system to be moderately challenging.

Lake Trail

The Lake Trail travels along the northern shore of Wildwood Lake and is an easy to moderate 14 km (8.7 mi) return hike. The trail treks through forest cover, open field and wetland habitat and returns along the same path back to the trailhead. The route is well marked by orange markers.

Willow Farm, Lakeview, Wimpey Trail (Map 27/F3) 🚶

Set amid the heart of the town of Aurora, this trail system spans some 3.5 km (2.2 mi) one-way connecting several different developments along the way. The trail is accessible from several local streets and is regarded as easy in difficulty. The route is a great way to further experience the outdoors around Aurora as it treks through some deciduous forest cover, open fields and subdivisions.

Windsor Area Trails (Map 1) 🚶 🚲 🏕

Devonwood Trail (C2)

The Devonwood Trail begins at the Devonwood Conservation Area, which is located in the southern portion of Windsor. The conservation area lies off the north side of Division Road (County Road 42). The trail is an easy 3 km (1.9 mi) one-way trek through the conservation grounds to a more developed area before ending near Fairlane Crescent and Conservation Avenue.

East Riverside Park Trail (D1)

East Riverside Park is located in the east end of Windsor off Little River Road. The trail is an easy 1.3 km (0.8 mi) loop through East Riverside Park. The trail travels around a pond providing viewing opportunities for waterfowl and other bird life.

Ganatchio Trail (D1)

The Ganatchio Trail is one of the longer urban trails found in Windsor as it stretches from Riverside Drive south all the way to Tecumseh Road. The 10.5 km (6.5 mi) trail is regarded as easy as it wanders through some treed areas within the Little River corridor. For a bit of variety, there is an easy 2 km (1.2 mi) side trail that branches off the main trail. The branch is found about half way along the main trail and travels north, meeting up with Bertha Street.

Little River Trail (D1)

This easy 2.6 km (1.6 mi) route travels along the meandering Little River. The trek begins at the E.C. Row Expressway and travels south to the rail tracks where you can retrace your steps back to the trailhead.

Riverfront Trail (A1)

The Riverfront Trail is the most popular urban trail in Windsor. It follows the scenic Detroit River from the Ambassador Bridge to Hiram Walker. The route passes through a series of connected parks and can be cycled as well as walked/hiked. If you have never visited Windsor, this is a route that is definitely worthwhile as it gives you a sense of the city along with a fantastic view across the river to Detroit in the USA.

Turkey Creek Trail (A2)

This trail can be picked up off the north side of Todd Lane (County Road 6) in the southeast part of the city. The easy route is a 4.6 km (2.9 mi) hike from Todd Lane east to Balmoral Street and back. The trail travels through The Spring Garden ANSI along an urban green space.

Wingham Community Trail (Map 23/G5) 🚶 🚲 🏕

This 2.5 km (1.6 mi) loop is an easy trail located in the town of Wingham. Parking and access to the trail is located off Minnie Street near the Maitland River. The trail begins by following the southern shore of the river along the old Canadian National Railway line. The trail continues to the Turnberry Floodplain Conservation Area before heading back to the trailhead along the old railbed. There are a number of rest benches and an old CNR Rail Bridge to cross.

Woodlands Arboretum Trail (Map 18/C1) 🚶

The Woodlands Arboretum is located northwest of the town of Clinton off the north side of Highway 8. This trail was established with the generous help of the Woodlands links Golf Course and actually crosses number 12 fairway as well as a few meadows and bogs. The easy 2.5 km (1.6 mi) trail begins at the parking area at the end of the public lane found west of the clubhouse access road. Be alert for oncoming golfers when crossing the fairway.

Winter Recreation

(Cross-country Skiing, Snowshoeing, Snowmobiling)

Cross-country Skiing & Snowshoeing

Southwestern Ontario has traditionally offered cross-country skiers a tremendous amount of variety. From established Nordic centres to rustic conservation areas there are many places to ski in the winter. Most of the systems offer ungroomed trails that are often track set by previous visitors.

The use of snowshoes is slowly becoming a popular alternative for winter travel. The new bear paw style shoes are merely an extension of your foot and allow you to travel virtually anywhere on snow. For those who prefer a more established route, many conservation areas and provincial parks have begun to promote their trail systems for snowshoeing. If you're looking to forge your own trail, larger trail systems such as parts of the Bruce Trail and any abandoned railway trail also make great snowshoeing destinations.

Although we have provided a good selection of trail networks below, the multi-use trail and park section of the book offers other alternatives. Rentals are also available on site at a few locations listed below as well as from retailers throughout Southwestern Ontario.

A.W. Campbell Conservation Area Trail (Map 11/F7)

The A.W. Campbell Conservation Area can be found by following County Road 72 (Nauvoo Road) south from the town of Watford to the Shiloh Line near the town of Alvinson. The trail system is comprised of two connected loops that combine to make a 3.3 km (2.0 mi) system. The route travels through a mix of meadow, floodplain and deciduous forest settings. Ski trails are not groomed, but are occasionally track set by other users.

Albion Hills Conservation Area Trails (Map 27/A4)

The Albion Hills Conservation Area offers 26 km (16 mi) of interconnected cross-country ski trails. The trails are well marked and traverse through a mixed forest and past several wetland areas. All trails are track set and one section is groomed for skate skiing. The routes vary from easy to difficult and there is also a warm up hut available at the trailhead area. Other outdoor fun that can be enjoyed at the area includes a skating rink and a fantastic toboggan hill. The conservation area is located near the village of Cedar Mills off County Road 50 (Queen Street). Equipment rentals are available and admission fees apply.

Bayview Escarpment Nature Reserve Trail (Map 35/B2)

This easy to moderate 7 km (4.3 mi) trail traverses along an old road through the nature reserve. The trail treks through some wooded sections and is suitable for both snowshoeing and cross-country skiing.

Bingeman's Ski Trail (Map 19/F4)

In the city of Kitchener, the Bingeman's Ski Trail area can be found off the north side of Victoria Street (Highway 7) near Natchez Road. The easy to moderate 8 km (5 mi) loop follows the Grand River throughout much of its length providing good views of the river environment. Bingeman's is a fully equipped ski area complete with a ski lodge and rentals.

Blue Mountain Nordic Centre (Map 31/G2)

Blue Mountain is the top rated Ontario downhill ski area that has finally developed a reputable system of cross-country ski trails. Found at the Collingwood Scenic Caves Nature Area, there are 21 km (13 mi) of groomed and track set trails ranging from easy to difficult available. The trails traverse through some mature forest stands and past several panoramic views of the area. Along with a warm up hut, snowshoeing opportunities also exist for visitors. Call (705) 446-0256 for more information.

Bronte Creek Provincial Park (Map 22/A5)

In the winter, this provincial park has a recreation complex complete with a lit skating rink. Also in the area is a tobogganing hill and almost 20 km (12 mi) of trails available for cross-country skiing. There are heated change areas and picnic shelters as well as ski and skate rentals available. Call (905) 827-6911 for more information.

Circle R Ranch Trails (Map 12/E6)

Located west of the city of London, the Circle R Ranch is home to a 20 km (12 mi) series of well mapped, marked and groomed cross-country ski trails. The trails wind their way through a mix of forest and rolling hills, a mix of easy to moderate terrain. There is also a heated lodge that offers ski rentals if required. Admission fees apply.

Clubine Forest Tract Trail (Map 28/C3)

The Clubine Forest Tract offers cross country skiers and snowshoers the opportunity to experience a well marked 2 km (1.2 mi) trail that spans through a mature forest plantation. The easy trail is not groomed, but is often track set by previous skiers.

Crawford Lake Conservation Area Trails (Map 21/F4)

The Crawford Lake Conservation Area is best known for its reconstructed Iroquoian Village, although the area also offers nearly 8 km (5 mi) of track set cross-country ski trails in winter. Another 4 km (2.5 mi) of the trails are available for snowshoeing. The conservation area is located southeast of Milton not far off the Guelph Line (County Road 1). A small admission fee is required.

Dundas Valley Conservation Area Trails (Map 15/E1)

West of Hamilton, the Dundas Valley Conservation Area continues to be a popular outdoor attraction during the winter. Some 40 km (24.8 mi) of trails are available at this park for both snowshoeing and cross-country skiing. Only 5 km (3.1 mi) of the trails are track set. A large toboggan hill is also a prime attraction to the area.

Duntroon Highlands Nordic Trails (Map 32/A4)

The Duntroon Highlands Nordic Centre is home to a collection of 16 km (9.9 mi) of groomed cross-country ski trails. Suitable for both traditional and skate skiing, the trails vary in difficulty from easy to moderate. The routes travel through a mixed forest and past a few fine lookout areas. Rentals are available and the warm up hut is particularly appealing on frosty days. Admission fees apply. For more information call (800) 263-5017.

Eugenia Falls Conservation Area Trail (Map 31/D5)

Located just north of the town of Flesherton, the Eugenia Falls are an impressive 30 m (98 ft) waterfall along the Beaver River and can be reached on skis. The easy 1 km (0.6 mi) loop trail traverses along the Cuckoo Valley through a mixed forest environment eventually meeting the falls.

Falls Reserve Conservation Area Trail (Map 23/B7)

Found along the north shore of the Maitland River, the Falls Reserve is home to an easy 3.2 km track set loop. The conservation area is located east of Goderich not far off the Londesboro Road (County Road 31).

Georgian Trail (Maps 31/D1-32/B2, 35/E5)

The Georgian Trail spans 32 km (19.9 mi) one-way between the towns of Meaford and Collingwood. The trail is accessible in over thirty areas, including off Highway 26 as well as in the towns of Meaford, Collingwood and Thornbury. A few of the attractions along the trail include trestle bridges, Craigleith Provincial Park and the Thornbury Fish Lock. Both cross-country skiers and snowshoers can utilize this trail in the winter. Ski trails are usually track set.

Goodwood and Secord Forest Tract Trails (Map 28/C3)

Northwest of Claremont, visitors can find the Goodwood Forest Tract off the west side of 3rd Concession Road, while the Secord Tract lies to the north off the east side of the 3rd Concession Road. Combined, the two forest tracts offer 5 km (3.1 mi) of suitable cross-country ski trails. The trails are generally moderate in difficulty and are well marked.

Greenwood Conservation Area Trail (Map 28/E5)

North of the town of Ajax, the Greenwood Conservation Area is home to 2 km (1.6 mi) of cross-country ski trails. The route follows Duffins Creek before skirting along the steep river valley. Cross-country skiers will find some sections moderate to difficult in nature.

Hanover Community Trail (Maps 24/D1, 30/D7)

Over the past few years, Hanover has reclaimed much of the old CP and CN rail beds in the area and has converted them into fantastic trail systems. Currently, there are about 11 km (6.8 mi) of easy trails that have been developed in and around the town. Most of the system skirt the edge of the charming Saugeen River providing a peaceful winter setting for both cross-country skiing and snowshoeing.

Hardwood Hill Management Unit Trail (Map 23/G3)

West of the small village of Teeswater, this management area lies near the corner of County Road 6 and Side Road 25 South. The management unit is home to an easy 1.2 km (0.7 mi) trail that is suitable for cross-country skiing and snowshoeing. The trail is not groomed.

Hay Swamp Trail (Map 18/C6)

Around Hay Swamp a series of old logging roads offer over 10 km (6.2 mi) of interconnecting routes. Cross-country skiing is the main winter use of the area, although it is possible to snowshoe as well. Vehicles, such as snowmobiles are not permitted in this fragile area. Donations to the Ausable Bayfield Conservation Area are always welcome for use of this outdoor area.

Headquarters Conservation Area Trails (Map 24/D1)

The Headquarters Conservation Area trails are quite popular during the winter with local cross-country skiers. The trail system is a 4.6 km (2.9 mi) loop route that has a number of connected shortcuts and is easy to moderate in difficulty. Snowshoeing is also quite popular at the conservation area, but please stay off the set ski tracks. A small entrance fee is requested and snowshoe rentals are available.

Heber Down Conservation Area Trail (28/F4)

The Heber Down Conservation Area lies to the north of the town of Whitby. The area is home to over 13 km (8.1 mi) of ski trails ranging from easy to difficult. A small fee is required for use of the trail system.

Hilton Falls Conservation Area Trails (Map 21/F3)

The Hilton Falls Conservation Area is a great place to escape in winter. The area offers 15.5 km (9.6 mi) of groomed ski trails that traverse through a forest setting to the site of a magnificent frozen waterfall. At the waterfall visitors can take a break by a fire before they head out on the remainder of their trek. Be sure to bring some marshmallows or hot dogs to cook over the fire.

Holland River Valley Trail (Map 27/F3)

In the town of Aurora, the Holland River Valley Trail travels north to south along the Holland River corridor. The Trail is an easy 8 km (5 mi) return route that meanders through the river valley. Skiers and snowshoers will enjoy the mix of forest cover, wetland and open field space along the route.

Joany's Woods Trail (Map 11/F2)

Visitors to Joany's Woods will find two secluded trails during winter. The Lookout Trail is an easy 3.2 km (2 mi) loop that traverses form the parking area through the quiet woods and past a few wetland areas. The Tulip Tree Trail is moderate in difficulty and spans 4.4 km (2.7 mi) over some challenging slopes. A conservation region pass is required for use of the trail system. Passes can be purchased at the Ausable Bayfield Conservation Region. Call (519) 235-2610 for more information.

Keppel Rail Trail (Maps 33/G3-34/C3)

The Keppel Rail Trail follows the old rail line between the settlements of Benallen, Shallow Lake and the village of Park Head. The multi-use trail stretches approximately 12.8 km (7.9 mi) one-way along gentle terrain. The route is open to cross-country skiers, snowshoers and snowmobiling during the winter.

Kirk Cousins Wildlife Area Trails (Map 13/A6)

Also known as the A'Nowaghi Forest Trails, this system offers an easy 5 km (3.1 mi) collection of interconnecting loops that skirt the ponds. The trails are suitable for non-groomed cross-country skiing and snowshoeing. Access to the management area is restricted to conservation region pass holders. Passes can be purchased at the Kettle Creek Conservation Authority. Call (519) 631-1270 for more information.

Kolapore Uplands Trails (Map 31/F4)

The Kolapore Demonstration Forest and surrounding area is home to a collection of approximately 60 km (37.3 mi) of interconnected trails that are used extensively by cross-country skiers during the winter. The trails range from easy to difficult as they travel through a mixed forest cover as well as past a few wetland and field areas.

Komoka Provincial Park Trail (Map 12/E5)

This park is home to three interconnecting ski/snowshoe trails that create a 6 km (3.7 mi) network. The trails provide views of the Thames River and are all generally easy to travel.

Kortright Centre for Conservation Trails (Map 27/D6)

Along with all of the wonderful educational displays and events, 14 km (8.7 mi) of groomed cross-country ski trails are available at the centre. The trails vary from easy to difficult and trek through a mature forest and past a few wetland areas. Admission fees apply.

Laurel Creek Conservation Area Trails (Map 20/C4)

Just outside the west end of the city of Waterloo lies the Laurel Creek Conservation Area. The area offers a 7.6 km (4.7 mi) collection of groomed cross-country ski trails for visitors to enjoy. There are three loops available; the beginner loop is 2 km (1.2 mi) in length, the intermediate loop stretches 4 km (2.5 mi) and the advanced loop covers 1.6 km (1 mi). Equipment rentals are available throughout the winter season. For more information call (519) 621-2761.

Lake Whittaker Conservation Area Trails (Map 13/E6)

Lake Whittaker is located southeast of the city of London and offers a collection of three trails totalling 6.5 km (4 mi). On the trail system, visitors will traverse around the glaciers created Lake Whittaker and past several interesting wetland areas. Portions of the system also pass through older tree plantations as well as sugar bush areas. The trails are not groomed and can be enjoyed by both skiers and snowshoers.

Longwoods Road Conservation Area Trails (Map 12/D7)

West of London, Longwoods Road offers a collection of 6.5 km (4 mi) of interconnected trails. The easy trails do have a few tougher areas for cross-country skiers. Snowshoeing is also a popular winter pastime. There is a small admission fee into the conservation area. For more information on costs and times the gate is open, call (519) 354-7310.

Loree Forest Trail (Map 31/G2)

The Loree Forest Tract lies along the Blue Mountain portion of the Bruce Trail. The forest is home to a secluded mix of trails that are utilized by hikers in the summer and cross-country skiers in the winter. The trails are found atop the Georgian Peaks Ski Area and are quite challenging in sections.

Maitland Woods Trail (Map 23/A7)

The Maitland Woods Trail is located in the southeast end of Goderich and is made up of three easy loop routes. The main loop trail is 3 km (1.9 mi) in length but there are also 1.5 km (0.9 mi) and 0.5 km (0.3 mi) loops. The trails are track set by previous users and no pets are permitted.

Mansfield Outdoor Centre (Map 32/E7)

For a small fee, this outdoor centre offers over 32 km (19.9 mi) of trails for cross-country skiing. 5 km (3.1 mi) of the trails are groomed for skate skiing, while the remaining trails are track set and maintained for classical skiing. There is a main building that has a small cafeteria and offers equipment rentals if needed. If you wish to stay more than one day at the centre, there are small rustic cabins available for weekend rental. The centre is located on Airport Road (County Road 18) south of the town of Stayner.

Maple Keys Sugar Bush Trail (Map 24/C7)

The Maple Keys Sugar Bush offers ungroomed trails for cross-country skiers and snowshoers to sample in winter. The short (0.8 km and 2 km) loops are often track set by other users and traverse through a scenic setting through the sugar bush forest.

Massie Trail (Map 34/F5)

The Massie Trail is located east of the town of Owen Sound and is a moderate 10 km (6.2 mi) trail. Skiers will enjoy the variety of terrain available along the route including some fine mature pine stands. There are hilly sections to be wary of. The Owen Sound Cross-Country Ski Club maintains the trails during the winter months.

Mountsberg Wildlife Centre Trails (Map 21/D4)

Besides the fabulous raptor and wildlife displays, the Mountsberg Wildlife Centre also has 12.5 km (7.8 mi) of groomed cross-country ski trails. Another 2 km or so of trails are also available for snowshoeing. Visitors can also enjoy skating on the nearby pond. Snowshoe rentals are available. For more information call (905) 854-2276.

Naftel's Creek Conservation Area Trail (Map 18/A1)

Between the towns of Goderich and Bayfield, the Naftel's Creek Conservation Area lies off the east side of Highway 21. The conservation area offers a moderate 3.2 km (2 mi) trail that loops through a mix of conifer trees and wetland areas. Three side trails are linked to the main trail and make for added adventure.

Pinehurst Lake Conservation Area Trails (Map 19/G7)

The Pinehurst Lake Conservation Area offers an extensive system of track set ski trails. The 12 km (7.5 mi) of trails can be interconnected and allow you to vary the difficulty and length of the route. A small fee is required to access the area and ski rentals are available.

Pinery Provincial Park (Maps 10/inset, 11/E1)

The Pinery is a great place for a winter outdoor adventure. The park offers four classical ski trails that total 27 km (16.8 mi) in length. There is also an 11 km (6.8 mi) skate skiing route designed for moderate skate skiing enthusiasts. The trails travel through mainly forested settings with periodic views of Lake Huron. Other winter activities that can be enjoyed at the park include winter camping, skating and tobogganing. Ski rentals are available on weekends.

Pleasure Valley Ski Trails (Map 28/D2)

North of Claremont, the Pleasure Valley Ski Area can be found off the east side of Brock Road (Count Road 1). The area offers over 22 km (13.7 mi) of maintained ski trails ranging from easy to difficult. There are plenty of facilities available for visitors, including a store, washrooms and first aid services. Summer visitors to Pleasure Valley can enjoy the trails on horseback. Fees for use of the area vary by activity and from season to season.

Point Pelee National Park Trails (Map 2/C7)

Point Pelee National Park is located south of the town of Leamington and offers a variety of outdoor activities during the winter months. Skating is available on the frozen ponds, while cross-country skiers will find ungroomed trails. A few of the trails can also be used for snowshoeing.

Port Burwell Provincial Park (Maps 7/G3, 8/E3)

Port Burwell Provincial Park is located south of the town of Tillsonburg but is not officially open during the winter. Locals and visitors alike often ski along the park roads when the snow falls. The park is quite secluded in the winter, making for a fine winter outdoor getaway.

Purple Woods Conservation Area Trail (Map 28/G2)

Located south of Port Perry, the Purple Woods Conservation Area is home of the spring Maple Syrup Festival. Visitors can enjoy the 4 km (2.5 mi) route along the conservation area's easy trail, experiencing the serenity of nature along the way. Cross-country skiing is permitted along the trail during the winter, although the route is not groomed.

Rondeau Provincial Park Trails (Map 3/F1)

Since Rondeau Provincial Park is located in the more temperate region of Southwestern Ontario along the shore of Lake Erie, snowfall can be limited during the winter. However, when sufficient snowfall exists, the many roads and trails of the park are available for cross-country skiing or snowshoeing.

Sauble Beach Ski Trails (Map 33/E1)

To reach the Sauble Falls Ski Trails, follow County Road 13 north past the Rankin River to the parking area off the east side of the road. From the parking area it is a short hike in to the heated chalet where you can get geared up. The trail system is maintained by local volunteers and is comprised of over 20 km (12 mi) of track set and groomed ski trails. The trails are quite scenic travelling through wooded areas and past a few wetland areas. A small fee applies for visitors in order to help maintain the area.

Saugeen River Trail (Map 23/B1)

Accessible from many points around the town of Walkerton, this easy trail follows the dykes of the Saugeen River. The main trail is about 5.5 km (3.4 mi) in length. Cross-country skiers and snowshoers use the ungroomed trails in winter.

Skyloft Ski Area (Map 28/E2)

South of Uxbridge, the Skyloft Ski Area is accessible off the 7th Concession Road. Along with downhill ski runs, the club offers over 10 km (6.2 mi) of cross-country ski trails. The trails range from easy to difficult and are regularly maintained throughout the winter season. A fee is required for use of the trails.

Stanley Trail (Map 18/B3)

The Stanley Trail is located west of the village of Varna and is approximately 4 km (2.5 mi) in length. The route is easy to moderate in difficulty and traverses from an open field into a mixed forest area. During the winter, the cross-country ski trails are occasionally track set.

Stoney Island Conservation Area Trails (Map 29/B7)

You can find the Stoney Island Conservation Area north of the town of Kincardine. Cross country skiers can enjoy an 8 km series of loop trails that lead through a mix of mature hardwood, hemlock and cedar forests. Portions of the trails also provide fine views of Lake Huron. The trails are groomed regularly for skate and traditional skiing.

Terra Cotta Conservation Area Trail (Map 26/F7)

The Terra Cotta Conservation Area can be found north of Georgetown via the 10th Line Road. The area is open year round, providing access to a 12 km (7.5 mi) trail system for cross-country skiing enthusiasts in the winter. The trails are groomed regularly and are generally easy in nature. During weekends, cross-country ski rental are available.

Valens Conservation Area (Map 21/C6)

The Valens Conservation Area is a great place for winter adventure. The conservation area offers ice fishing hut rentals, skating on the reservoir, winter camping and cross-country skiing. Over 10 km (6.2 mi) of trails are groomed or track set allowing visitors to explore the area. For rentals and more information call (905) 525-2183.

Walker Woods (West Forest Tract) Trail (Map 28/D2)

Walker Woods is located south of Uxbridge and is home to a 6 km (3.7 mi) trail system that is ideal for cross-country skiing in the winter. The trail is generally easy to travel, although there are a few hills and tricky sections along the route. All trails are well marked and make a great place to get some outdoor exercise.

Wasaga Beach/Blueberry Plains Nordic Centre (Map 32/E2)

At Wasaga Beach Provincial Park, the Blueberry Plains Nordic Centre offers over 27 km (16.8 mi) of groomed and track set ski trails. The trails wind their way through the park and range from easy to difficult. A portion of the trails are also open for snowshoeing. Visitors will appreciate the warm up hut and there are ski and snowshoe rentals available. There is a small access fee for the trails.

Wingham Community Trail (Map 23/G5)

Located in the town of Wingham is an ungroomed 2.5 km (1.6 mi) loop trail. The easy trail begins by following the southern shore of the Maitland River along the old Canadian National Railway line. The trail loops near the Turnberry Floodplain Conservation Area before heading back to the trailhead.

Snowmobiling

The Ontario Federation of Snowmobile Clubs (OFSC) is a powerful organization that has brought together snowmobile clubs from around Ontario in an effort to standardize and expand snowmobiling trail opportunities. To date, the OFSC trail system spans over 49,000 km from one corner of the province to the other. All users travelling on an OFSC trail must have a valid trail permit, which can be picked up at most local snowmobile retailers and outdoor stores. OFSC provincial trail permits for the 2003 season were $150, although there is often a significant discount offered if you purchase your permit before December 1st of each year. Trail systems are patrolled by Trail Wardens who enforce permit usage. All proceeds from permits go directly into creating the safest and best trail system in North America.

Grey/Bruce Trails (Maps 29-31, 33-39)

The Owen Sound and Bruce Peninsula region offers some of the best snowmobile trails in the province. The region lies in a heavy snow belt area formed mainly from lake effect off the Georgian Bay. The region has a well established TOP trail system and is often open in late November. The beautiful rolling hills along the Niagara Escarpment in this part of the province make for some interesting snowmobiling.

Huron Trails (Maps 11, 18, 23, 24, 29, 30)

The area lying inland along Lake Huron south of the Bruce Peninsula is another heavy snowfall area that offers some fantastic powder throughout the winter. Snowmobilers can travel from town to town along the Lake Huron shoreline enjoying the many sights along the way. While much of the terrain in the region is made up of farmland and open fields, the brisk winds form Lake Huron can make even a modestly cold day quite cold on a sled.

London, Kitchener/Waterloo Trails (Maps 12-14, 18-20)

The cities of Kitchener/Waterloo and London have a good established trail system throughout the area. The main obstacle to a good sledding in this part of the province is snow. Often there is little snow until well into January and even then the season can be limited. Some years, decent snowfalls can be found regularly, while other years there is very little even though there's plenty to the north.

Lake Erie Shoreline Trails (Maps 1-3, 5-9, 15-17)

The Lake Erie shoreline region is quite temperate compared to most of Ontario, especially in the more southern reaches near Leamington and further south. Trail systems have been established and in good years riders can get up to two months of decent riding in. However, some years the trails are only open for a few days at a time and consistency can really limit riding time.

North of Metro Toronto Trails (Maps 26-28, 32)

In the Lake Simcoe region north of Metro Toronto snowmobilers can enjoy a fine group of trails. Snowfall can be a factor at times, although there are usually two good months a year available to ride in this region. Lake Simcoe itself is shown in our Cottage Country edition but there are other fine trails to explore in this book. In particular, look for the trails around Alliston and Wasaga Beach, when snow is available.

Service Providers

Accommodations

Bed and Breakfast by the Lake

Open all year. Overlooking Lake Erie. Beautiful sandy beach. Air conditioned. TV. Full breakfast. No smoking inside. VISA
Attraction: Lighthouse Theatre

30 Elm Park, Port Dover, ON
N0A 1N0

Christine Ivey, John Baker
519-583-1010
www.bbcanada.com/bbbylake

Jordan Valley CampGround

Exit 57 QEW. Explore historic village of Jordan, picturesque shops, local vintages & cuisine. Families enjoy parkland setting, nature trails, and canoeing. Relax, Explore, Rejuvenate.

3902 21st Street
Jordan, Ontario, L0R 1S0
tel/fax: **905-562-7816**
jvc@campingniagara.com
www.campingniagara.com

Maison Tanguay B&B

Open all year, fishing, hiking, cycling, golf, cross country skiing, beautiful sunsets, delicious full breakfasts.

46 Nelson St. West
Goderich, On, N7A 2M3
519-524-1930
www.bbcanada.com/686.html

Moeke's Ankerstee

Open All Year.

Hiking, biking, diving, skidoing, getting back to nature.

Full Cooked Breakfasts.

479 Dyers Bay Rd.
Miller Lake, On, N0H 1Z0

tel: **519-795-7769**
fax: **519-795-7231**

Renn's Nest B&B

Situated at the base of Mt. Nemo on Niagara Escarpment. Bruce Trail runs along the top of Mt. Nemo. Warm Christian hospitality extended with a full breakfast.

5292 Walkers Line, R.R. #2
Milton, On, L9T 2X6
905-319-0938
www.bbcanada.com/2831.html

jkren@bserv.com

Rochester Place Resort

"Your Leisure Headquarters
on the
North Shore of Essex County"

CAMPING, BOATING, FISHING,
GOLFING, DINING

1-800-563-5940
www.rochesterplace.ca

Tours & Guides

Grey County Tourism

Welcome to Ontario's premier four seasons destination on the southern shores of Georgian Bay! Hike 250 Km of the Bruce Trail on the Niagara Escarpment, paddle the Saugeen River Watershed, experience the Beaver Valley fall colours, or seek the alpine thrills of the Blue Mountains. Grey County is beautiful...naturally.

595 9th Ave. East, Owen Sound, ON

toll free 1-800-567-GREY (4739)

Rawhide Adventures

Ontario's working cattle ranch. Great horses, unbelievable scenery. No head to tail riding. Help work the cows or just enjoy the escarpment. B&B next to the Bruce Trail.

R.R. #3 Shelburne ON

L0N 1S7

519-925-0152
www.Rawhide-Adventures.on.ca

Steve Bauer Bike Tours

Providing luxurious fully supported cycling adventures for enthusiasts of all levels, in Canada, Europe, Central America & Cuba.

P.O. Box 342
Beamsville, On, L0R 1B0

905-563-8687
www.stevebauer.com

Important Numbers

Ministry of Natural Resources
General Inquiry ....(800) 667-1940

.... (800) 667-1840 (French)

....www.mnr.gov.on.ca

OutdoorsCard
Customer Service ....(800) 387-7011

Aurora,
Greater Toronto Area............. 905) 713-7400

Aylmer....................................(519) 773-9241

Chatham ....(519) 354-7340

Clinton ....(519) 482-3428

Guelph..................................(519) 826-4955

Owen Sound ....(519) 376-3860

Vineland ....(905) 562-4147

Invading Species Hotline ....(800) 563-7711

Sportfish Contaminant-
Monitoring Program ....(800) 820-2716

Parks
Ontario Parks (Reservations) ...(888) 668-7275

.... www.OntarioParks.com

Bruce Peninsula
National Park ....(519) 596-2233

Bruce Trail ....(800) 665-4453

Poaching Violations
Crime Stoppers ....(800) 222-8477

Tourism Ontario
Resorts Ontario ....(705) 325-9115

Travel Ontario ....(800) ONTARIO

Southwestern Ontario Mapkey

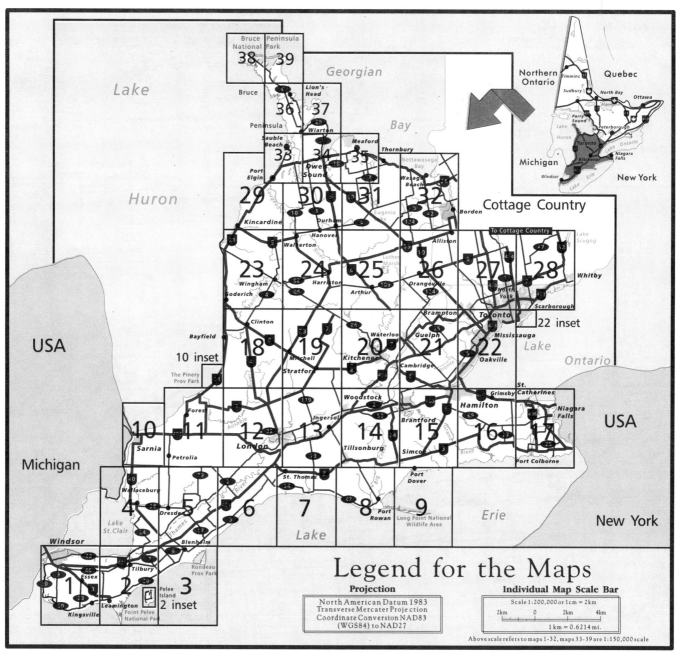

Legend for the Maps

Projection

North American Datum 1983
Transverse Mercater Projection
Coordinate Conversion NAD83
(WGS84) to NAD27

Individual Map Scale Bar

Scale 1:200,000 or 1cm = 2km

2km   0   2km   4km

1 km = 0.6214 mi.

Above scale refers to maps 1-32, maps 33-39 are 1:150,000 scale

Recreational Activities:

Anchorage / Marina
Beach
Boat Launch
Campsite / Limited Facilities
Campsite / Trailer Park
Campsite (trail / boat access)
Canoe Access Put-in / Take-out
Cross Country Skiing
Diving
Downhill Skiing
Fishing
Float Plane
Golf Course
Hiking Trail
Horseback Riding
Mountain Biking
Motorbiking / ATV
Paddling (canoe / kayak)
Picnic Site
Portage
Snowmobiling

Miscellaneous:

Airport / Airstrip
Beacon
Cabin / Lodge / Resort
Forestry Lookout (abandoned)
Gate
Highways
  Trans-Canada
  County Road / Sec Hwy
Interchange
Lighthouse
Marsh
Microwave Tower
Mine Site (abandoned)
Parking
Point of Interest
Portage (meters) .... P 50
Ranger Station
Town Village, etc
Travel Information
Viewpoint
Waterfalls

Line Definition:

Highways
County Roads
Paved Secondary Roads
Paved City Roads
Secondary Roads
2wd / Side Roads
Unclassified / 4wd Roads
Trail / Old Roads
Long Distance Trail
Snowmobile Trails
Canoe Routes
Powerlines
Pipelines
Railways

Provincial Park /   Conservation Area/   City
National Park   Natural Area

Restricted Area /   Swamps   First Nations   USA
Private Property

© Mussio Ventures Ltd.

Windsor

See Map 2

See Inset Map on Page 2

2km 0 2km 4km

1

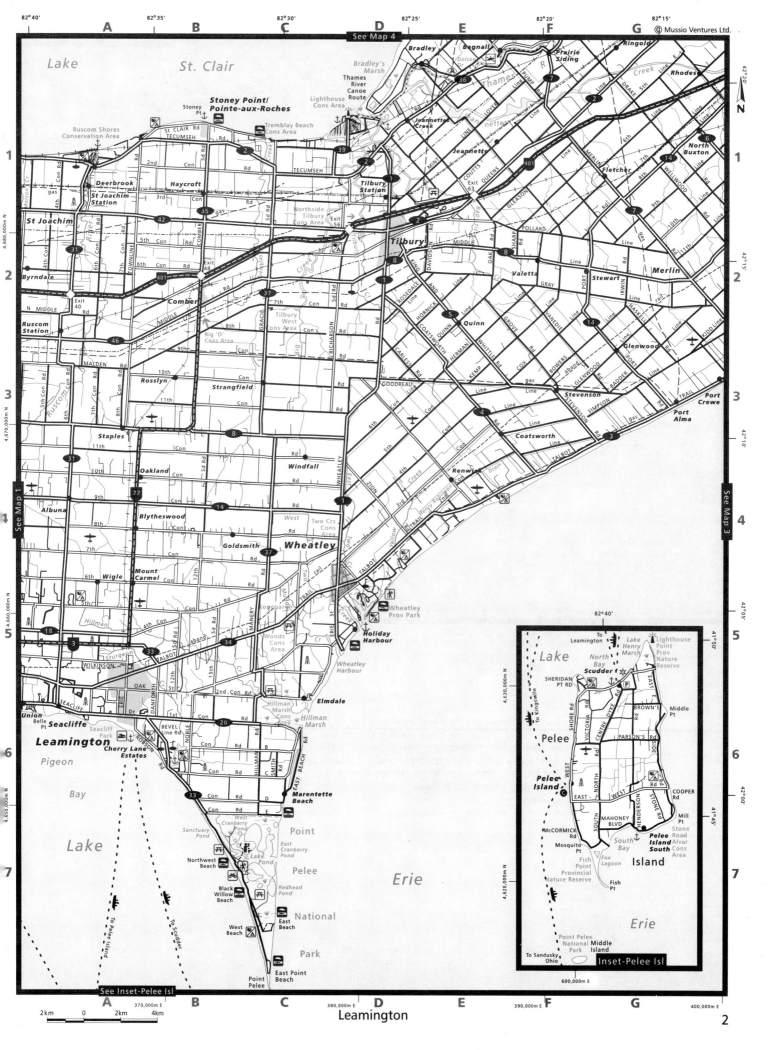

Mussio Ventures Ltd.

Lake St. Clair

Stoney Point/
Pointe-aux-Roches

Ruscom Shores
Conservation Area

Bradley

Bagnall

Prairie
Siding

Ringold

Rhodes

North
Buxton

Thames R

Bradley's
Marsh

Thames
River
Canoe
Route

Tremblay Beach
Cons Area

Lighthouse
Cons Area

Jeannettes
Creek

TECUMSEH
St CLAIR Rd

Stoney
Pt

Deerbrook

Haycroft

St Joachim
Station

St Joachim

Byrndale

Ruscom
Station

Comber

Rosslyn

Strangfield

Staples

Oakland

Windfall

Albuna

Blytheswood

Goldsmith

Wigle

Mount
Carmel

Wheatley

TECUMSEH

Tilbury
Station

Northside
Tilbury
Cons Area
Exit 56

Tilbury
West
Cons Area

Big 'O'
Cons Area

Jeannette

Jeannettes
Creek

Tilbury

Valetta

Merlin

Quinn

Quinn

Glenwood

Fletcher

Stewart

Coatsworth

Renwick

Port
Crewe

Port
Alma

Malden

Wheatley
Prov Park

Holiday
Harbour

Wheatley Harbour

Elmdale

Hillman
Marsh
Cons Area

Hillman Marsh

Woods Cons
Area

Seacliff

Union

Belle

Seacliffe

Seacliff
Park

Leamington

Cherry Lane
Estates

Pigeon

Bay

Marentette
Beach

West
Cranberry
Pond

Sanctuary
Pond

East
Cranberry
Pond

Point

Northwest
Beach

Lake
Pond

Redhead
Pond

Black
Willow
Beach

Pelee

Lake

Erie

West Beach

National

East
Beach

Park

East Point
Beach

Point
Pelee

Inset-Pelee Isl

Lake

Pelee

Pelee
Island

To
Leamington

Scudder

North
Bay

Lake
Henry Marsh

Lighthouse
Point Prov
Nature
Reserve

SHERIDAN
PT RD

BROWN'S

Middle
Pt

PARSON'S

McCORMICK
Rd

Mosquito
Pt

MAHONEY
BLVD

South
Bay

Fox
Lagoon

COOPER
Rd

Mill
Pt

Pelee
Island
South

Stone
Road
Alvar
Cons
Area

Island

Fish
Point
Provincial
Nature Reserve

Fish
Pt

To Sandusky
Ohio

Point Pelee
National
Park

Middle
Island

Erie

To Kingsville

To Pelee Island

To Scudder

2km   0   2km   4km

Leamington

2

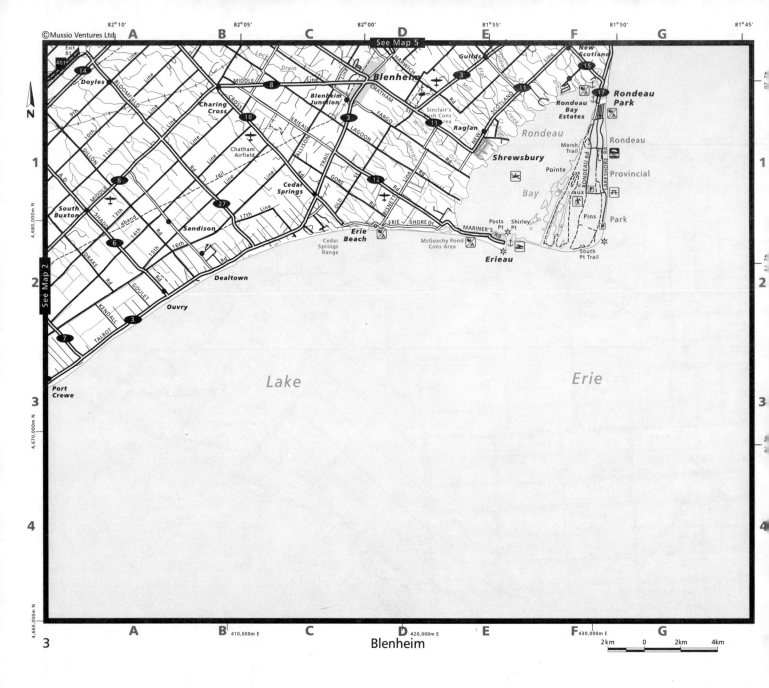

Rondeau Provincial Park was established in 1894 as Ontario's second provincial park and is one of the most popular destinations in Southwestern Ontario. In addition to one of the largest tracts of Carolinian forest in Ontario, the park protects a vast wetland area that is home to hundreds of birds and other wildlife. In the spring and fall, bird watchers are treated to an incredible display as thousands of migrating birds from around North America use the wetlands as a stopover on their long journeys.

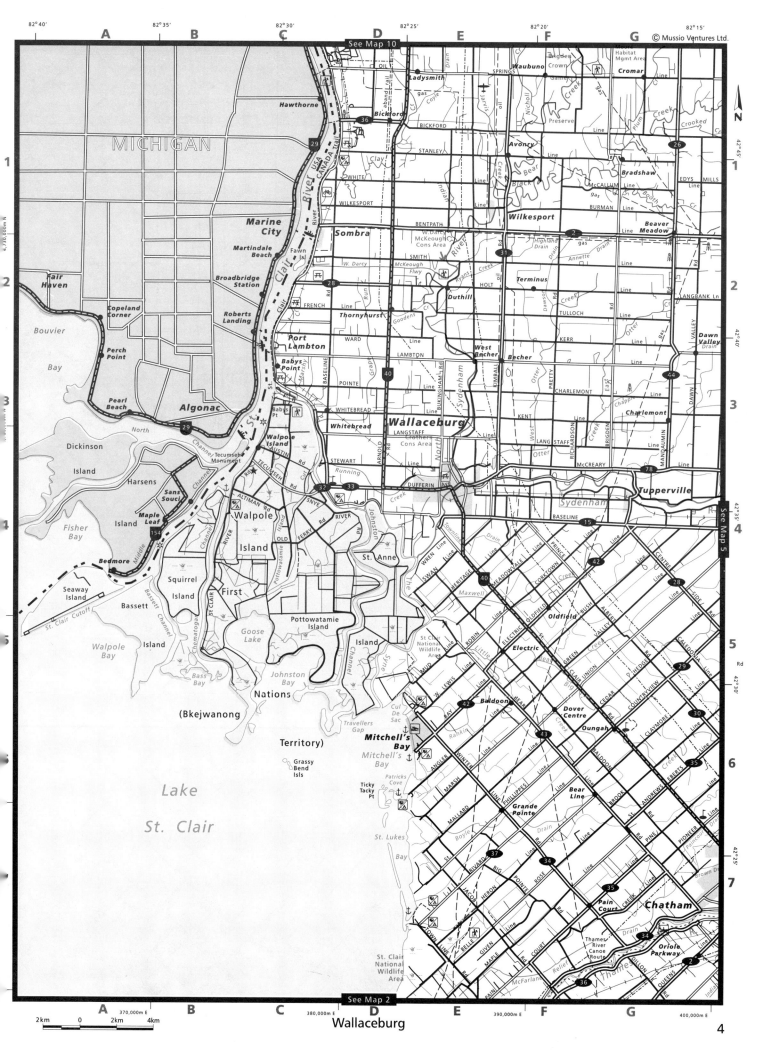

© Mussio Ventures Ltd.

Wallaceburg

4

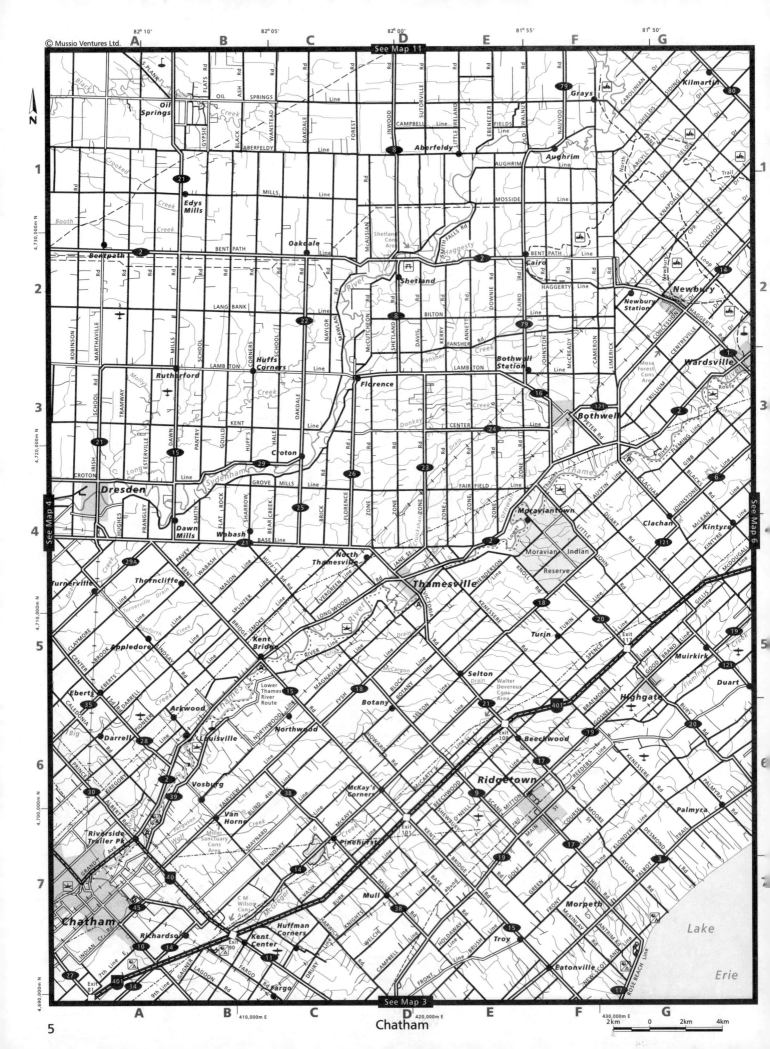

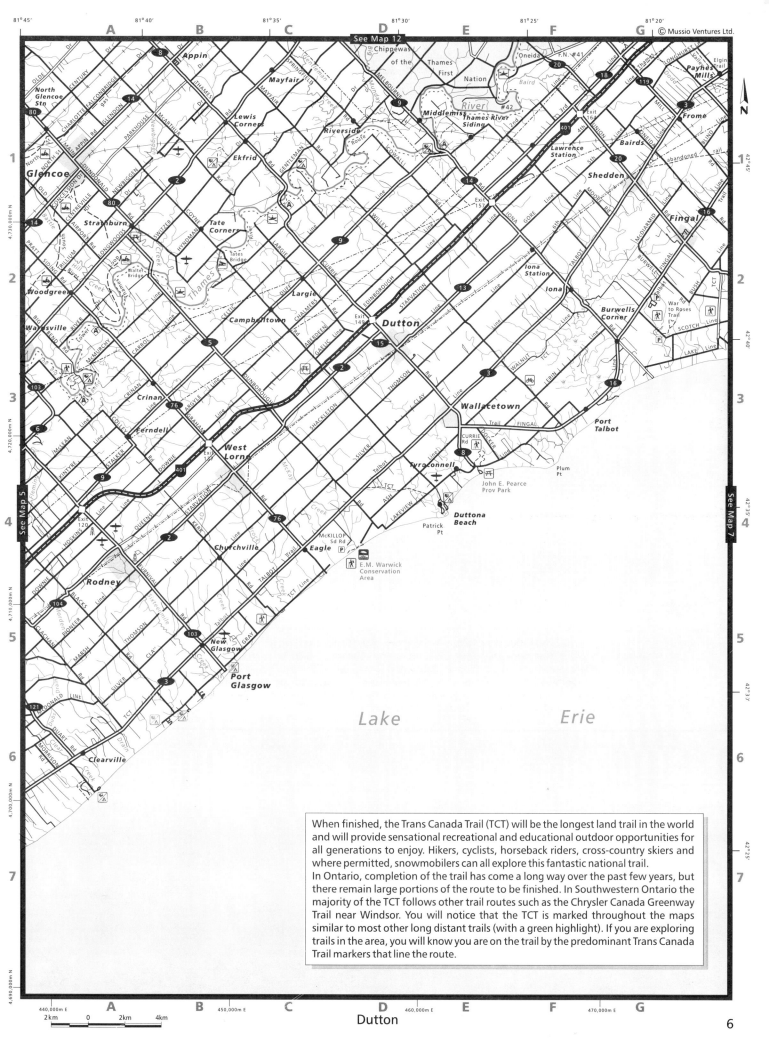

© Mussio Ventures Ltd.

81°45' 81°40' 81°35' 81°30' 81°25' 81°20'

A B C D E F G

Appin

Mayfair

North Glencoe Stn

Lewis Corners

Ekfrid

Riverside

Glencoe

Strathburn

Tate Corners

Tates Bridge

Woodgreen

Walters Bridge

Largie

Campbelltown

Largie

Crinan

Ferndell

West Lorne

Rodney

Churchville

Eagle

New Glasgow

Port Glasgow

Clearville

Middlemiss

Thames River Siding

Lawrence Station

Dutton

Wallacetown

Tyrconnell

Duttona Beach

Patrick Pt

Plum Pt

John E. Pearce Prov Park

E.M. Warwick Conservation Area

McKILLOP Sd Rd

Chippewas of the Thames First Nation #42

River

Baird

Oneida F.N. #41

Shedden

Bairds

Fingal

Frome

Paynes Mills

Iona Station

Iona

Burwells Corner

War to Roses Trail

Port Talbot

Lake   Erie

When finished, the Trans Canada Trail (TCT) will be the longest land trail in the world and will provide sensational recreational and educational outdoor opportunities for all generations to enjoy. Hikers, cyclists, horseback riders, cross-country skiers and where permitted, snowmobilers can all explore this fantastic national trail.

In Ontario, completion of the trail has come a long way over the past few years, but there remain large portions of the route to be finished. In Southwestern Ontario the majority of the TCT follows other trail routes such as the Chrysler Canada Greenway Trail near Windsor. You will notice that the TCT is marked throughout the maps similar to most other long distant trails (with a green highlight). If you are exploring trails in the area, you will know you are on the trail by the predominant Trans Canada Trail markers that line the route.

See Map 5

See Map 7

2km 0 2km 4km

440,000m E 450,000m E 460,000m E 470,000m E

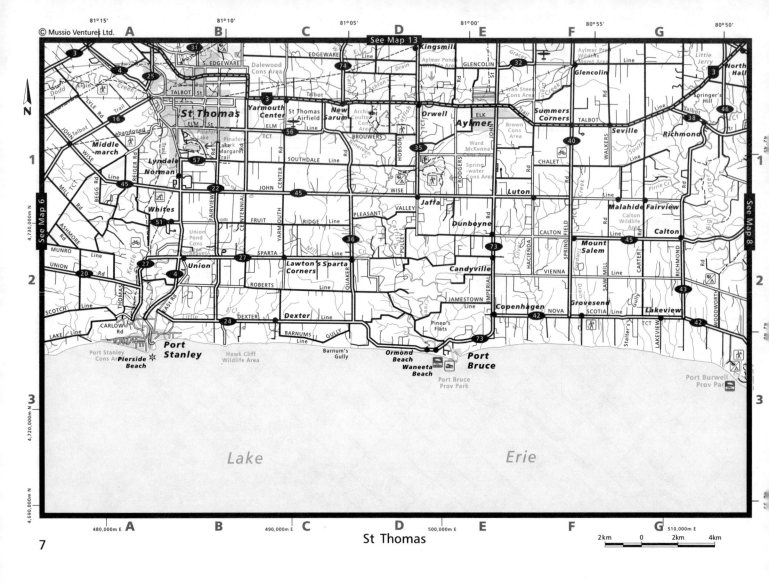

© Mussio Ventures Ltd.

81°15' 81°10' 81°05' 81°00' 80°55' 80°50'

A **B** **C** **D** **E** **F** **G**

See Map 6

See Map 8

Lake *Erie*

7

A **B** **C** **D** **E** **F** **G**

480,000m E 490,000m E 500,000m E 510,000m E

4,730,000m N
4,720,000m N
4,690,000m N

St Thomas

2km 0 2km 4km

In the early 1800's, the **Talbot Trail** was one of the first roads built in the region. The road was originally constructed from Fort Malden, which is now known as Amhurstburg, to St. Thomas. Today, the route continues further east following Highway 3 for most of its route. The trail was named after Colonel Thomas Talbot, who was instrumental in establishing this transportation link that helped create many of the settlements throughout the region.

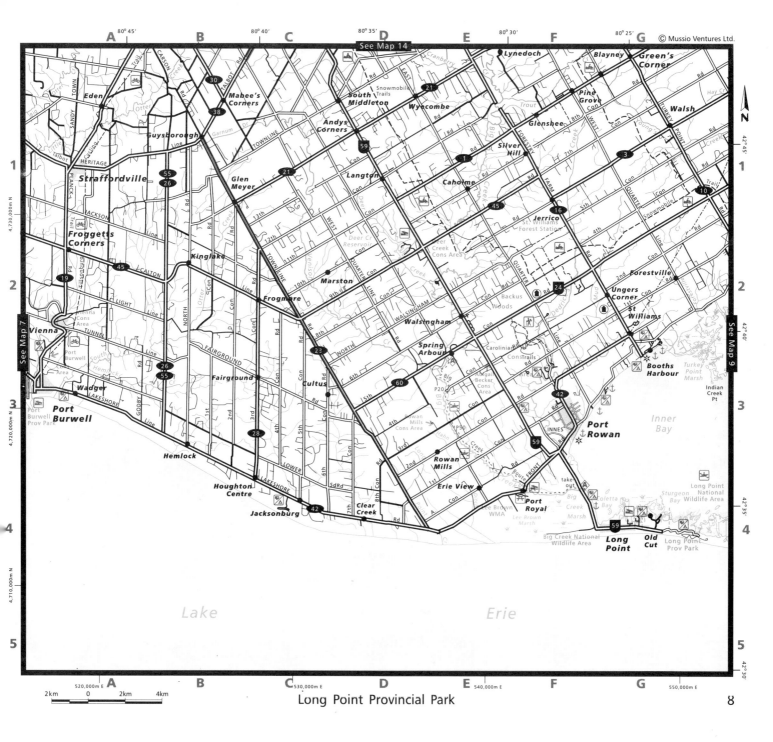

© Mussio Ventures Ltd.

Long Point Provincial Park provides access to the 40 kilometre (24.8 mile) long sandspit formation that juts out into Lake Erie. The sandspit is protected by the Long Point National Wildlife Area and is an important migratory birding area. During the spring and fall, the point is inundated with migratory birds that create an impressive display.

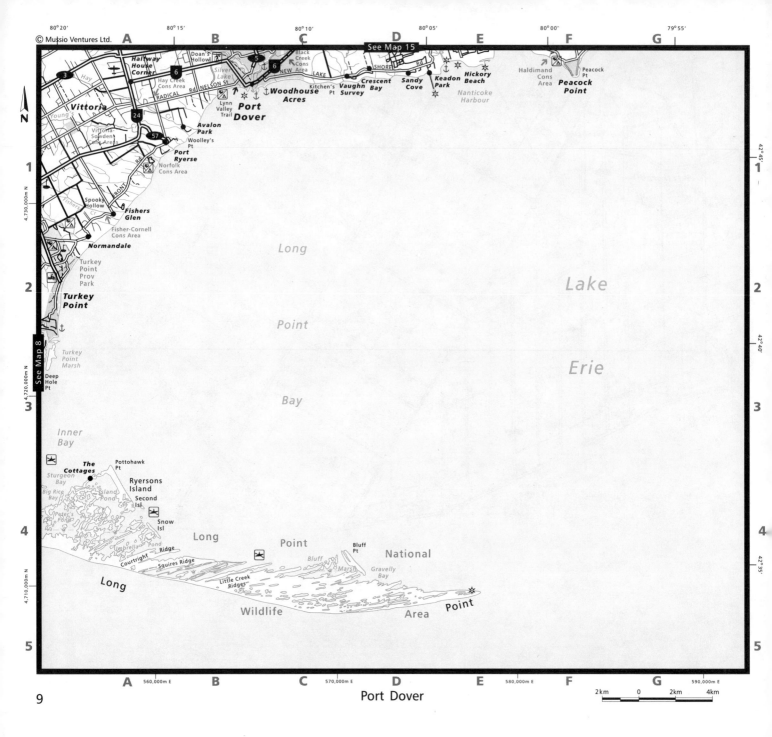

© Mussio Ventures Ltd.

80°20'   80°15'   80°10'   80°05'   80°00'   79°55'

A   **B**   **C**   **D**   **E**   **F**   **G**

Halfway
House
Corner

Doan's
Hollow

Hay Creek
Cons Area

Black
Creek
Cons
Area

See Map 15

Haldimand
Cons
Area

Peacock
Pt

Vittoria

RADICAL   Rd   NELSON St

Silver
Lake

NEW

LAKE

SHORE   Rd

Kitchen's
Pt

Vaughn
Survey

Crescent
Bay

Sandy
Cove

Keadon
Park

Hickory
Beach

Nanticoke
Harbour

**Peacock
Point**

Lynn
Valley
Trail

**Port
Dover**

**Woodhouse
Acres**

Vittoria-
Sowden
Cons Area

**Avalon
Park**

Woolley's
Pt

**Port
Ryerse**

Norfolk
Cons Area

1   **1**

42°45'

4,730,000m N

Spooky
Hollow

**Fishers
Glen**

Fisher-Cornell
Cons Area

Normandale

Turkey
Point
Prov
Park

Long

Lake

2   **2**

42°40'

**Turkey
Point**

Turkey
Point
Marsh

Point

Erie

See Map 8

4,720,000m N

Deep
Hole
Pt

Bay

3   **3**

42°40'

**Inner
Bay**

**The
Cottages**

Pottohawk
Pt

Sturgeon
Bay

**Ryersons
Island**

Island
Pond

Big Rice
Bay

**Second
Isl**

Peter's
Pond

Snow
Isl

Long

Point

Bluff
Pt

National

4   **4**

42°35'

4,710,000m N

Umbrella
Pond

Courtright   Ridge

Squires Ridge

Little Creek
Ridges

Bluff
Marsh

Gravelly
Bay

Long

Wildlife

Area   **Point**

5   **5**

A   560,000m E   **B**   **C**   570,000m E   **D**   **E**   580,000m E   **F**   **G**   590,000m E

Port Dover

2km   0   2km   4km

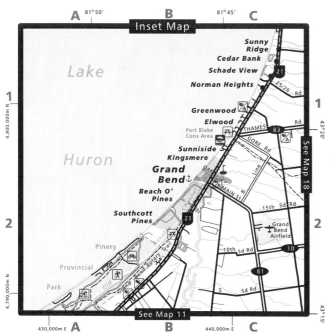

See Map 18

Inset Map

Lake
Huron

Sunny Ridge
Cedar Bank
Schade View
Norman Heights

Greenwood
Elwood

Port Blake Cons Area

Sunniside
Kingsmere

Grand Bend

Beach O' Pines

Southcott Pines

Pinery

Provincial

Park

Grand Bend Airfield

See Map 11

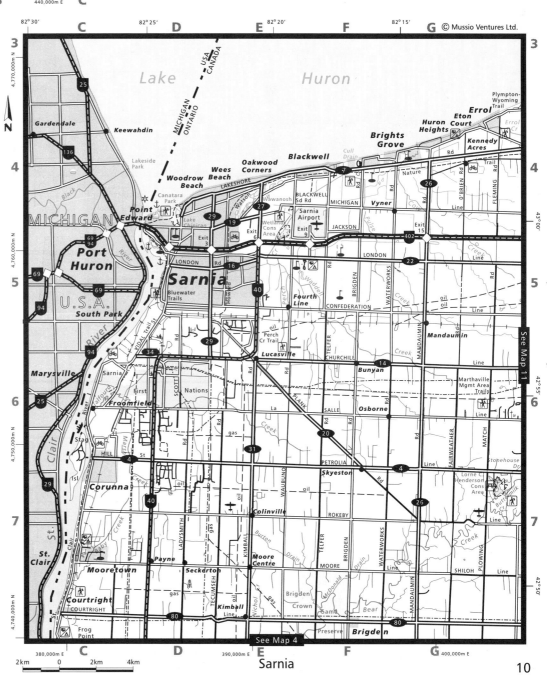

© Mussio Ventures Ltd.

Lake   Huron

Plympton-Wyoming Trail

Gardendale
Keewahdin

Errol

Eton Court

Huron Heights

Brights Grove

Kennedy Acres

Lakeside Park

Woodrow Beach
Wees Beach

Oakwood Corners

Blackwell

Cull Drain

Nature

MICHIGAN

Point Edward

Canatara Park

Lake Chipican

LAKESHORE

Wawanosh

BLACKWELL Sd Rd

MICHIGAN

Vyner

Sarnia Airport

Port Huron

U.S.A.

South Park

Sarnia

Bluewater Trails

LONDON

Exit 3

Exit 6

Wetland Cons Area

Exit 9

JACKSON

Exit 15

402

LONDON

Fourth Line

CONFEDERATION

BRIGDEN

WATERWORKS

Marysville

Sarnia

First

Nations

SCOTT

Lucasville

CHURCHILL

TELFER

Mandaumin

Bunyan

Marthaville Mgmt Area Trails

Froomfield

Stag Isl

HILL

Osborne

Skyeston

PLANK

La SALLE

PETROLIA

ROKEBY

WATERWORKS

FAIRWEATHER

MATCH

Stonehouse Dr

Lorne C Henderson Cons Area

Corunna

Colinville

WAUBUNO

Payne

Seckerton

Moore Centre

KIMBALL

LADYSMITH

TECUMSEH

MOORE

TELFER

BRIGDEN

Brigden Crown

Nichol

McDonald Drain

Bear

MANDAUMIN

SHILOH

PLOWING

St. Clair

Mooretown

Courtright

COURTRIGHT

Frog Point

Kimball

Brigden

Preserve

See Map 4

2km 0 2km 4km

Sarnia

See Map 11

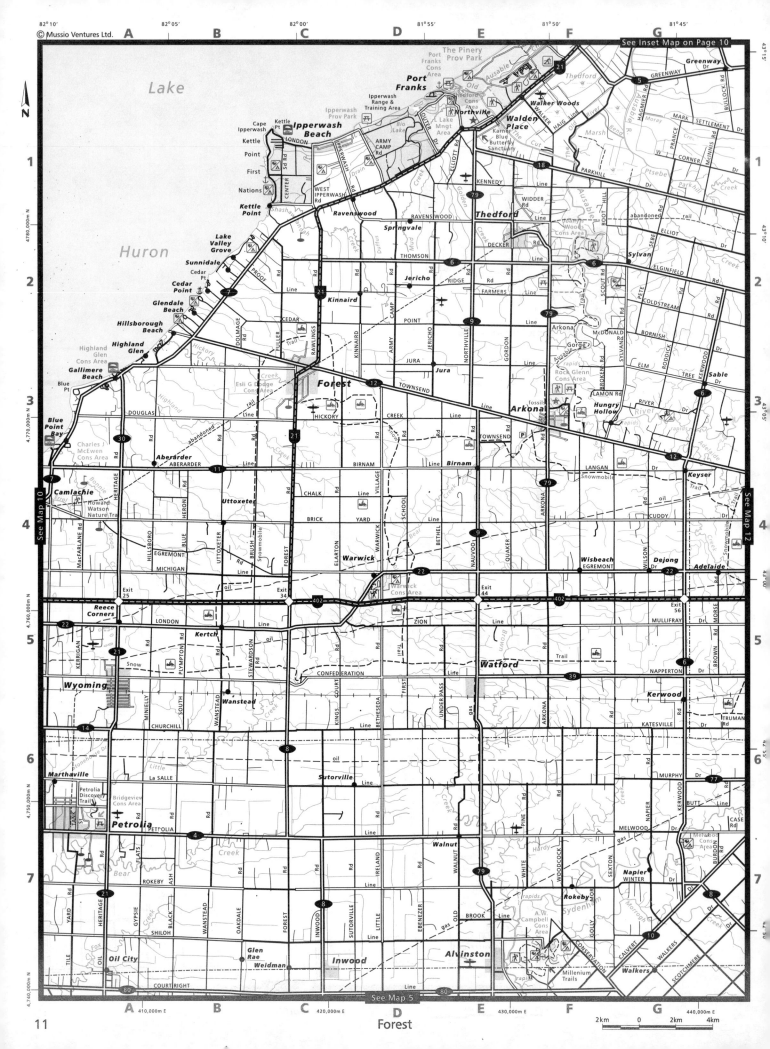

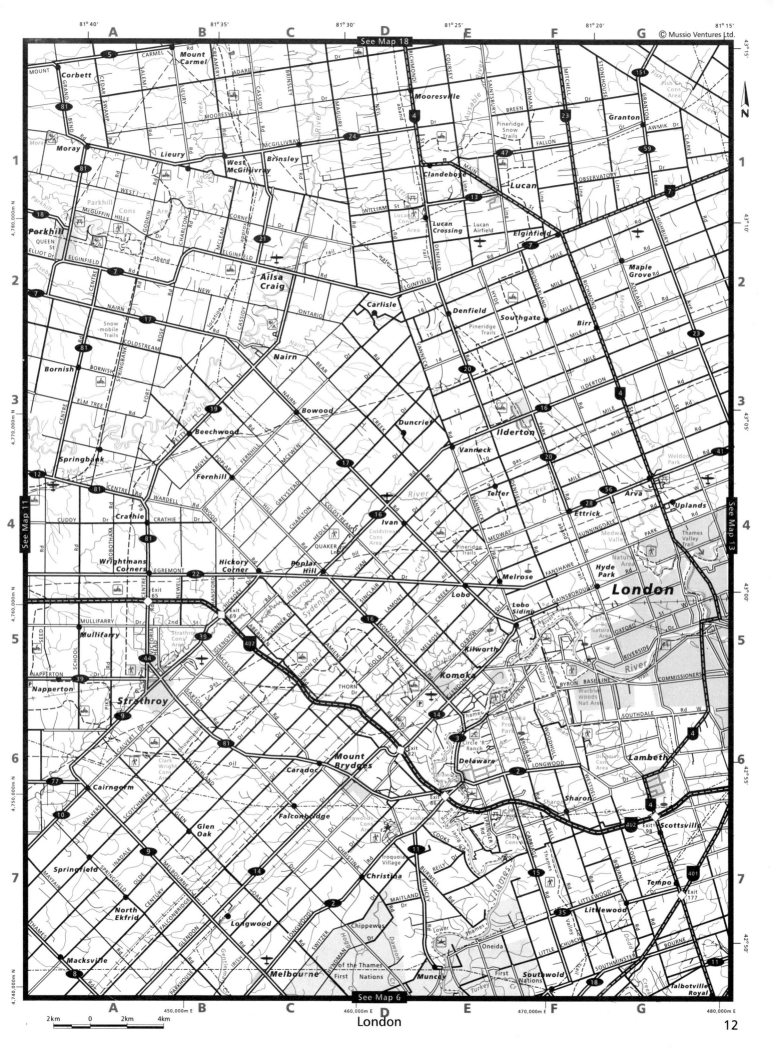

© Mussio Ventures Ltd.

London

12

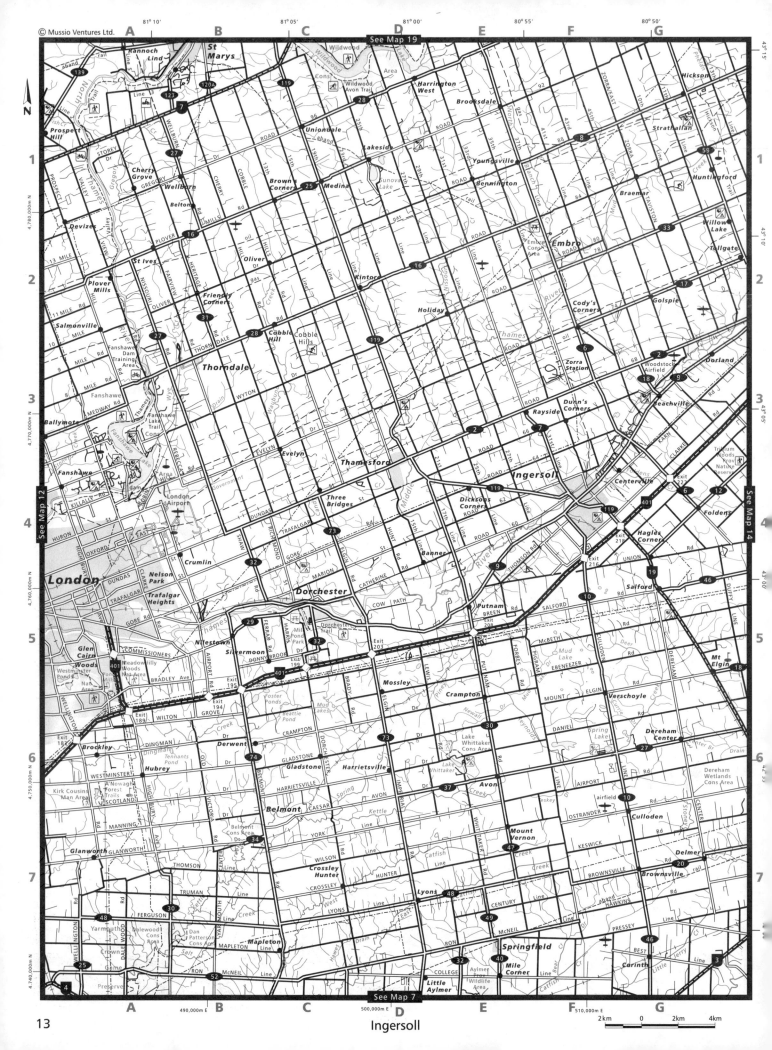

© Mussio Ventures Ltd.

See Map 19

See Map 12

See Map 14

See Map 7

Ingersoll

2km   0   2km   4km

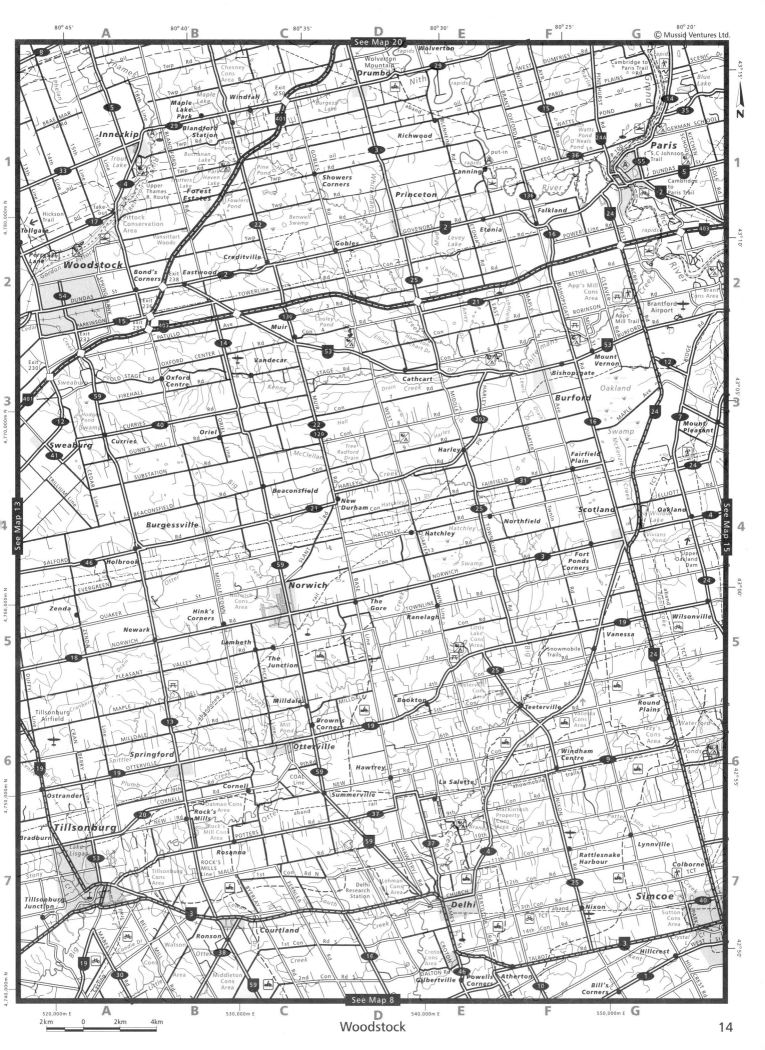

© Mussio Ventures Ltd.

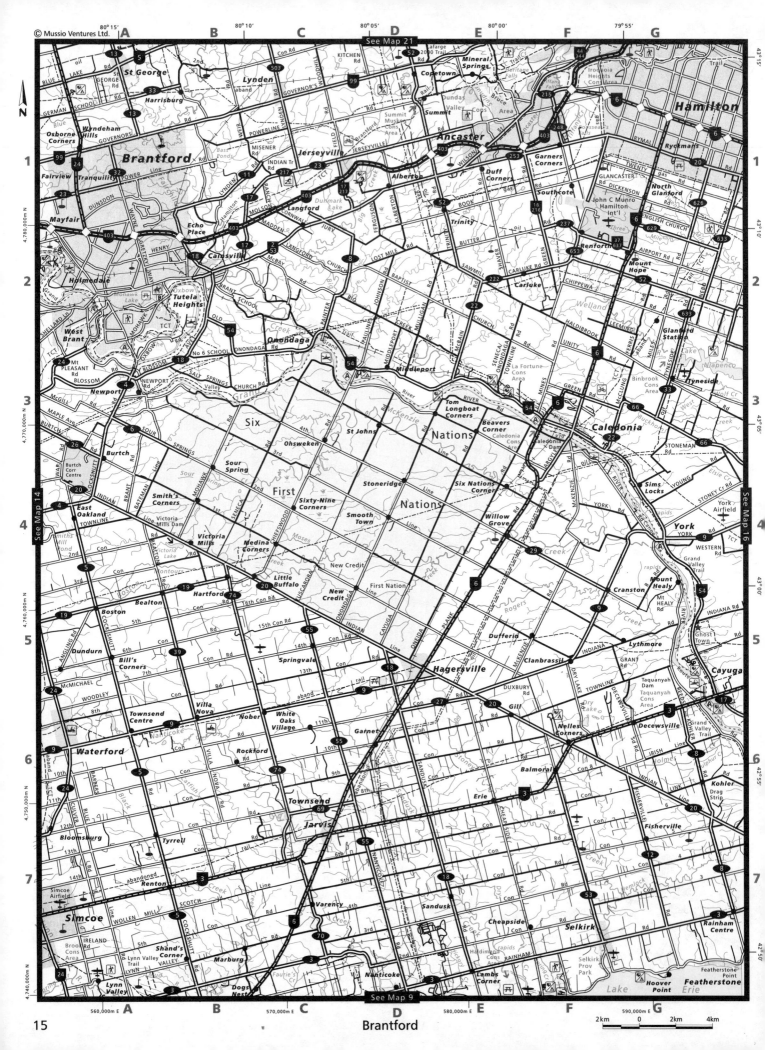

© Mussio Ventures Ltd.

See Map 14

See Map 16

See Map 9

Brantford

2km 0 2km 4km

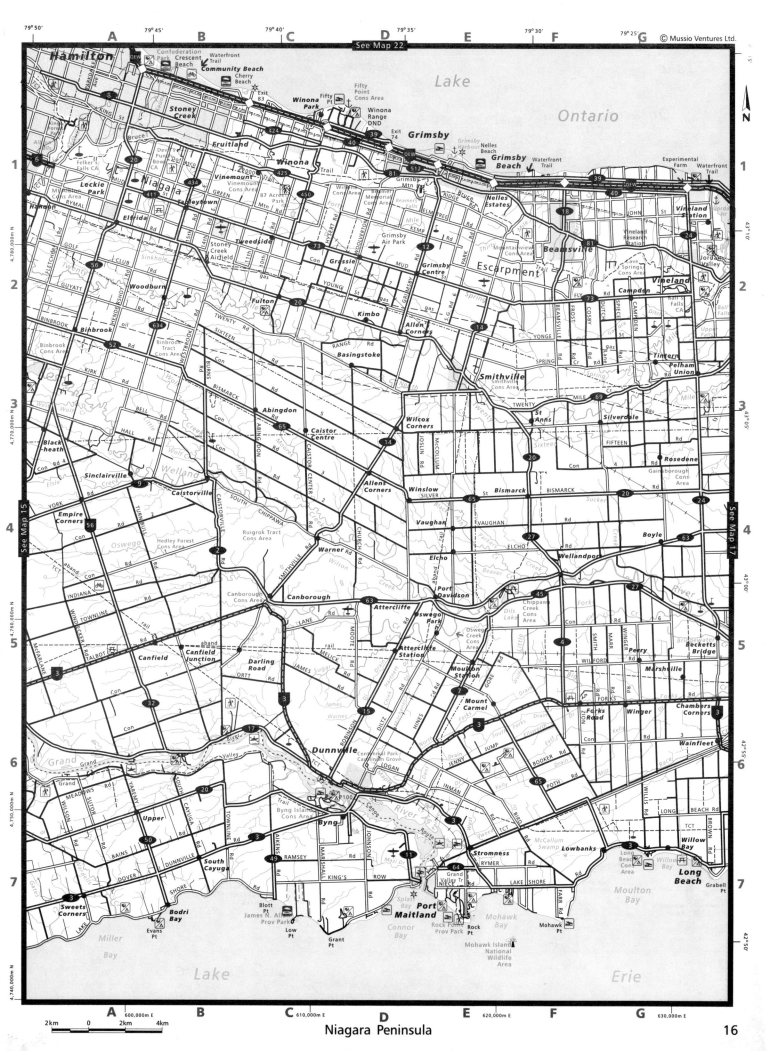

Niagara Peninsula

16

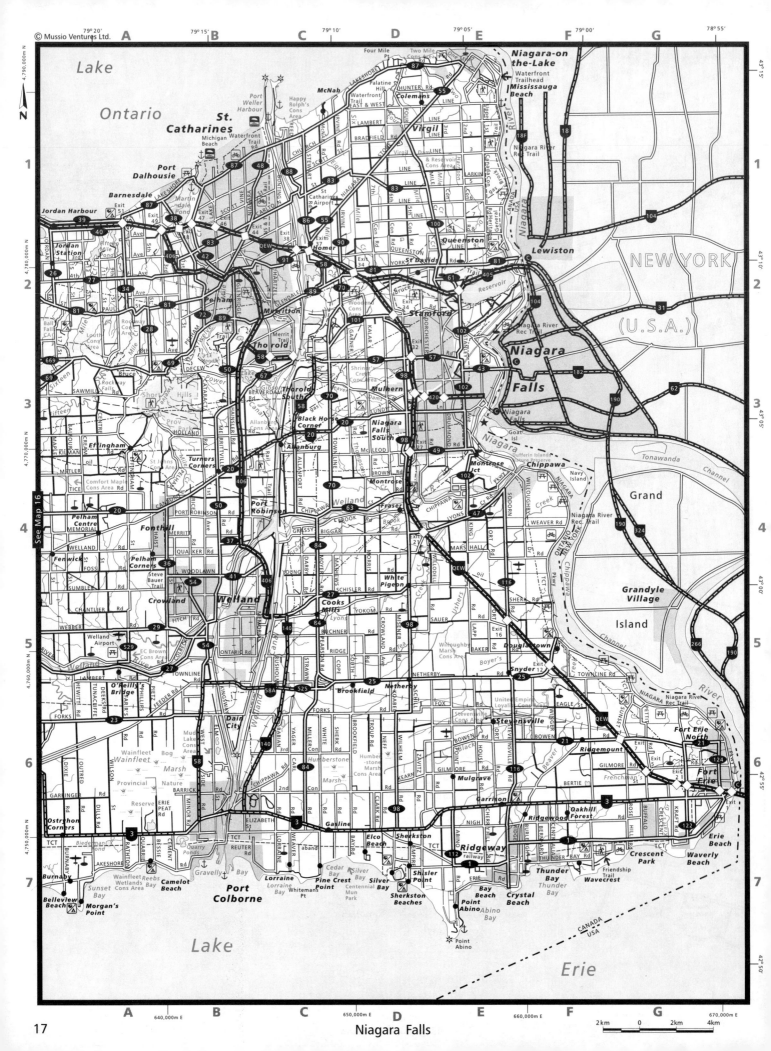

Niagara Falls

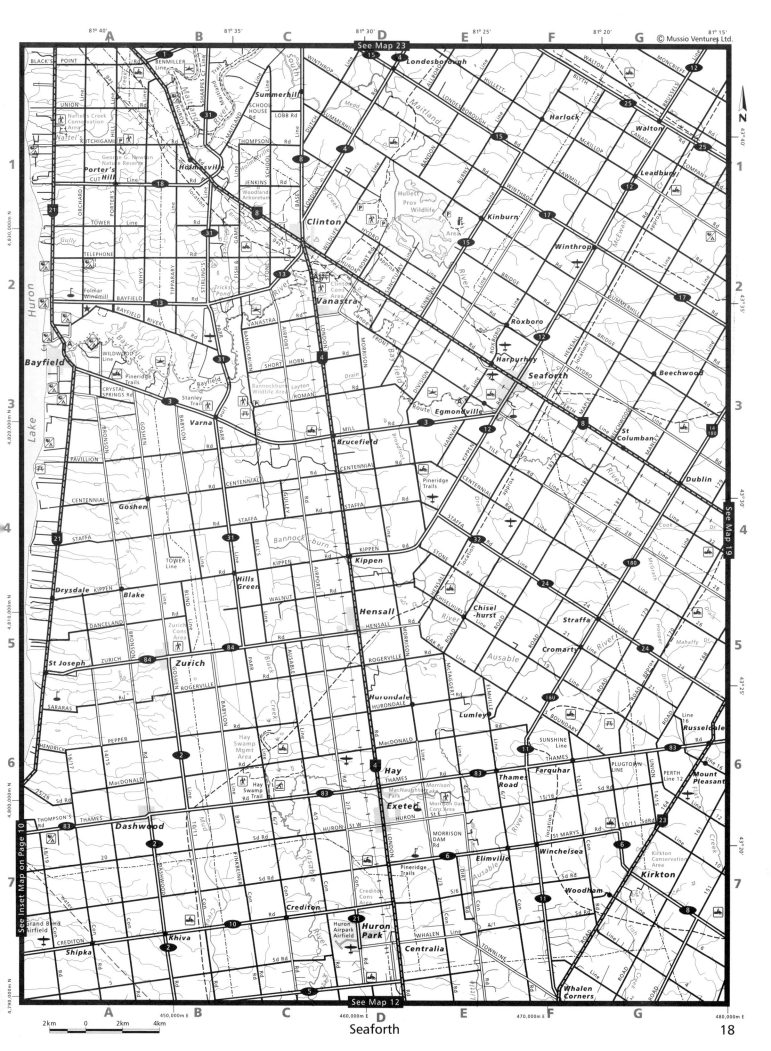

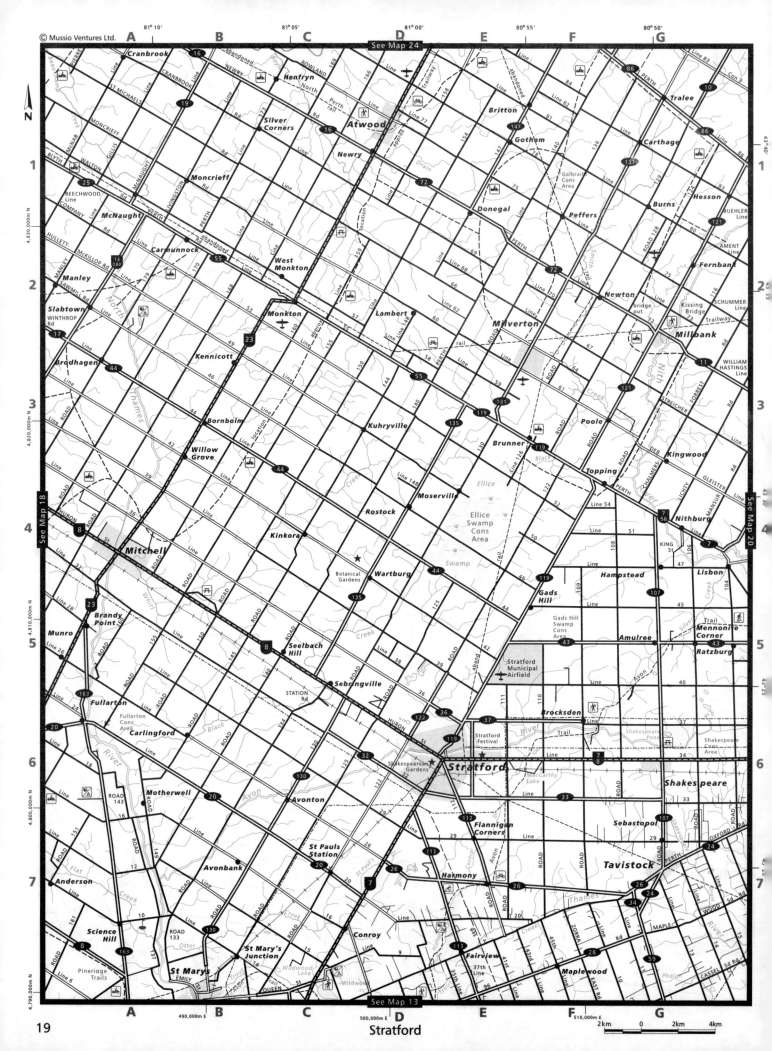

© Mussio Ventures Ltd.

Stratford

See Map 18
See Map 20
See Map 13

2km 0 2km 4km

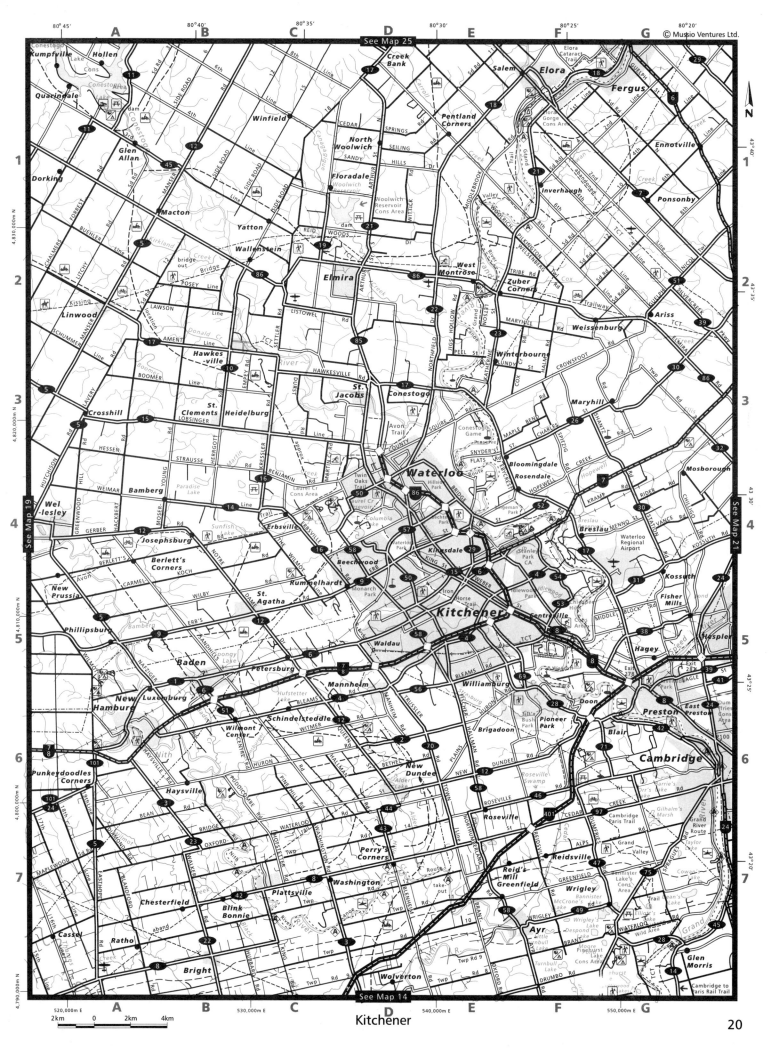

© Mussio Ventures Ltd.

Kitchener

20

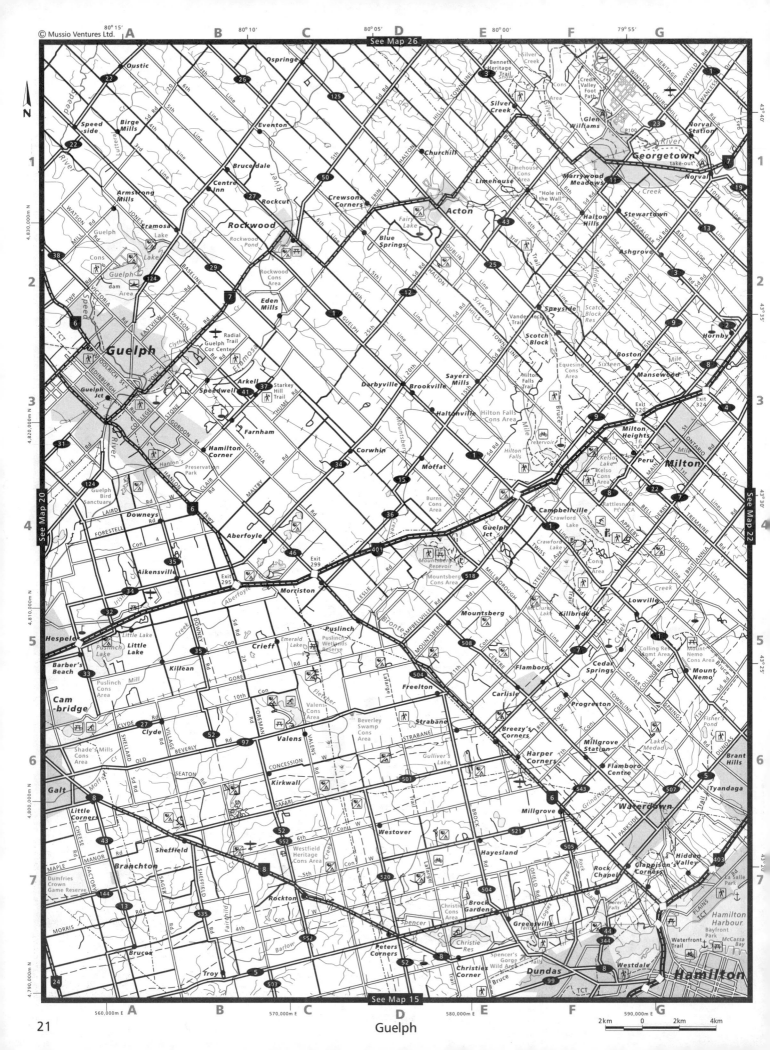

Guelph

© Mussio Ventures Ltd.

Brampton

North York

Mount Pleasant

Northwood Park

Peel Village

Mount Charles

York

Del Ray

Forest Hill

Moore Park

Amber Heights

Springbrook

Huttonville

Devry West

Hanlant

Lester B. Pearson International Airport

Eringate

Thorncrest Village

Silverhorne

Oakwood

The Annex

Yorkville

Churchville

Meadowvale Village

Brittania

Burnhamthorpe

Humber Valley

High Park

The Kingsway

Parkdale

Toronto

Whaley's Corners

Meadowvale Station

Meadowvale South

River View

Streetville

Alderwood

Mimico

Etobicoke

New Toronto

Long Branch

Sunnyside Beach

Humber Bay Park

Toronto City Center Airport

Toronto Island Park

Toronto Islands

Mugg's Isl

Long Pond

Agerton

Hornby Station

Drumquin

Snider

Sherican Homelands

Park Royal

Dixie

Mississauga

Cooksville

Mississauga Valley

Cooksville

Lorne Park

Port Credit

Lakeview

JC Saddington Park

Marie Curtis Park

Lake Ontario

Omagh

Boyne

Trafalgar

Clearview

Birchwood

Clarkson

Jack Darling Memorial Park

Rattray Marsh Cons Area

refinery

Lake Ontario

Glenorchy

Falcorwood

Horton Heights

Charnwood

Castle Green

Clearview

Lakeside Park

Ennisclare Park

Oakville Heritage Trails

Ash

Sunningdale

Oakville Harbour

Oakville

Palermo

Zimmerman

Bronte Creek Prov Park

Tansley

Orchard

Sheldon

Bronte

Bronte Harbour

Oakville Heritage Trails

Palmer

Appleby

Clarksdale

Dynes

Shoreacres

Port Nelson

Burlington

North York

Bennington Heights

Moore Park

Parkview Hill

Oakridge

Birchmount Park

Cliffside

Bluffer's Park

Scarborough Bluffs

Woodbine Heights

Birch Cliff

Riverdale

Don Vale

The Beaches

Balmy Beach

Waterfront Trail Ashbridge's Bay Park

Lake Ontario

Maple

Burlington Beach Beachway Park

Toronto Harbour

Mugg's Isl

Terry Gap

Outer Harbour

Aquatic Park

Burlington Beach Hamilton Harbour

Toronto Island Park

Toronto Islands

Hamilton

Hamilton Beach

Waterfront Trail

Mississauga

See Map 27
See Map 28
See Map 16
See Map 21
See Map 22
See Inset below

2km 0 2km 4km

22

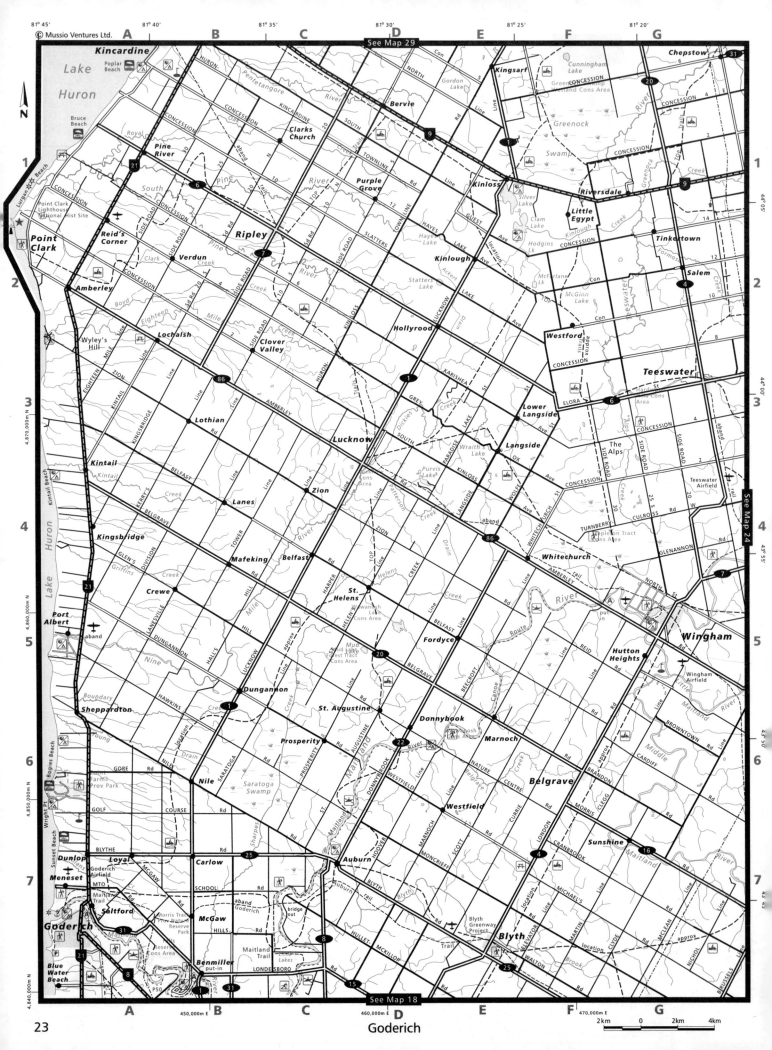

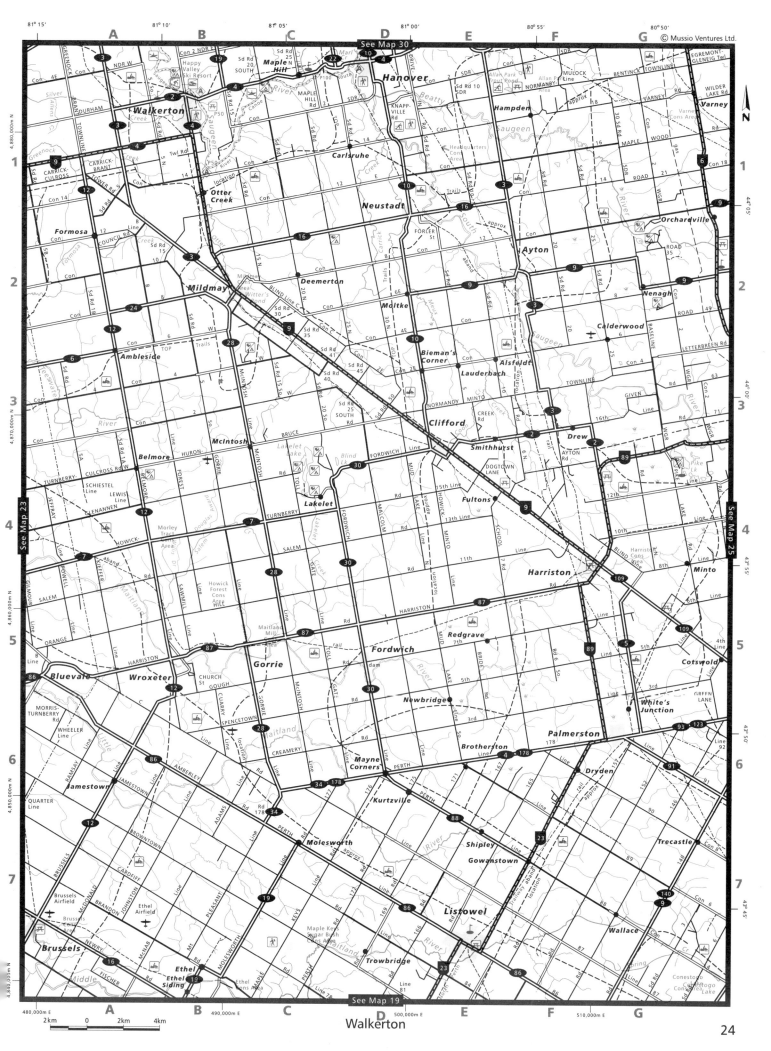

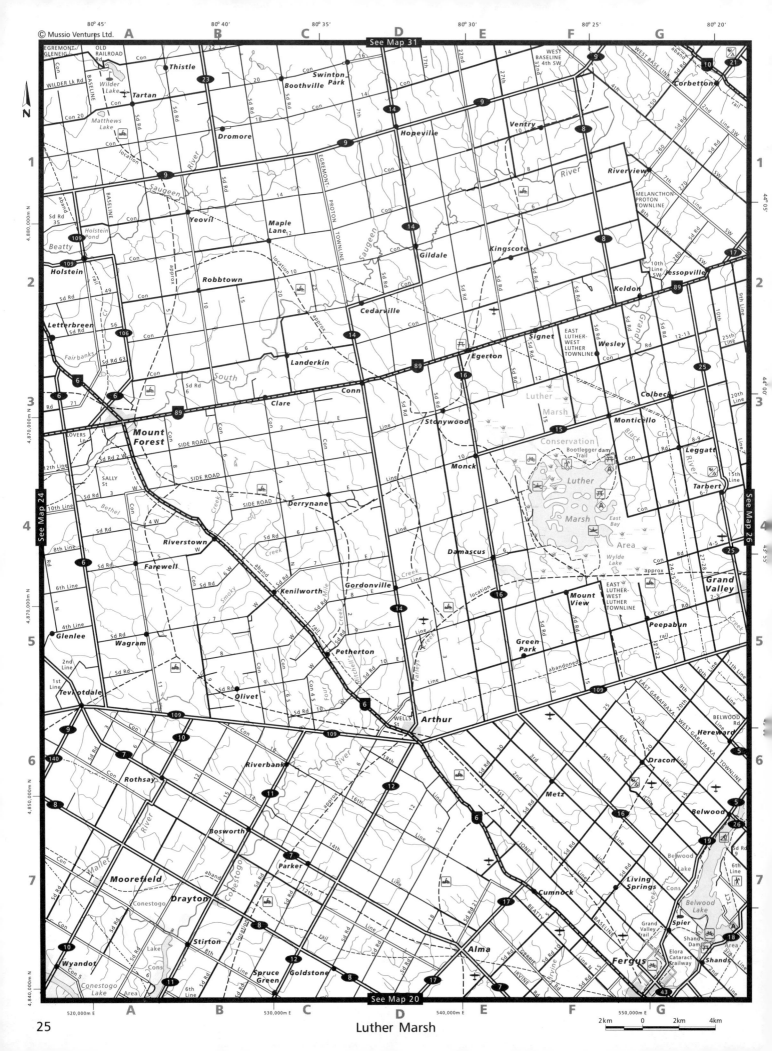

© Mussio Ventures Ltd.

See Map 31

See Map 24

See Map 26

25

Luther Marsh

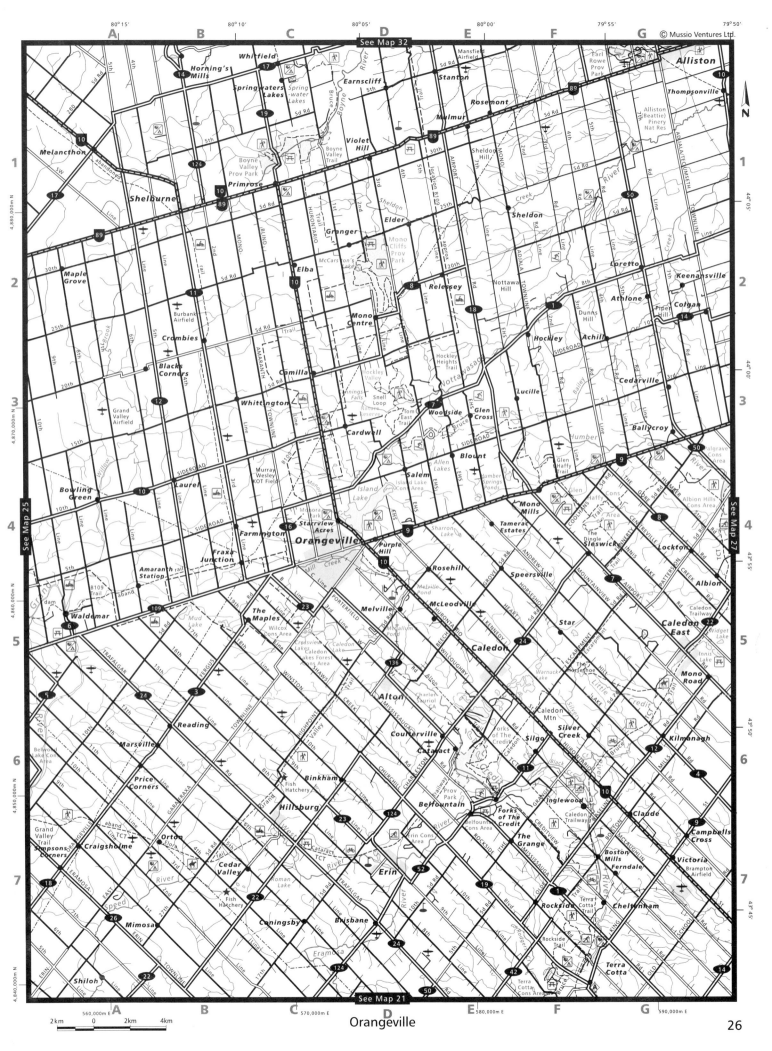

© Mussio Ventures Ltd.

See Map 25

See Map 27

2km 0 2km 4km

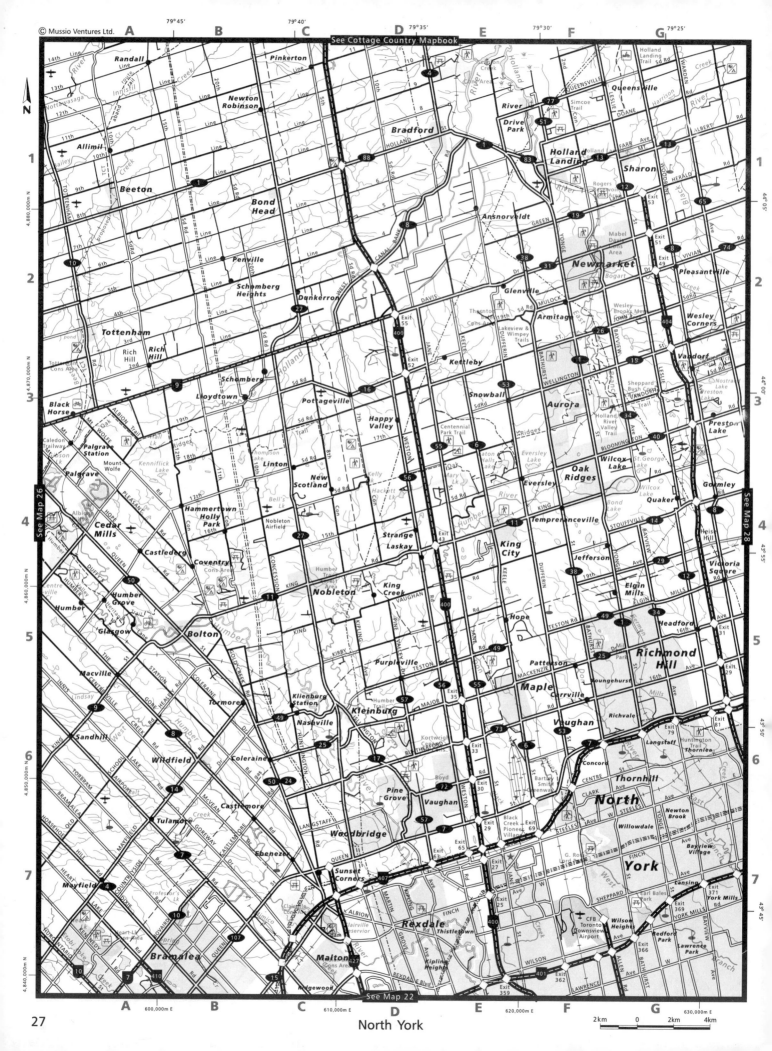

© Mussio Ventures Ltd.

27

North York

2km 0 2km 4km

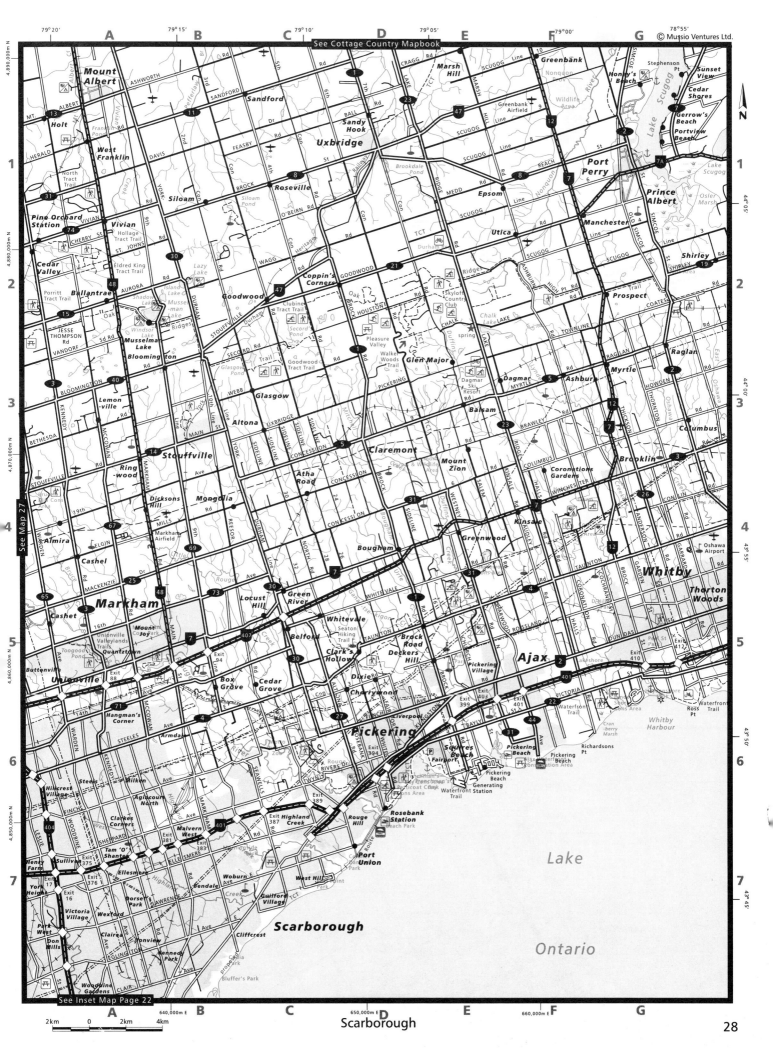

© Mussio Ventures Ltd.

N

2km 0 2km 4km

See Inset Map Page 22

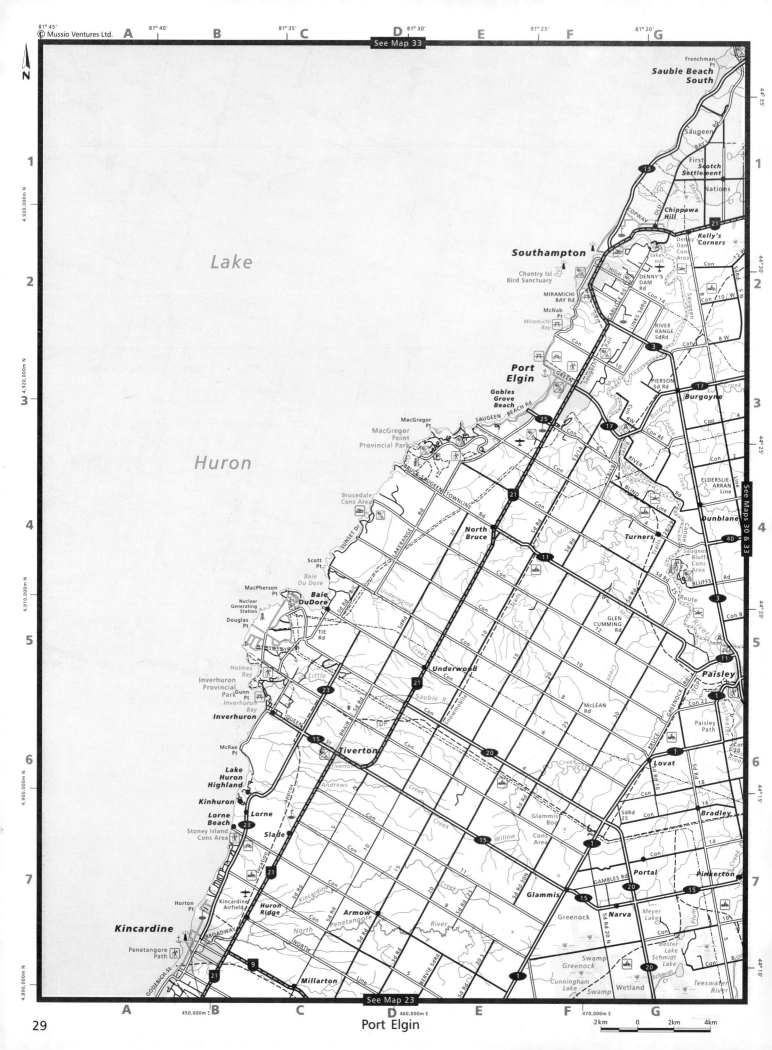

© Mussio Ventures Ltd.

Lake

Huron

Southampton

Chantry Isl
Bird Sanctuary

**Port
Elgin**

Gobles
Grove Beach

MacGregor
Pt

MacGregor
Point
Provincial Park

Brucedale
Cons Area

Scott
Pt

Baie
Du Dore

MacPherson
Pt

**Baie
DuDore**

Nuclear
Generating
Station

Douglas Pt

TIE
Rd

Holmes
Bay

Inverhuron
Provincial
Park

Gunn
Pt

Inverhuron
Bay

Inverhuron

McRae
Pt

Tiverton

**Lake
Huron
Highland**

Kinhuron

**Lorne
Beach**

Lorne

Slade

Stoney Island
Cons Area

Horton
Pt

Kincardine
Airfield

**Huron
Ridge**

Kincardine

Penetangore
Path

BROADWAY

GODERICH ST.

Sauble Beach
South

Frenchman
Pt

Saugeen

BAY

First
Settlement

Scotch
Settlement

Nations

Chippawa
Hill

Kelly's
Corners

DENNY'S
DAM
Rd

Denny
Dam
Area

RIVER RANGE
SdRd

PIERSON
Sd Rd

Burgoyne

ELDERSLIE-
ARRAN
Line

Dunblane

Saugeen
Bluffs
Cons
Area

BLUFFS

**North
Bruce**

Turners

GLEN
CUMMING
Rd

Paisley

Paisley
Path

Underwood

McLEAN
Rd

Lovat

Glammis Bog
Cons
Area

Bradley

Portal

Pinkerton

Glammis

GAMBLES Rd

Narva

Greenock

Meyer
Lake

Bester
Lake

Schmidt
Lake

Swamp
Greenock

Cunningham
Lake

Swamp

Wetland

Teeswater
River

Armow

Millarton

Penetangore
River

North

29

Port Elgin

See Map 33

See Map 23

See Maps 30 & 33

2km 0 2km 4km

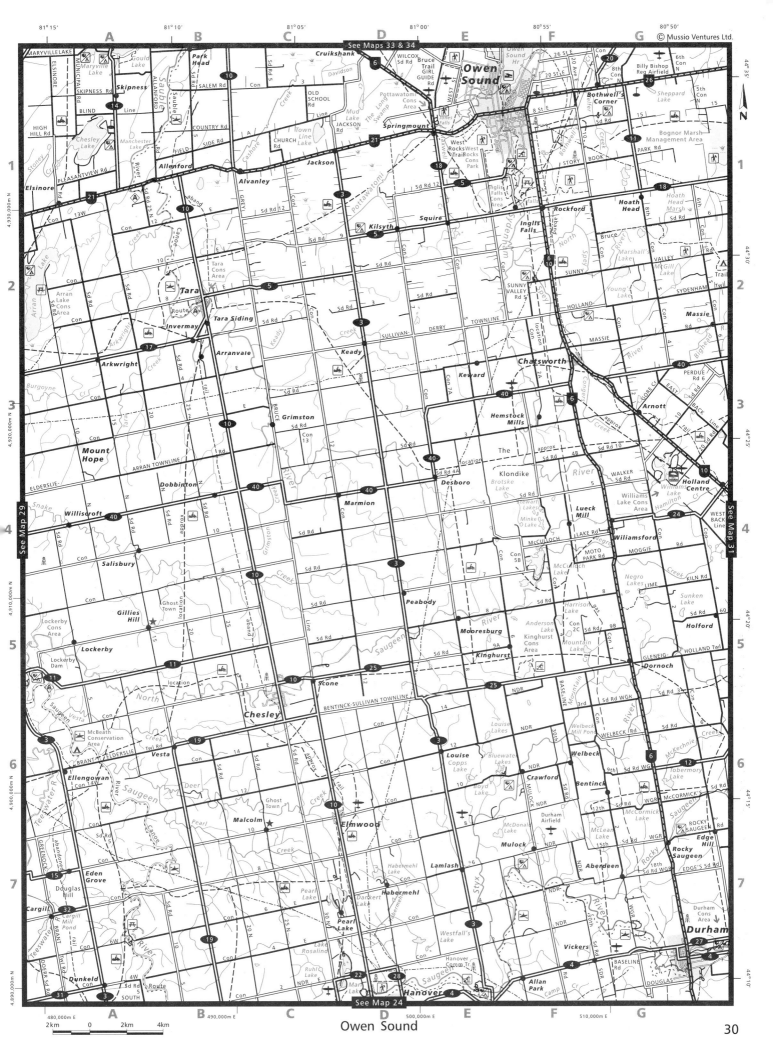

© Mussio Ventures Ltd.

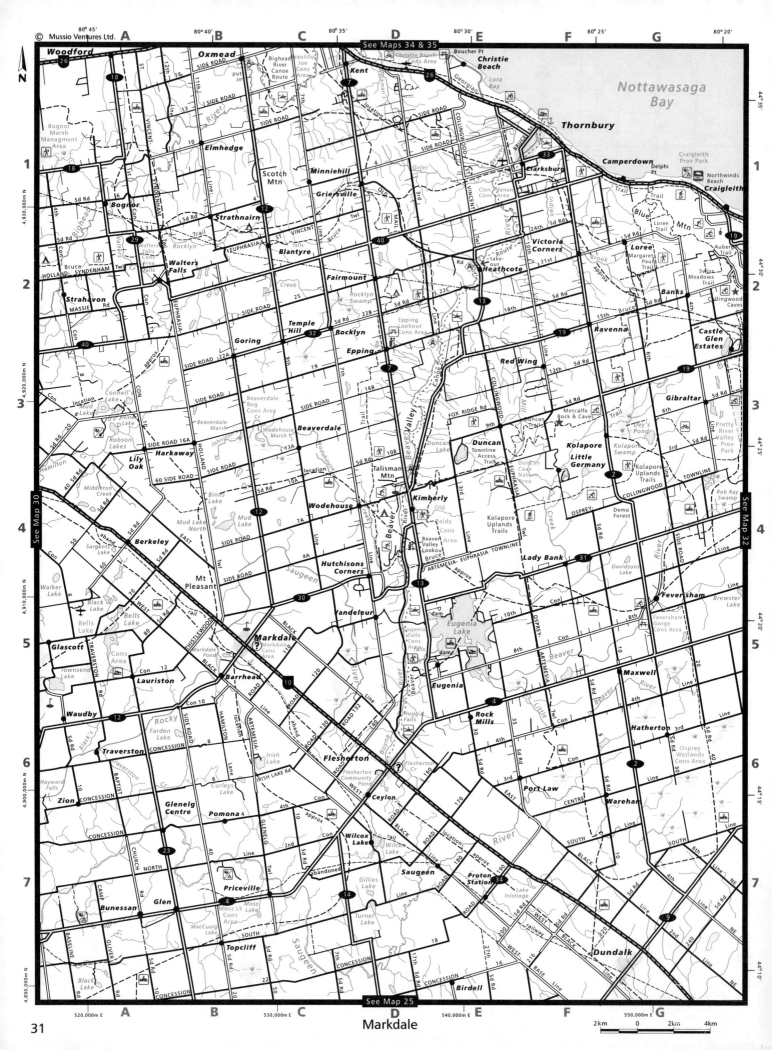

© Mussio Ventures Ltd.

Nottawasaga Bay

See Map 30

See Map 32

Markdale

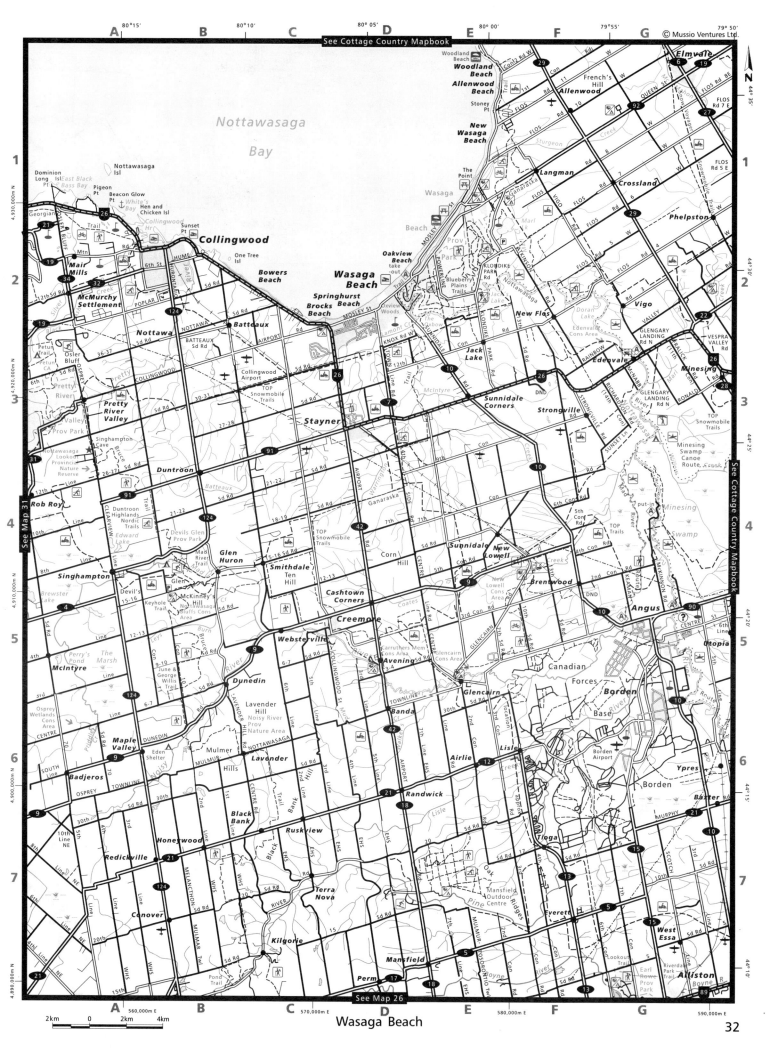

© Mussio Ventures Ltd.

Nottawasaga
Bay

Woodland
Beach
Allenwood
Beach

French's
Hill
Allenwood

Elmvale

New
Wasaga
Beach

The Point

Langman

Crossland

Phelpston

Dominion
Long Isl East Black
Pt Bass Bay
Pigeon Pt
Beacon Glow
White's Hen and
Bay Chicken Isl
Sunset Pt

Collingwood

Mair
Mills

McMurchy
Settlement

One Tree
Isl

Bowers
Beach

Wasaga
Beach

Oakview
Beach
take-out

Springhurst
Brocks Beach
Beach

Oxview
Woods

Klondike
Park

Bluebird
Plains Trails

Jack
Lake

Vigo

Glengary
Landing

New Flos

Edenvale

Vespra
Valley
Rd

Minesing

Nottawa

Osler Bluff
CA

Petun
Trail

Pretty
River
Valley
Prov Park

Batteaux

Collingwood
Airport

Stayner

Sunnidale
Corners

Strongville

Minesing
Swamp Canoe
Route

Nottawasaga
Lookout
Provincial
Nature Reserve

Singhampton
Cave

Duntroon

TOP
Snowmobile
Trails

TOP
Snowmobile
Trails

Rob Roy

Duntroon
Highlands
Nordic Trails

Devils Glen
Prov Park

Glen
Huron

Smithdale
Ten Hill

Corn
Hill

Sunnidale
New
Lowell

New
Lowell
Cons Area

Brentwood

Minesing
Swamp

Singhampton

Devil's

Glen

McKinney's
Hill
Nottawasaga
Bluffs Cons
Area

Cashtown
Corners

Angus

Utopia

McIntyre

Perry's
Pond

The
Marsh

Websterville

Creemore

Avening

Glencairn

Carruthers Mem
Cons Area

Glencairn
Cons Area

Canadian

Forces

Maple
Valley

Dunedin

June &
George
Willis Trail

Lavender
Hill
Noisy River
Prov
Nature Area

Banda

Glencairn

Borden

Base

Badjeros

Osprey
Wetlands
Cons Area
CENTRE

Eden
Shelter

Mulmer
Hills

Lavender

Airlie

Lisle

Borden
Airport

Ypres

Borden

Black
Bank

Randwick

Baxter

Honeywood

Ruskview

Tioga

Redickville

Terra
Nova

Mansfield
Outdoor
Centre

Oak

Everett

West
Essa

Conover

Kilgorie

Mansfield
Pine
Ridges

Earl
Rowe
Prov Park

Alliston

Perm

2km 0 2km 4km

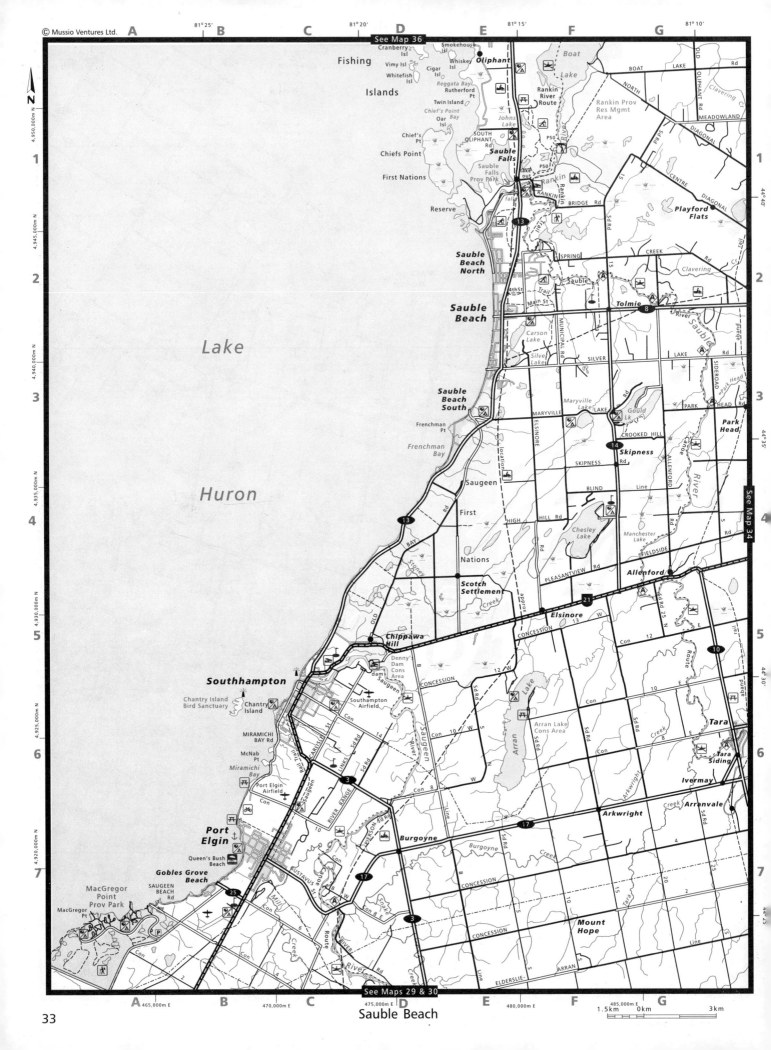

© Mussio Ventures Ltd.

33

Sauble Beach

See Map 36
See Map 34
See Maps 29 & 30

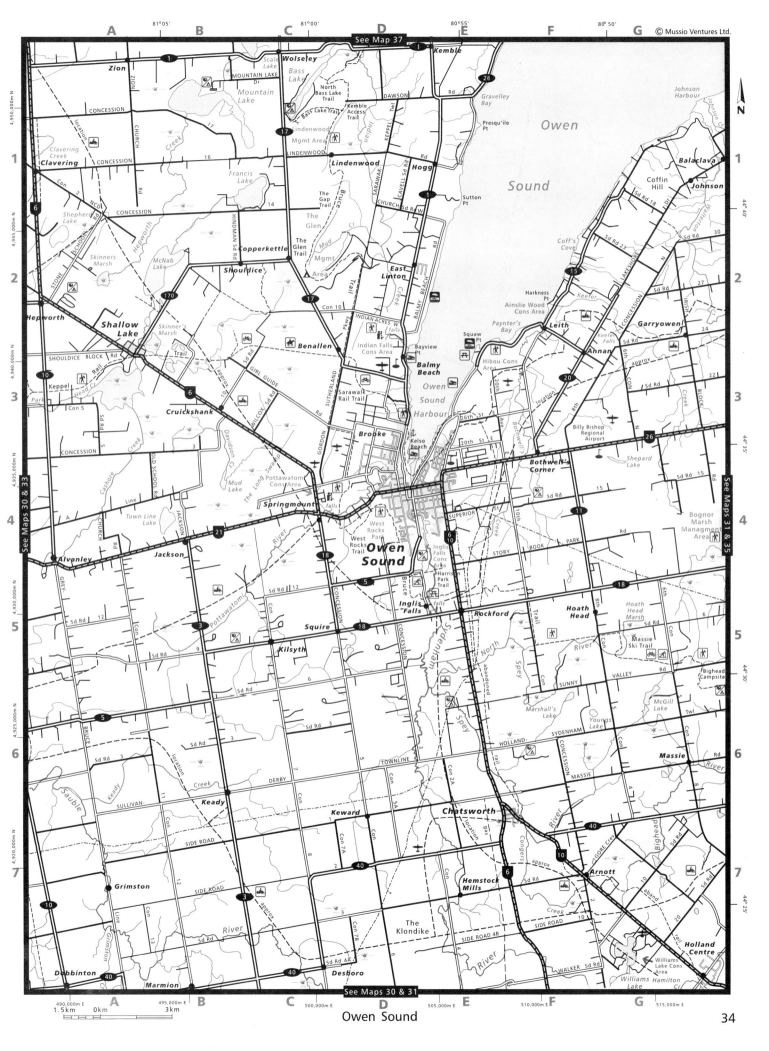

© Mussio Ventures Ltd.

Owen Sound

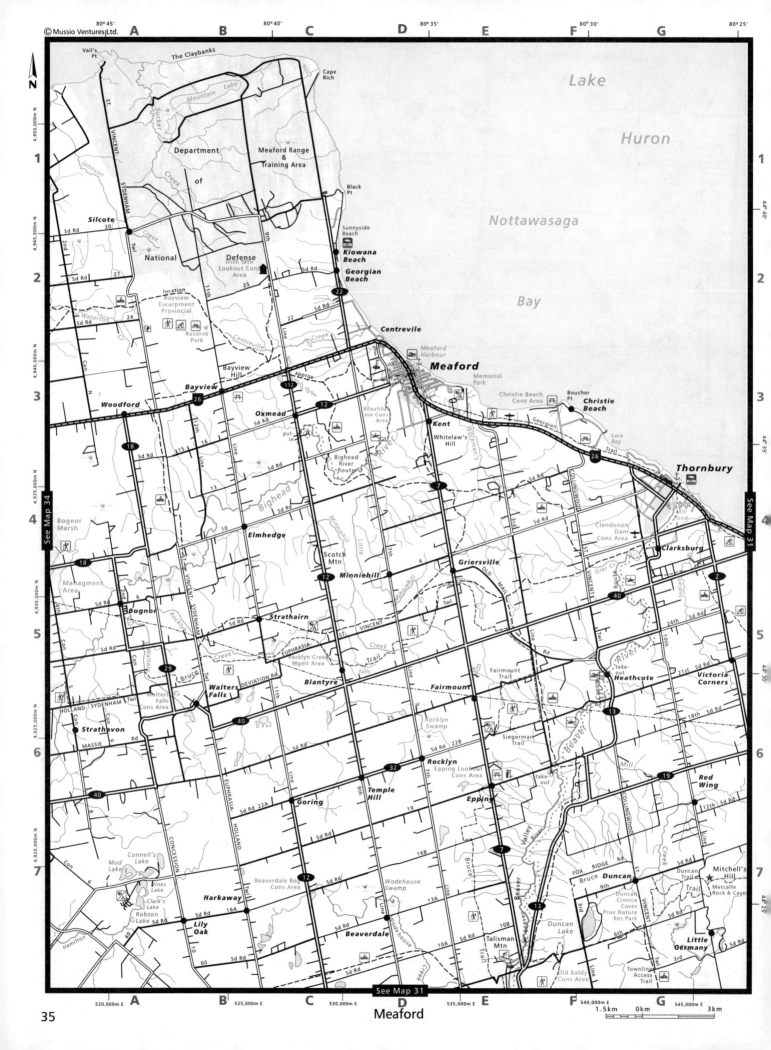

© Mussio Ventures Ltd.

Lake

Huron

Nottawasaga

Bay

Meaford

Thornbury

Christie Beach

Clarksburg

Heathcote

Victoria Corners

Red Wing

Duncan

Little Germany

Mitchell's Hill

Silcote

Woodford

Bayview

Oxmead

Kiowana Beach

Georgian Beach

Centreville

Kent

Elmhedge

Minniehill

Griersville

Strathairn

Blantyre

Fairmount

Bognor

Walters Falls

Strathavon

Rocklyn

Epping

Temple Hill

Goring

Harkaway

Lily Oak

Beaverdale

See Map 34

See Map 31

0 km   1.5 km   3 km

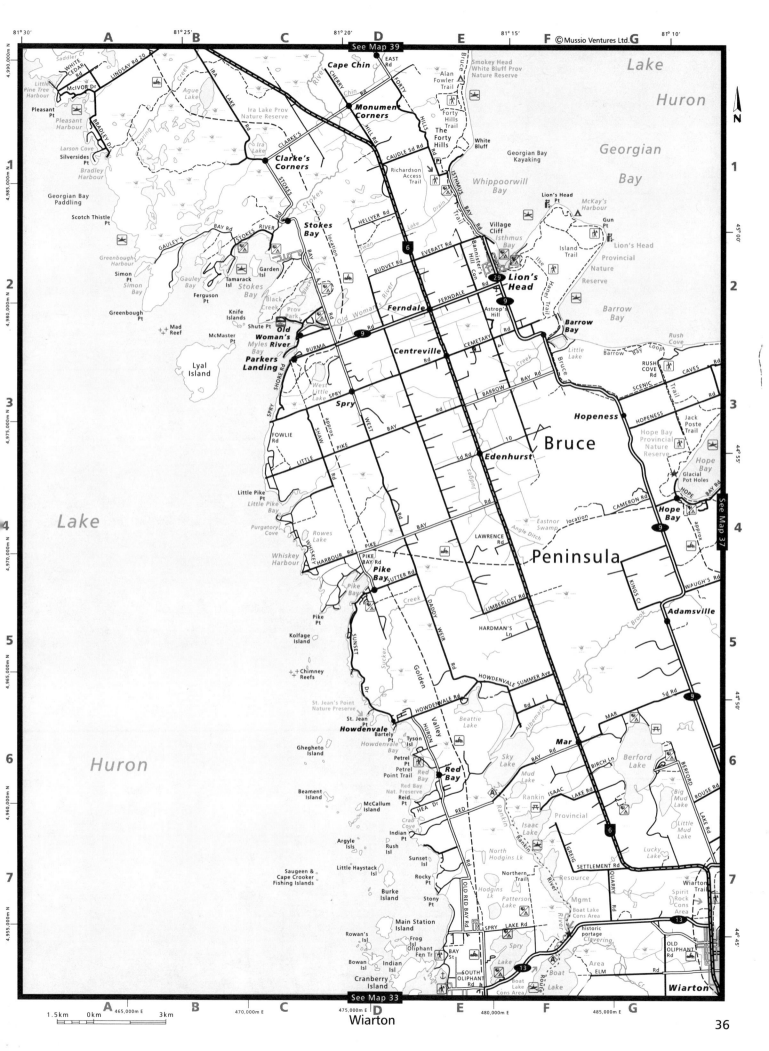

© Mussio Ventures Ltd.

Lake
Huron

Georgian
Bay

Bruce

Peninsula

Lake

Huron

Wiarton

36

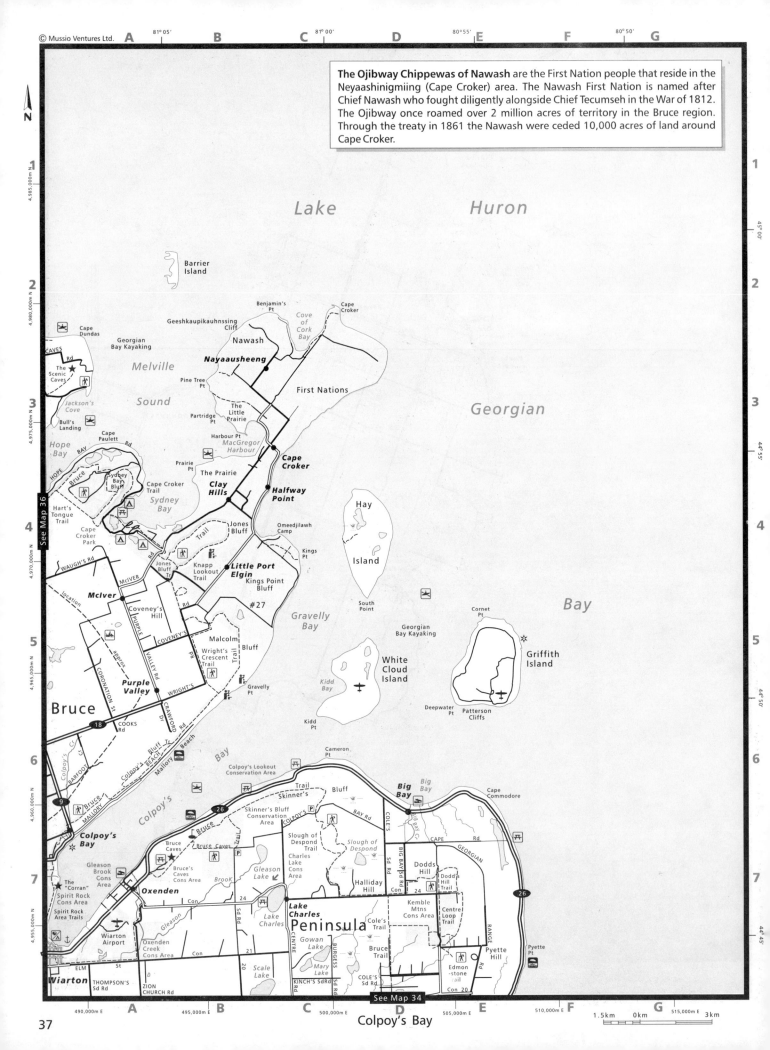

© Mussio Ventures Ltd.

The Ojibway Chippewas of Nawash are the First Nation people that reside in the Neyaashinigmiing (Cape Croker) area. The Nawash First Nation is named after Chief Nawash who fought diligently alongside Chief Tecumseh in the War of 1812. The Ojibway once roamed over 2 million acres of territory in the Bruce region. Through the treaty in 1861 the Nawash were ceded 10,000 acres of land around Cape Croker.

Lake   Huron

Barrier
Island

Cape Dundas

CAVES Rd

The Scenic
Caves

Jackson's
Cove

Bull's
Landing

Cape
Paulett   Rd

Hope
Bay

BAY

HOPE

Bruce

Sydney
Bay
Bluff

Hart's
Tongue
Trail

Cape
Croker
Trail

Sydney
Bay

Cape
Croker
Park

Georgian Bay Kayaking

Melville

Sound

Geeshkaupikauhnssing
Cliff

Benjamin's
Pt

Cove
of
Cork
Bay

Cape
Croker

Nawash

Nayaausheeng

First Nations

Georgian

Bay

Pine Tree
Pt

The
Little
Prairie

Partridge
Pt

Harbour Pt

MacGregor
Harbour

Prairie
Pt

The Prairie

Clay
Hills

Cape
Croker

Halfway
Point

Jones
Bluff

Omeedjilawh
Camp

Hay

Island

Kings
Pt

Little Port
Elgin

Kings Point
Bluff

#27

Gravelly
Bay

South
Point

Georgian
Bay Kayaking

Cornet
Pt

Griffith
Island

Jones
Bluff
Tr

Knapp
Lookout
Trail

WAUGH'S Rd

location

McIVER

McIver

Coveney's
Hill

COVENEY'S

Malcolm

Wright's
Crescent
Trail

Bluff

Gravelly
Pt

Kidd
Bay

White
Cloud
Island

Deepwater
Pt

Patterson
Cliffs

Bruce

Purple
Valley

CORONATION ST.

approx

VALLEY Rd

WRIGHT'S

CRAWFORD Dr

Rd

18

COOKS
Rd

Kidd
Pt

Cameron
Pt

Big
Bay

Big
Bay

Cape
Commodore

Colpoy's

Cr

BARFOOT

Bruce

MALLORY

9

Colpoy's
Bay

The
"Corran"

Spirit Rock
Cons Area

Spirit Rock
Area Trails

Wiarton
Airport

Gleason
Brook Cons
Area

Oxenden

Bruce
Caves

Gleason
Brook

Oxenden
Creek
Cons Area

Wiarton

ELM

St

THOMPSON'S
Sd Rd

ZION
CHURCH Rd

Colpoy's   BEACH   Mallory Beach

Bluff Jr.

Bay

Colpoy's Lookout
Conservation Area

Trail

Skinner's

Bluff

Skinner's Bluff
Conservation
Area

Slough of
Despond
Trail

Charles
Lake
Cons
Area

Bruce
Caves
Cons Area

Gleason
Lake

24

Con

Gleason

Lake
Charles

Con

Slough of
Despond

Halliday
Hill

Lake
Charles

Peninsula

Gowan
Lake

Mary
Lake

Scale
Lake

BURGESS

CENTRE

21

20

KINCH'S SdRd

COLE'S
Sd Rd

Con 20

Bruce
Trail

Cole's
Trail

COLE'S
Sd Rd

Cole's   Trail

BAY Rd

COLPOY'S

P

P

P

BAY Rd

COLE'S

Sd Rd

BIG BAY   Sd Rd

Big Bay Cr

Dodds
Hill

Dodd's
Hill
Trail

Kemble
Mtns
Cons Area

24

Con

CAPE

GEORGIAN   Rd

RANGE

26

Centre
Loop
Trail

Edmon-
stone
Trail

Pyette
Hill

Pyette
Pt

See Map 36

See Map 34

Colpoy's Bay

37

1.5 km   0 km   3 km

490,000 m E   495,000 m E   500,000 m E   505,000 m E   510,000 m E   515,000 m E

81° 05'   81° 00'   80° 55'   80° 50'

45° 00'

44° 55'

44° 50'

44° 45'

4,985,000 m N

4,980,000 m N

4,975,000 m N

4,970,000 m N

4,965,000 m N

4,960,000 m N

4,955,000 m N

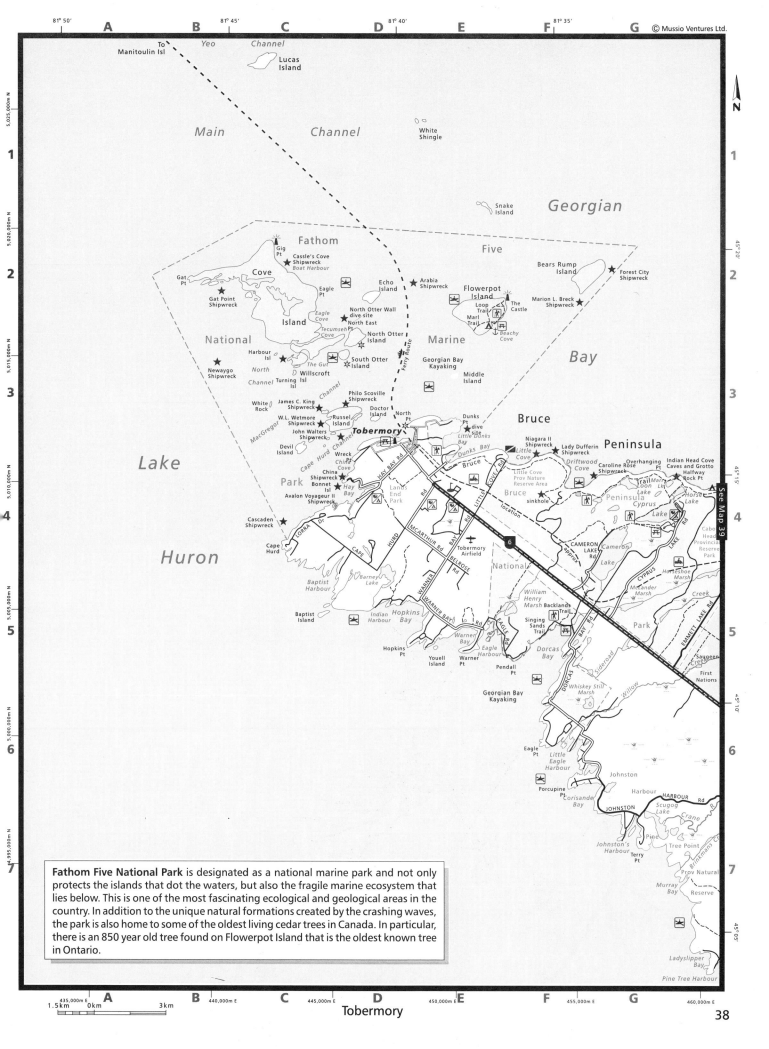

Main *Channel*

Georgian

Five

Marine

Bay

Fathom

Cove

Island

National

Bruce

Peninsula

Park

Lake

Huron

Yeo Channel

To
Manitoulin Isl

Lucas
Island

White
Shingle

Snake
Island

Gig
Pt

Cassle's Cove
Shipwreck
Boat Harbour

Gat
Pt

Eagle
Pt

Echo
Island

Arabia
Shipwreck

Bears Rump
Island

Forest City
Shipwreck

Flowerpot
Island

Loop
Trail

Marl
Trail

The
Castle

Marion L. Breck
Shipwreck

Gat Point
Shipwreck

*Eagle
Cove*

North Otter Wall
dive site

North East

*Tecumseh
Pt*

Beachy
Cove

North Otter
Island

Georgian Bay
Kayaking

National

Harbour
Isl

Willscroft

The Gut

South Otter
Island

Middle
Island

Newaygo
Shipwreck

*North
Channel*

Turning
Isl

Ferry Route

White
Rock

James C. King
Shipwreck

Philo Scoville
Shipwreck

Dunks
Pt

dive
site

Niagara II
Shipwreck

Lady Dufferin
Shipwreck

*Driftwood
Cove*

Overhanging
Pt

Indian Head Cove
Caves and Grotto
Halfway
Rock Pt

W.L. Wetmore
Shipwreck

Russel
Island

Doctor
Island

North
Pt

*Little Dunks
Bay*

Dunks Bay

Little
Cove

Caroline Rose
Shipwreck

MacGregor

John Walters
Shipwreck

Tobermory

Little Cove
Prov Nature
Reserve Area

Devil
Island

Wreck

Cape Hurd Channel

*China
Cove*

Hay
Bay Rd

Bruce

Little

Cove Rd

sinkhole

Trail

Loon

Lk

Peninsula

Cyprus

Horse
Lake

China
Shipwreck

Bonnet
Isl

Hay
Bay

*China
Cove*

Lands
End
Park

Bruce

Cameron
Lake

Lake

Avalon Voyageur II
Shipwreck

LORRA
Dr

HURD

MCARTHUR Rd

BAY
Rd

location

approx

CAMERON
LAKE
Rd

Cameron
Lake

CYPRUS

McLander
Marsh

Horseshoe
Marsh

Cascaden
Shipwreck

CAPE

Rd

Tobermory
Airfield

BELROSE
Rd

National

6

Horseshoe
Lake

Cabot
Head
Provincial
Reserve
Park

Cape
Hurd

Barney
Lake

WARNER
BAY

William
Henry
Marsh

Backlands
Trail

Park

CYPRUS

DORCAS

EMMETT LAKE Rd

*Baptist
Harbour*

*Indian
Harbour*

Hopkins
Bay

Rd

Singing
Sands
Trail

Saugeen
Creek

Baptist
Island

WARNER BAY

Warner
Bay

Eagle
Harbour

Dorcas
Bay

First
Nations

Hopkins
Pt

Youell
Island

Warner
Pt

Pendall
Pt

Whiskey Still
Marsh

Willow

Georgian Bay
Kayaking

Eagle
Pt

Little
Eagle
Harbour

Johnston

Harbour

HARBOUR
Rd

Porcupine

*Corisande
Bay*

JOHNSTON

Scugog
Lake

Crane
R

Pine

Tree Point

Brinkmans Cr

*Johnston's
Harbour*

Terry
Pt

Prov Natural

Murray
Bay

Reserve

*Ladyslipper
Bay*

Pine Tree Harbour

See Map 39

Fathom Five National Park is designated as a national marine park and not only protects the islands that dot the waters, but also the fragile marine ecosystem that lies below. This is one of the most fascinating ecological and geological areas in the country. In addition to the unique natural formations created by the crashing waves, the park is also home to some of the oldest living cedar trees in Canada. In particular, there is an 850 year old tree found on Flowerpot Island that is the oldest known tree in Ontario.

1.5km   0km   3km

Tobermory

38

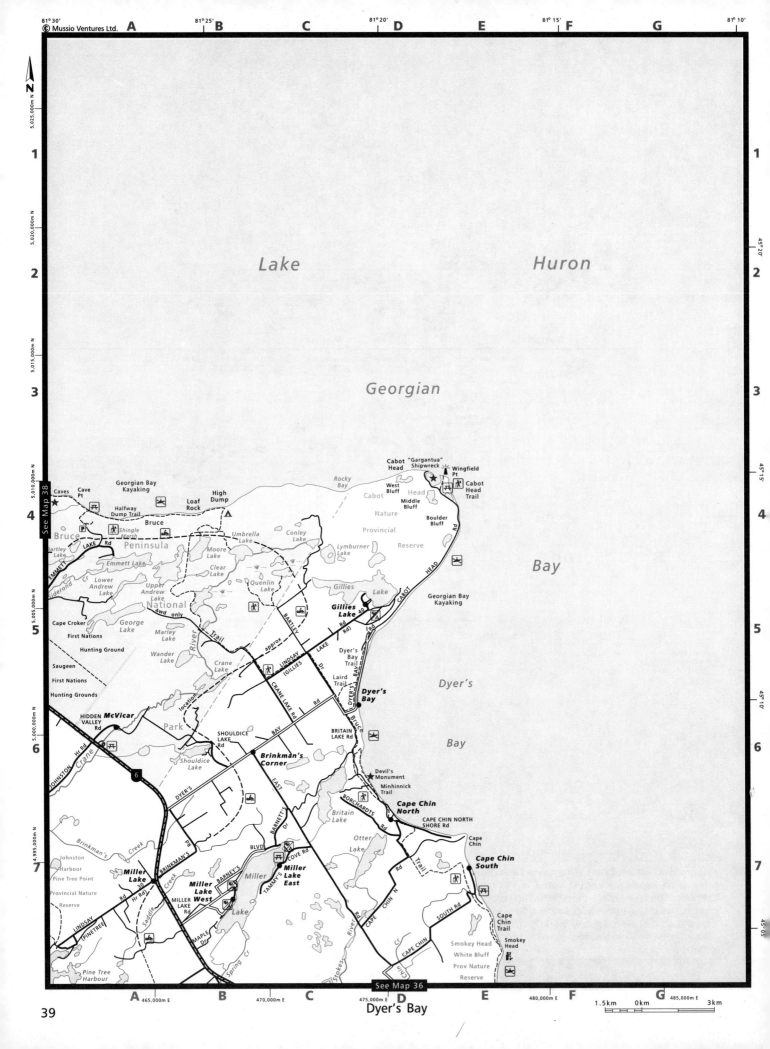

Dyer's Bay

Index

Ontario Mapbook Series

Algonquin Region

Eastern Ontario

Near North Ontario

FISHING ONTARIO

Fishing Ontario
Muskoka

Cottage Country

To obtain your book see your local
outdoor retailer, bookstore or contact:

Backroad Mapbooks
5811 Beresford Street
Burnaby, B.C.
V5J 1K1, Canada
P. (604) 438-3474
F. (604) 438-3470

orders@backroadmapbooks.com

Published By:

www.backroadmapbooks.com

Fishing Ontario
Kawarthas

Western Canada
Book Series

Fishing BC
Cariboo

Volume II:
Vancouver Island

Fishing BC
Lower Mainland

Volume IV:
The Kootenays

Fishing Ontario
Eastern Ontario

...and much more!

For a complete list of titles visit us at **www.backroadmapbooks.com**
or call us toll free   **1-877-520-5670**

AVAILABLE
ONLINE
-Individual Lake Charts
-Customized Map Orders
-Book Updates
-Online Shopping

www.backroadmapbooks.com